ENACTING
Alberta School Leaders'
PROFESSIONAL
PRACTICE
COMPETENCIES:
A Toolkit

GEORGE J. BEDARD, PʜD

and

CARMEN P. MOMBOURQUETTE, EᴅD

UNIVERSITY OF LETHBRIDGE

Faculty of Education

LETHBRIDGE, ALBERTA

◆ FriesenPress

Suite 300 - 990 Fort St
Victoria, BC, Canada, V8V 3K2
www.friesenpress.com

ISBN
978-1-4602-7671-6 (Hardcover)
978-1-4602-7672-3 (Paperback)
978-1-4602-7673-0 (eBook)

1. Education, Leadership
2. Education, Professional Development
3. Education, Research

Distributed to the trade by The Ingram Book Company

As professors, researchers, and authors we have been blessed by the support and guidance of our families, friends, and colleagues. For these many blessings we would like to dedicate this book to the principals who so kindly gave of their time during our conversations with them; to the our colleagues who continually strive to better the lives of students through their work with current and future teachers and with the many school leaders who work so tirelessly to make their schools places of great learning; and to our families whose love and support keeps us going.

—Carmen Mombourquette & George Bedard

Testimonial for *Enacting Alberta School Leaders' ProfessionalPractice Competencies: A Toolkit*

The authors have provided not only an articulate and compelling case for the establishment of professional practice standards for Alberta's school leaders but also a valuable resource for aspiring and veteran practitioners. The personal testimonies shared are not only informative but also truly inspirational. In giving voice to those leaders whose performance has made a profoundly positive difference in the lives of their students, Dr. Bedard and Dr. Mombourquette have provided an impetus for a province-wide professional dialogue. This book will serve to expand the collective wisdom of today's leaders and to accelerate the development of a new generation of school leaders, something that is critical and long overdue.

—R. G. (Bob) Garneau, EdD
Senior Manager
Leadership Excellence Branch
Alberta Education

Many provinces, states and countries have developed research-based professional standards for school principals. While there are similarities among all these standards, the most important differences are how these standards address the local educational contexts. The Alberta professional practice competencies are research-based, align with provincial regulations and reflect the fact that Alberta principals are members of the teaching profession. The case studies in this book provide evidence that Alberta principals incorporate distributed leadership strategies, support collaborative teams and work to develop a shared responsibility for student learning with the teachers in their school. With this study Dr Bedard and Dr Mombourquette provide a window onto the status of the Principal Quality Practice Guideline approved for voluntary implementation in 2009. Their research indicates that while the leadership practices of the principals in this study aligned with the provincial competencies, few school districts have incorporated the competencies into district programming for leadership development and principal induction.

—Jacqueline Skytt
Executive Staff Officer of the Alberta Teachers' Association,
Professional Development (retired)

TABLE OF CONTENTS

CHAPTER 1:

Introduction

About the Book

This book is an empirical study of how 10 Alberta principals conceived and implemented (enacted) the *Professional Practice Competencies for School Leaders*. We divide the book into the following sections:

- an introduction (rationale for the book, and policy background);
- a theoretical framework for Alberta's School Leadership Professional Practice Competencies (a literature review);
- a discussion of methodology;
- our interviews with 10 experienced and successful school principals;
- findings of our study (a descriptive summary);
- an analysis chapter where we juxtapose key findings with the framework literature;
- and we end with some conclusions that return us to the research questions posed for the study.

The principals lead the following types of schools: elementary, middle, junior/senior high, high school, and a First Nations school. The names we assign to the voices are not their real names, and we have taken care to remove identifiers, all in keeping with social science norms. We chose these 10 interviews from a sample of 27 principals whom we interviewed over a period of about 18 months. We decided to present the interviews of the 10 principals because we wanted to let their own voices take centre stage, and because they are telling a story, a narrative, that shows how they manage to implement each competency and relate them to each other. We were also curious about the type of mentorship they have received, prior to and during their principalships. We preface their replies about competencies with a question about mentorship.

The principals talk about how they address the competencies in their schools. You will note in the description of their years of service that they began their teaching and leadership careers *before* the introduction of the competencies. From what they tell us, we can surmise their leadership practices pre-competencies were pretty much aligned with the seven competencies. In other words, the seven competencies are a manifestation of what "good principals" should know and do, and be inclined to do, as part of their professional practice. Both authors of this text were participants in the original stakeholders' committee and the later leadership framework committee, and we recognize that the unanimous support the stakeholders gave to the competencies was founded on their knowledge of what separates strong and effective principals from others who are less accomplished. In other words, the dimensions or competencies are not some ideal fantasy of unobtainable goals, but rather reflections of universally acknowledged good practices that have wide and deep support in Alberta.

A Not Yet Official Policy

The roles and responsibilities of school-level leadership are complex, all-consuming, ever evolving, and, historically speaking, not clearly defined (Mombourquette, 2013). Schools themselves are harbingers of the escalating social, political, and economic change that is increasingly defining the 21st century. We have seen rise of the term *21st Century Learning* as a catch-all for what many people see as the way forward for schools in their attempts to educate current and future generations of children. We have come to know that school-level leadership plays a critical, if indirect, role in student learning. This viewpoint argues that principal leadership has the second greatest effect on student learning within the confines of the school building (Leithwood & Jantzi, 2008).

A perceived mismatch between the policy and regulatory expectations for principals, and the lack of standards for principal preparation and evaluation, prompted the Alberta government to respond to a provincial commission on education recommendation

(Alberta Learning, 2004)[1] that dealt specifically with the need to recognize and support the leadership role of principals. Recommendation: 76 advocates for the province to "develop a quality practice standard and identify the knowledge, skills and attributes required for principals" (Alberta Learning, 2003, p. 14).

In 2005, shortly after the Learning Commission Report was published, a stakeholders[2] meeting was called and the Framework Committee that was formed went to work on developing a set of standards for Alberta school principals. The work of this stakeholder committee culminated in publication of *The Principal Quality Practice Guideline: Promoting Successful School Leadership in Alberta* (Alberta Education, 2009).

Included in the Guideline were the following seven competencies or standards of school principal leadership:

1. Fostering Effective Relationships,
2. Embodying Visionary Leadership,
3. Leading a Learning Community,
4. Providing Instructional Leadership,
5. Developing and Facilitating Leadership,
6. Managing School Operations and Resources, and
7. Understanding and Responding to the Larger Societal Context.

Each competency was expanded through the use of *Descriptors* so as to give principals solid examples of what "the job" looked like in practice (see **Appendix A**).

---

1   The title of the Ministry of Education, as it is known in many Canadian provinces, has changed more than once in Alberta. In 2004, for example, it was Alberta Learning; not long after that, the present use of Alberta Education came into effect.

2   The stakeholder committee consisted of representatives from the following organizations: Alberta Home and School Councils' Association (AHSCA), Alberta School Boards Association (ASBA), Alberta Teachers' Association (ATA), Alberta Teachers' Association-Council of School Administration (CSA), Association of Independent Schools and Colleges in Alberta, Alberta Association of Public Charter Schools, College of Alberta School Superintendents (CASS), Council on Alberta Teaching Standards (COATS), La Fédération des conseil scolaires francophone de l'Alberta, Concordia University College, Campus St. Jean, The King's University College, University of Alberta, University of Calgary, University of Lethbridge, and Alberta Education.

However, what was not included in the *Guideline* was a link to the literature in the field, nor, in essence, a theoretical justification for the articulation of the competencies enumerated within; hence, we felt the need to develop a theoretical framework in this book. The *Guideline* invokes a mandate, one that amounts to a moral imperative, for Alberta school principals: "The principal is an accomplished teacher who practices quality leadership in the provision of opportunities for optimum learning and development of all students in the school" (Alberta Education, 2009, p. 4).

Jurisdictions throughout the English-speaking Commonwealth are establishing standards of practice for their principals and others involved in school leadership: Ontario established its framework in 2012 (Leithwood, 2012); the British Columbia Principal and Vice Principal Association updated their guidelines in 2013 (BCPVPA, 2013); New South Wales adopted standards in 2005 (New South Wales, 2005); the Professional Development Council of the Australian Principals Associations produced five leadership propositions in 2003 (Australian Principals Association, 2003); while England adopted its first version of leadership standards in 1997, updated them in 2004, and to some degree revised them again in 2010 (Doughty, 2013). The Alberta competencies share a strong degree of commonality with iterations of the ISLLC standards that inform educational leadership preparation in the United States.[3] We acknowledge that, particularly in the United States, the intent and effects of the standards of practice movement has been subject to some criticism (English, 2006), but our wider purpose here is to explore from an Albertan perspective the seven competencies of educational leadership as prospective policy, including relevant tools and the support for each competency in current literature.

We must underscore that the *Guideline* is presently not mandated provincially like the *Teacher Quality Standard*, or empowered by an order-in-council, regulation, or statute like the School Act (this may happen in the future). Recent evidence found by Mombourquette (2013) indicates that some districts in this province make little, if any, use of the competencies in the selection, preparation, development, supervision, and evaluation of school leaders. However, in other research on district[4] leadership prac-

---

3   See http://www.ccsso.org/documents/2014/Draft%202014%20ISLLC%20Standards%2009102014.pdf.

4   In Alberta, the intermediary agencies that oversee a number of publicly funded schools are called either districts or divisions. Their statutory designation is "authorities" and they are also commonly referred to as school boards or central

tices in three high-performing districts, we noted the competencies were core to their working cultures (Bedard, Mombourquette, & Aitken, 2013).

REFERENCES

Alberta Education. (2009). *Principal quality practice guideline: Promoting successful school leadership in Alberta.* (LB2831.926.C2 A333 2009). Edmonton, AB: Alberta Education. Retrieved from http://education.alberta.ca/admin/resources.aspx

Alberta Learning. (2003). *Every child learns, every child succceeds: Report and recommendations.* (LC91.2.A3.A333 2003). Edmonton, AB. Retrieved from http://education.alberta.ca/department/ipr/commission.aspx

Alberta Learning. (2004). *Progress Report: Government's response to Alberta's Commission on Learning.* Edmonton, AB: Government of Alberta.

Australian Principals Association. (2003). *Leaders lead: Strengthening the Australian school.* Hindmarsh, South Australia: Australian Principals Associations Professional Development Council.

BCPVPA. (2013). *Leadership standards for principals and vice-principals in British Columbia.* Victoria, BC: British Columbia Principals and Vice Principals Association.

Bedard, G., Mombourquette, C., & Aitken, A. (2013). Calgary Catholic School District. In J. Brandon, P. Hanna, & K. Rhyason (Eds.), *Vision in action: Seven approaches to school system success* (pp. 165-231). Edmonton, AB: College of Alberta School Superintendents.

Doughty, J. (2013). Leadership standards. *Paper presented at the International Conference.* London, England.

English, F. W. (2006). The unintended consequences of a standardized knowledge base in advancing educational leadership preparation. *Educational Administration Quarterly, 42*(3), 461-472. doi: 10.1177/0013161x06289675

Fullan, M. (2003). *The moral imperative of leadership.* Thousand Oaks, CA: Corwin.

Leithwood, K. (2012). *The Ontario leadership framework 2012* (pp. 1-65). Toronto, ON: The Institute for Education Leadership.

---

offices. Superintendents are the chief educational officers at this level, supported by specialized educators and administrative staff. Each division or district is accountable to locally elected boards of trustees and to Alberta Education. In Canada K-12 education is largely within the constitutional powers accorded to each province, with the federal government playing a much less pronounced role. In Alberta, the funding model and curriculum policy are highly centralized at the provincial level. Forty-two districts are public (secular), seventeen are separate (Roman Catholic), and four are francophone. Other authorities oversee charter and private schools that may or may not receive some public funding.

Leithwood, K., & Jantzi, D. (2008). Linking leadership to student learning: The contributions of leader efficacy. *Educational Administration Quarterly, 44*(4), 496-528. doi: 10.1177/0013161x08321501

Mombourquette, C. (2013). Principal leadership: Blending the historical perspective with the current focus on competencies in the Alberta context. *Canadian Journal of Educational Administration and Policy, 1*(147), 1-19.

New South Wales. (2005). *School leadership capability framework*. Sydney: Department of Education and Training.

CHAPTER 2:

Developing a Theoretical Framework

In this chapter, we do not take the position that the seven competencies or dimensions are all encompassing, and we do not render an opinion on whether or not they are the final word regarding what constitutes school leadership. Instead, we follow a process whereby we provide concise theoretical support for each competency, dimension, or standard, as they are called in different countries, and which we have found in the available literature from the field of educational leadership. Referenced in this chapter is various literature which we located during extensive database searches throughout much of 2013 and early 2014. We utilized key word searches as well as a type of snowball search, using article references to find relevant sources of information for our study. For the comprehensive literature that attends to a recent iteration of the American ISLLC standards, see Taylor et al., 2012.

Prior to tackling the theoretical framework for the competencies themselves, we first want to present a rationale for the role of mentorship in the development of school leaders. We recognize that various elements contribute to the acquisition of knowledge, skills, and attributes required of the position. A school leader's beliefs and perceptions influence the way in which leadership is manifested (Lapointe, Poirel, & Brassard, 2013; Urick & Bowers, 2013). Context also plays a role in leadership style (Camburn, Rowan, & Taylor, 2003). In addition, Orr and Orphanos (2011) note the importance of graduate studies and their connection to principal effectiveness. Yet mentorship and the supports received by new principals also play an important role, according to Duncan and Stock (2010). Hansford and Ehrich (2005) identify the following as positive outcomes for principal mentees: supports gained, greater levels of empathy noted, counselling availability, shared ideas, problem-solving help, professional development enhancements, and a sense of improved confidence in one's ability to do what has become a very demanding job.

The Seven Competencies of Alberta School Leadership

The *Guideline* is explicit that the following order of the competencies should not be construed as a hierarchy in which some competencies trump or subsume other ones. Rather, the competencies are presented in a mutually re-enforcing relationship. In doing so, we would suggest that the intent is to illustrate that the implementation of any one competency usually requires attendance to other competencies as well.

Fostering Effective Relationships

"The principal builds trust and fosters positive working relationships, on the basis of appropriate values and ethical foundations, within the school community—students, teachers and other staff, parents, school council and others who have an interest in the school" (Alberta Education, 2009, p. 4).

Goddard (2003) refers to the blending of relational networks, norms, and trust as structural and functional forms of social capital. A positive social capital perspective necessitates the need for teachers to act with fairness, dignity, and integrity. Widely shared teacher-based social capital influences student achievement (Goddard, Tschannen-Moran, & Hoy, 2001). Sharing leadership was also found important by Adams and Forsyth (2013). Additionally, teacher job satisfaction, internalization, and identification are influenced by principal leadership style (Aydin, Sarier, & Usyal, 2013). Principal leadership style plays a key role in supporting student achievement through interactions with teachers (Wahlstrom & Seashore-Louis, 2008). When these interactions are based on positive relationships, achieved through shared leadership practices, and based on mutual trust, teacher efficacy is increased, and so too is student achievement (Tschannen-Moran, 2003).

Schools throughout Alberta have become increasingly diverse in terms of language, ethnicity, religion, sexual orientation, and student learning abilities. Promoting an inclusive school culture that respects and honours diversity is enshrined in provincial documentation and goals for education (Alberta Education, 2011). Principals must be attuned to the needs of students and to those of teachers who have to work within these increasingly diverse environments. They must pay attention to the school as a cultural entity, where relationship building is valued and supported when principals:

- treat the school as whole rather than attending to the fragmented parts;
- work with school district leadership to blend district and school-based initiatives;
- have the ability to communicate a compelling rationale to school stakeholders;
- know that secondary and elementary schools need to differentiate the support systems put in place to support diversity; and
- use data extensively for tracking progress with instructional improvements (Elfers & Stritikus, 2013; Higgins-Norman, Goldrick, & Harrison, 2009).

With the moral imperative of school leadership in Alberta being provision of opportunities for optimum learning and development of all students, the competencies have built in a requirement for principals to demonstrate responsibility for all students and to act in their best interests. Research from New Zealand (Timperley, 2011a) points out the importance of both declarative and procedural types of principal knowledge, knowing what needs to be done, actively communicating the same, and establishing measurable benchmarks that address key concerns about student achievement. The principal plays a key role in not only building healthy relationships with teachers who directly influence student learning, but through community building actions that also directly impact students (McNeely et al., 2002).

A key element of transformational leadership is the leader's ability to build and sustain healthy relationships with school staff (Leithwood & Jantzi, 2005). Being a transformational leader implies modelling, promoting, and communicating a vision and mission that is inclusive in nature and clearly focused on student learning needs. Following a multifaceted approach in which distributed leadership is enacted, continual inquiry in instructional practices is the norm, and collective decision making is used to enhance student achievement (Copland, 2003). Printy and Marks (2006) add further evidence as to the importance of strong principals sharing instructional leadership roles with teachers, and in clarifying how this impacts student achievement.

To achieve an environment that supports shared instructional leadership resulting in healthy relationships and increased student achievement, research indicates the importance of effective communication, facilitation, and problem-solving skills, and the degree to which the principal is accessible to the teachers for advice (Friedkin & Slater, 1994).

The competencies identify the likelihood of conflict occurring within the school community and indicate that principals must develop support processes for dealing with relationships and dissension. Canadian researchers Kutsyuruba, Walker, and Noonan (2011) contend that trust is an integral aspect of human relationships and when broken must be restored through the efforts of the principal. Important are: spending the time and effort required, and handling issues in a timely manner in a way that is not only sincere but perceived to be as well.

The final *Descriptor* associated with the building relationship competency is "adhering to a professional standard of conduct" (Alberta Education, 2009, p. 4). In Alberta, principals, like all of the publicly funded teachers, are members of the Alberta Teachers' Association ("Teaching Profession Act," 2000). Teachers in Alberta are subject to the professional responsibilities enumerated in the *Code of Professional Conduct*. The *Code* lays out areas of conduct in relationship to pupils, school authorities, colleagues, and the profession.[5]

Embodying Visionary Leadership

"The principal collaboratively involves the school community in creating and sustaining shared school values, vision, mission and goals" (Alberta Education, 2009, p. 4).
School vision and its influence on student learning gains is well documented in the literature.[6] We detail some of the nuances associated with the complex issue of vision and the role it plays within a principal's leadership mandate.

The principal needs to be "guided by an educational philosophy that is based on sound research, personal experiences, and ongoing reflection" (Alberta Education, 2009, p. 4). In addition, the principal needs to be effective in communicating this educational philosophy to the stakeholders in the school community. Key to this *Descriptor* is the belief held by the principal about education and the ability of all students to learn. Bandura

---

5   For further details on the *Code of Professional Conduct* see https://www.teachers.ab.ca/About%20the%20ATA/ UpholdingProfessionalStandards/ProfessionalConduct/Pages/CodeofProfessionalConduct.aspx.

6   See Bottoms & Schmidt-Davis, 2010; Chappuis, Chappuis, & Stiggins, 2009; Gronn, 2002; Lambert, 2005; Marzano, Waters, & McNulty, 2005; Murphy, Elliott, Goldring, & Porter, 2007; Naseer, 2011; Seashore-Louis, Dretzke, & Wahlstrom, 2010; Waters, Marzano, & McNulty, 2003; Ylimaki, 2006.

(1993) and Tschannen-Moran (2009) speak of belief in terms of efficacy, or one's belief in making a difference in the lives of others. Hallinger and Heck (1996) note the principal's need to be guided by an educational philosophy, leading to the establishment of goals, based on perceived needs within the school community. These goals impact the principal's influence on student achievement.

Vision-related research recognizes that educators do not perform their critical function of supporting student achievement in isolation from a wider organizational context. Alberta's publicly funded schools are organized within school districts. The principal needs to be cognizant of the vision and mission for education provided by the district, and through the district to the Province of Alberta. Research by Bedard, Mombourquette, and Aitken (2013) demonstrates the importance of aligning school, district, and provincial goals for education. Knapp, Copland, Honig, Plecki, and Portin (2010) found that aligning school goals and district goals around learning improvement produced sustainable change and student achievement gains when a district-wide focus on student learning was emphasized. This entailed, among other things, a re-design of district level services to support the work of the schools (Honig, 2012).

The principal meaningfully engages the school community (teachers, support staff, parents, students, and members of the community at large) in identifying and addressing areas for school improvement. Copland (2003) refers to the importance of the principal playing a key role in framing questions that will lead the community's efforts in the quest of finding better ways to meet student learning needs. Often the literature engaging the community is centred on the concept of distributed leadership. Leithwood, Mascall, and Strauss (2009) indicate that distributing leadership does not diminish demand for leadership by the principal, but rather, increases it in scope and depth.

The competency of *Embodying Visionary Leadership* acknowledges the important role played by the principal in understanding the culture of the school. Instructional leadership is highly related to school culture, and has a significant influence upon all factors associated with it (Sabin, 2011). The connection between leadership and creation of a common school culture depends on the presence and cohesiveness of an interacting group of individuals (Turan & Bektas, 2013). Furthermore, Turan and Bektas (2013) found it was important to allow school principals the freedom to work with teachers to form a school culture. School culture matters when student learning is at question (Seashore-Louis & Wahlstrom, 2011). Principals provide support by facilitating identification and preservation of what is of value while also attending to cultural factors that do not support student learning. When done right, the instructional leadership of the principal blends with the culture of the school and together they form a powerful force for positively impacting student learning (Seashore-Louis & Wahlstrom, 2011).

Existing school culture may enhance student learning or drag it down. School culture in and of itself does not necessarily mean a positive or negative influence. It can be either (Deal & Peterson, 2009). For school culture to be a force for positive impact on student learning the principal needs to facilitate change and promote innovation consistent with current and future school community needs. School culture plays a positive role when buttressed by a number of factors: a strong sense of community; a focus on learning and setting high expectations for all students; and exhibiting care for the well-being of teachers, staff, students, and members of the larger community (Griffin & Green 2013).

Embodying Visionary Leadership requires principals to analyze a wide range of data to determine progress towards achieving school goals. Ylimaki (2006) provides a variety of definitions for the term *vision*. She notes the most often-used definition relates to a principal's ability to see and articulate a compelling future for the school (Bennis & Nanus, 1985; Westley & Mintzberg, 1989). Ylimaki also notes that the other prominent definition is based on the development of goals for an improved future for the school as an organization (Boyd, 1992; DuFour & Eaker, 1998). The former definition is leader driven, while the latter is based more on the collective development of the way forward. In either case, data play an important role in making sure the vision is actualized and impacts student learning.[7]

The final *Descriptor* for *Visionary Leadership* speaks to the need to communicate and celebrate school accomplishments so as to inspire continuous growth. Waters et al. (2003) identified 21 specific leadership responsibilities that are significantly correlated with student achievement. Included are:

- *Culture* – fostering shared beliefs and a sense of community and cooperation;
- *Focus* – establishing clear goals and keeping these goals at the forefront of the school's attention;

---

7   See Barnes, Camburn, Sanders, & Sebastion, 2010; Bowers, 2009; Copland, 2003; Datnow, Park, & Wohlstetter, 2007; Knapp, Copland, & Swinnerton, 2007; Luo, 2008.

- *Communicate* – establishing strong lines of communication with teachers and students;
- *Outreach* – advocating and being a spokesperson for the school to all stakeholders, and
- *Affirm* – recognizing and celebrating school accomplishments and acknowledging failures.

Leading a Learning Community

"The principal nurtures and sustains a school culture that values and supports learning" (Alberta Education, 2009, p. 5).

In many ways *Leading a Learning Community* cuts to the heart of what school leadership is about: providing opportunities for optimum learning and development of all students in the school. Spillane, Halverson, and Diamond (2001) provide an analytical lens to explore the required principal leadership dimensions for teacher learning within a professional learning community. Included in the dimensions are physical capital, human capital, and social capital. Physical capital is defined as a resource, such as the appropriate allocation of funding; human capital is teacher knowledge, skills, and expertise; and social capital is relations among individuals built on trust, collaboration, and a sense of obligation (Richmond & Manokore, 2011).

Many researchers support the idea that the principal plays a key role in establishing and maintaining a school culture that supports student learning.[8] Not as well researched is the understanding that the principal should promote and model life-long learning for students, teachers, other staff, and self. However, the work of Timperley and various colleagues (Timperley, 2011a, 2011b; Timperley, Wilson, Barrar, & Fung, 2007; Timperley, Wilson, & Fung, 2008) supports the active involvement of the principal alongside teachers as they collectively strive to improve student learning.

---

8   See Adams, 1999; Barnes et al., 2010; Bloom & Owens, 2013; Camburn, Rowan, & Taylor, 2003; Darling-Hammond, Meyerson, La Pointe, & Orr, 2009; Donaldson, 2013; Fullan, 2010; Hallinger & Heck, 2010a, 2010b; Heck & Hallinger, 2009; Knapp, Copland, Honig, Plecki, & Portin, 2010; Lambert, 2005; Leithwood & Jantzi, 1990; Leithwood & Jantzi, 2008; Leithwood & Mascall, 2008; Moolenaar et al., 2010; Murphy, Smylie, Mayrowetz, & Seashore-Louis, 2009.

Fostering a culture of high expectations for students, teachers, and other staff was an idea supported and promoted by Dewey (1959) and has since been well researched (Brown, Anfara, & Roney, 2004; Hallinger & Murphy, 1986; Hays, 2013; Jacobson, Brooks, Giles, Johnson, & Ylimaki, 2007; Pascopella, 2009; Podsakoff, MacKenzie, Moorman, & Fetter, 1990; Reynolds, 1999) and shown to be effective in increasing student learning gains in both low- and high-achieving schools. Miron (1997) noted that high expectations, when applied equally to all students, prevented discrimination. Donaldson (2013) found that the principal influences school-wide expectations for student achievement through the hiring process and placement of teachers within the school community.

In recent years we have seen a change in teacher professional development practices and a renewed interest in the value of developing teacher knowledge, skills, and attitudes so as to improve pedagogy leading to improved student learning. Timperley (2011b) speaks to the need to move from teacher professional development, which she connotes to be something that is done to teachers, to a process of teacher professional learning, which she maintains is driven by teachers' desire to improve their own practices. The role played by the principal in implementing high quality teacher professional development and professional learning is noted by Gumus (2013) who found active principal involvement is key if the processes are to impact student learning. Additionally, Youngs and King (2002) maintain that the full value of teacher professional development as a means of building school capacity is only actualized when all staff participate in ongoing activities addressing "teachers' knowledge, skills, and dispositions; professional community; and program coherence" (p. 647).

Leading a Learning Community also extends to reaching out to the community and facilitating meaningful parental involvement that includes keeping parents informed about their child's learning and development (Young, Austin, & Growe, 2013). Epstein and Sanders (2006) developed a framework for parent/school affiliation. They describe six types of involvement that educators could/should engage in with parents: parenting, communicating, volunteering, learning at home, decision making, and collaborating with the community. Henderson and Mapp (2002) provide the research base for increased parent involvement in schools when they note: "When schools, families, and community groups work together to support learning, children tend to do better in school, stay in school longer, and like school more" (p. 7). Gordon and Seashore Louis (2009) link active involvement of parents to principal leadership style and level of acceptance of distributed leadership. Scholarship on parent–principal relationships also attends to the challenges that can be created when parents become active in the life of the school. Principals need to pay attention to tensions that can arise and, like much associated with school leadership, develop a vision, goals, and implementation plan for active and positive involvement of parents (Horvat, Curci, & Partlow, 2010).

Providing Instructional Leadership

"The principal ensures that all students have ongoing access to quality teaching and learning opportunities to meet the provincial goals of education" (Alberta Education, 2009, p. 5).

When the term *instructional leadership* is entered into Google Scholar as the search parameter, no less than 478,000 articles, books, and other sources appear. In 2014 alone more than 3900 references are included. The Alberta *Education Act* emphasizes that the first duty of a principal is to "provide instructional leadership in the school" (Education Act, 2012, p. 123). But what is *instructional leadership?*

Leithwood, Jantzi, and Steinbach (1999) describe instructional leadership from the perspective of leader focus. Principals need to focus attention on teachers' behaviours in their work directly affecting student growth and development. They also address instructional leadership from the broader context of organizational variables like school culture and other influences on teacher/student work. Hallinger and Heck (1997) conceptualize instructional leadership in terms of category (defining school mission, managing instructional programs, promoting school climate) and of mode of impact (direct, mediated, and reciprocal). Leithwood, Jantzi, and Steinbach (1999) and Hallinger and Heck (2010b) differentiate the direct and indirect influences of the principal regarding student achievement. Direct influences include shaping the school's direction through vision, mission, goals, and offering greater opportunities for others to share in their creation. Indirect influences relate to a number of actions undertaken by the principal as they work with teachers. The third conceptualization comes from Blase and Blase (1998) who value a blend of supervision, staff development, and curriculum development. Like Timperley (2011b), Blase and Blase support the idea that the principal is an important variable in teacher professional development, working alongside teachers to promote improved practices.

Southworth (2002) adds to these conceptualizations of instructional leadership by addressing three of the approaches shown effective in improving the quality of teaching and learning:

1. Modelling, with heads (principals) using their own teaching, and even assemblies, as an exemplar, and working alongside staff in classrooms;
2. Monitoring, with heads looking at teachers' weekly plans and pupils' work and reviewing test data; and
3. Professional dialogue, taking all opportunities to discuss teaching and learning in staff meetings, developing curricular policies, reviewing pupil data, probing teachers' assumptions, and promoting ideas. (p. 4)

The first *Descriptor* in the *Instructional Leadership* competency necessitates that the principal "demonstrate a sound understanding of current pedagogy and curriculum" (Alberta Education, 2009, p. 5). Hattie (2012) provides the most current meta-analysis of what research says about high-yield teaching strategies. Proven teacher influences on student learning include: feedback to students, instructional quality, direct instruction, class environment, challenge of goals, peer tutoring, mastery learning, and questioning (Hattie, 2003). Marzano et al. (2005) present strategies for school leaders to follow when working with teachers to incorporate high-yield teaching strategies. In addition to working with teachers collectively, principals need to differentiate and individualize how they work with teachers to build instructional capacity (May & Supovitz, 2011).

Alberta has adopted a curriculum standards approach to student achievement. Grades 1 to 12 curriculum standards are articulated in a Provincial Program of Studies. Grade 3, 6, and 9 students write Provincial Achievement Tests, and Grade 12 students write Diploma Exams in core subject areas. In addition, students in the province also participate in various international assessments, and other items best described as standardized tests. Once a year, Alberta Education provides all publicly funded schools with a report card of sorts referred to as the Accountability Pillar (Alberta Education, 2012). Various types of data go into this report: student achievement results, information gleaned from surveys of students, teachers, and parents, along with items like graduation rates. Principals, according to the competencies, need to "implement strategies for addressing standards of student achievement" (Alberta Education, 2009, p. 5) leading to improved

Accountability Pillar results. These strategies are usually a combination of the principal's direct and indirect influences.

Brown & Green (2014) identify seven strategies used by school leaders to successfully turn around high-poverty, low-performing schools. These include: leadership, collaboration, professional development, school organization, data analysis, curriculum alignment, and student intervention. Other strategies also note the importance of identifying what students need to know, how to get them to know it, and when they have learned it (ten Bruggencate, Luyten, Scheerens, & Sleegers, 2012). Sammons, Gu, Day, and Ko (2010) highlighted strategies and actions school principals can adopt to raise pupil attainment by paying attention to standards for student learning. A growing body of evidence supports reform around developing essential curriculum standards, standards-based criterion-referenced tests, and standards-based extended learning opportunities that impact student learning (Mason, Mason, Mendez, Nelsen, & Orwig, 2005). However, the reliance upon the use of standards in curriculum, particularly when defined through centralized government departments, is contested by a number of scholars and teacher organizations (Miller, 2013).

Included in this competency is the requirement for principals to "ensure that student assessment and evaluation practices throughout the school are fair, appropriate, and balanced" (Alberta Education, 2009, p. 5). Numerous researchers have connected the power of fair, appropriate, and balanced student assessment practices to student learning gains.[9] Learning-focused leadership, student learning assessment, and school improvement, when interwoven, provide a framework for an aligned and coherent approach to developing and implementing strategies that can have a positive influence on sustained improvement in a school (Aitken, 2009; Webber et al., 2009).

Principals need to "implement effective supervision and evaluation to ensure that teachers consistently meet the Alberta Teaching Quality Standard"[10] (Alberta Education, 2009, p. 5). At the heart of this *Descriptor* lies the belief that student learning can increase through direct work with teachers and improvement of their practice. We find considerable evidence to support the idea that teachers and teaching in schools

---

9   See Black & Wiliam, 2010; Bowers, 2009; DeVito & Thomas, 2010; Guskey, 2007; Halverson, 2010; Joint Advisory Committee, 1993; Marynowski, 2013; Webber, Aitken, Lupert, & Scott, 2009.

10   See http://www.education.alberta.ca/department/policy/standards/teachqual.aspx.

is key to school improvement endeavours (Lewis, 2008; Seashore-Louis, Dretzke, et al., 2010).

What is at question in this *Descriptor* is whether or not teacher supervision and evaluation lead to better teachers, teaching, and hence student learning. Murphy, Hallinger, and Heck (2013) indicate there is little direct or indirect evidence to support the notion that evaluation of teachers by the principal leads to school improvement and in turn better student learning. They favour what is referred to in the Alberta context as teacher supervision, in which the principal: provides feedback to teachers (Hattie, 2009); develops communities of practice in which teachers share goals, work, and responsibilities for student outcomes (Wahlstrom & Seashore-Louis, 2008); offers abundant support for the work of teachers (Leithwood & Jantzi, 2005); and creates systems in which teachers have the opportunity to routinely develop and refine their skills (Bryk, Sebring, Allensworth, Luppescu, & Easton, 2010).

Principals are to "ensure appropriate pedagogy is utilized in response to various dimensions of student diversity" (Alberta Education, 2009, p. 5). Albertan schools are becoming increasingly diverse communities. Preparing school leaders for the challenge of ensuring that diversity is attended to requires ongoing needs assessment, consensus building, curriculum enhancements, and providing faculty with a voice in establishing school communities of practice (Lalas & Morgan, 2006). Once in place, leadership for diversity works to promote student learning (Riehl, 2000; Waters et al., 2003).

Within the literature there is considerable support for the understanding that principals need to "ensure that students have access to appropriate programming based on their individual learning needs" (Alberta Education, 2009; Salisbury, 2006; Salisbury & McGregor, 2002). Capper, Frattura, and Keyes (2000) offer the following focal points for inclusive schooling: shift from providing separate programs for a few students to providing excellent educational services for all students; channel the standards movement into proactive teaching and assessment to ensure student success; and use funding and the law to support excellent services for all. The principal is one of the actors who can use these as levers for inclusive schooling. At the same time there is evidence that inclusionary practices may be inhibited by the lack of principal preparation, support, and understanding (Goodley, 2010; Mittler & Mittler, 2000; Viachou, 2004).

This competency also encourages principal leadership in school-based technologies. Principals need to "recognize the potential of new and emerging technologies, and enable their meaningful integration in support of teaching and learning" (Alberta

Education, 2009, p. 5). Schrum and Levin (2013) provide a clear description of the challenges current school leaders face trying to move their schools towards 21st century technologies. They also note the skills required for leveraging technology to improve student engagement and achievement. The main focus of technology use should be on integrating it into the teaching and learning processes and developing the capacities of principals and teachers towards this end.

Tapping into community resources is another *Descriptor*. The principal "ensures that teachers and other staff communicate and collaborate with parents and community agencies, where appropriate, to support student learning and to support the use of community resources to enhance student learning" (Alberta Education, 2009, p. 5)"[11] What is noted in the literature is that schools cannot be expected to single-handedly do all the work of addressing the most pressing barriers facing students and their families. Areas typically mentioned to expand the initiatives for improving community involvement include: program and service strategies related to academic learning, youth development, parent and/or family engagement and support, health and social services, and community partnerships (Anderson-Butcher et al., 2008).

Developing and Facilitating Leadership

"The principal promotes the development of leadership capacity within the school community: students, teachers and other staff, parents, and school council for the overall benefit of the school community and education system" (Alberta Education, 2009, p. 5).

This competency recognizes that while the formal responsibility is vested in the office of the principal, the actual work of meeting a multitude of tasks associated with school improvement requires the proactive involvement of a number of important actors. This means that the principal needs to "demonstrate informed decision making through open dialogue and consideration of multiple perspectives" (Alberta Education, 2009, p. 5). Core to the principal's development and facilitation of leadership in others is the active involvement of school stakeholders in ethical decisions made for the school and

---

11   See Adelman & Taylor, 2005; Anderson-Butcher et al., 2008; Blank, Melaville, & Shah, 2003; Doll & Lyon, 1988; Hatch, 1998; Henderson & Mapp, 2002; Keith, 1996; Millican & Bourner, 2011; Nzinga-Johnson, Baker, & Aupperlee, 2009; Roth, Brooks-Gunn, Murray, & Foster, 1998; Sanders, 2008; Sommerville & McDonald, 2002.

the processes through which those decisions are arrived at. However, principals should not be swayed by collective decisions that at their heart subvert the very notion of core values and practices serving the interests of students and their parents. The principal needs to ensure that decisions do not favour some students and teachers, as the case may be, at the expense of others (Frick, Faircloth, & Little, 2013). This requires the principal to understand the importance of role modelling and making visible the key aspects in decision making, such as the values and goals that undergird them. The principal's influence in the decision making process is highly correlated to how often teachers seek their professional advice and guidance (Moolenaar et al., 2010).

The principal attends to the requirement to "promote team building and shared leadership among members of the school community" (p. 6), and to "facilitate meaningful involvement of the school community, where appropriate, in the school's operation using collaborative and consultative decision making strategies" (p. 6). In numerous sections of this chapter we have highlighted the value of distributed leadership. In this section we note the work of Harris (2012) when she addresses the implications arising from the use of the distributed leadership model. She addresses how the role of the principal is affected and changed as leadership is more widely shared within the school. When power is distributed we tend to see a move away from positional leadership, building a high degree of reciprocal trust. Harris also notes the likelihood of improved student learning when leadership is distributed. Canadian researchers Sackney and Walker (2006) relate the importance of principals building leadership capacity in others by developing a learning community culture that builds trust, collaboration, risk taking, reflection, shared leadership, and data-based decision making.

The final *Descriptor* for this competency changes the conversation a little when it suggests that the principal must "identify and mentor teachers for future educational leadership roles" (p. 6). Youngs' (2007) demonstrated, at least at the elementary level, that mentoring does make a difference. Youngs found that principals should promote school cultures in which experienced teachers are actively involved in the induction of newer teachers.

Managing School Operations and Resources

"The principal manages school operations and resources to ensure a safe and caring, and effective learning environment" (Alberta Education, 2009, p. 6).

The first *Descriptor* listed for managing school operations and resources is: "The principal effectively plans, organizes, and manages the human, physical and financial resources of the school and identifies the areas of need" (Alberta Education, 2009, p. 6). In a comprehensive review of the field of educational leadership and management, Hallinger (2005) found that the management side of educational leadership continued to be valued, and was deemed instrumental in ensuring that the core function of school was to maximize student learning. Schools are organizations that need a certain level of management in order to function and perform responsibilities connected to student learning (Leithwood, 2009; Leithwood, Day, Sammons, Hopkins, & Harris, 2006; Murphy, 2005; Murphy et al., 2007; Seashore-Louis, Leithwood, Wahlstrom, & Anderson, 2010; Silins & Mulford, 2002). What is open for debate is whether or not these functions need to be distributed, and the level of teacher involvement in their delivery. Somech (2010) maintains we are debating the wrong question. She indicates that participative decision-making needs to be considered in terms of the practical implications for schools. When so considered there may be times when participation is unnecessary, and others in which it is shown to be the most effective way to move forward. Furthermore, she maintains that participative decision-making makes a statement about how to treat and motivate teachers as resources for the school's success.

The final *Descriptor* cuts to the heart of the core requirement of the school, with student learning being the driving force for effective and efficient school operation. The principal "utilizes teaching, learning, and student development to guide management decisions and the organization of learning" (Alberta Education, 2009, p. 6). There are a number of models that blend management type decisions with student learning (Breiter & Light, 2006; M. Brown, Boyle, & Boyle, 2000; Burnett, 2007; Goker, 2006; Parmigiani, 2012). In addition, research is also starting to point to the role teachers want to play in school management processes. The more decisions were perceived as directly affecting students and teachers, the more they should be involved in the decision making process (Jasmin-Olga & Chatziioannidis, 2013).

Understanding and Responding to the Larger Societal Context

"The principal understands and responds appropriately to the political, social, economic, legal and cultural contexts impacting the school" (Alberta Education, 2009, p. 6).

In this final *Competency* we are reminded that the school and the community context matters, influencing the role of the principal, and in turn being influenced by the principal.[12]

The first *Descriptor* states that the "principal advocates for the needs and interests of children and youth" (Alberta Education, 2009, p. 6). Often in the literature this item is defined in terms of the principal's role in relation to diversity issues. A number of researchers note the need to adopt a more receptive type of leadership to respond to the needs of students as their needs are identified. By responding in this way principals are "challenged to look beyond their own interests, values, and perspectives that might otherwise get in the way of achieving a mutually satisfying resolution to a problem" (Zaretsky, 2004, p. 283). In this regard, the disposition to accommodate practices that recognize diversity are often associated with passion, persistence, and commitment to social justice (Jacobson, 2011). In Canada, issues of ethnicity, race, language, religion, and sexual orientation often frame various perspectives on diversity.

"Knowledge of local, national, and global issues and trends related to education" (Alberta Education, 2009, p. 6) describe yet another set of dynamic contextual variables that principals need to understand and, if appropriate, respond to. Presumably, the framing of these issues requires some heavy lifting on the part of Ministry and districts as to long term trends of various types and how they may impact local schooling issues.

Embedded in this competency is a reference to the role of vision—the principal "assesses and responds to the unique and diverse community needs in the context of the school's vision and mission" (Alberta Education, 2009, p. 6). This usually involves the participation of parents and community members to ascertain what the needs are and how the school should respond to them (Johnson, 2007; Ladky & Peterson, 2008).

The final *Descriptor* speaks to advocacy. The principal "advocates for the community's support of the school and the larger education system" (Alberta Education, 2009, p. 6). This item highlights the external influence of the principal. This competency encourages the principal to help shape parent and community views about education and the role it plays in shaping public perception. Khalifa (2012) notes that the principal's

---

12   See Biyd, 1985; Boyd, 1992; Goldring, Huff, May, & Camburn, 2008; Klar & Brewer, 2013; ten Bruggencate et al., 2012; Walker & Shuangye, 2007.

role of community leader, when coupled with high visibility within the community and advocacy for community causes, leads to trust and rapport between the school and community.

Riehl (2008) makes the point that schools are serving a more heterogeneous student population now than ever before. Reihl drew in normative, empirical, and critical literatures to review the role of principals in responding to the needs of diverse students. Three tasks were highlighted: fostering new meanings about diversity, promoting inclusive school cultures and instructional programs, and building relationships between schools and communities.

Concluding Statement

The literature documented in this analysis support the seven competencies of leadership found in *The Principal Quality Practice Guideline: Promoting Successful School Leadership in Alberta* (Alberta Education, 2009). The sources cited above are by no means exhaustive, but we do think that they provide a sturdy foundation to enrich understandings about how the competencies are grounded in empirical research and the big ideas, concepts, and strategies from the field of educational leadership. As such, for the purposes of this study, they provide a theoretical framework that structured our conversations with the ten principals in our interviews. Finally, we will return to some of this literature when we examine the narratives of the principals as to how they enacted the competencies in their own contexts. These enactments, or espoused practices, we would argue, are grounded in defensible theories of action.

REFERENCES

Adams, J. P. (1999). Good principals, good schools. *Thrust for Educational Leadership, 29*(1), 8.

Adelman, H., & Taylor, L. (2005). *The school leader's guide to student learning supports: New directions for addressing barriers to learning.* Thousand Oaks, CA: Corwin.

Aitken, E. N. (2009). Effective leadership and assessment working together for school improvement: Hitching the horse to the cart. *International Journal of Learning, 16*(3), 151-165.

Alberta Education. (2009). *Principal quality practice guideline: Promoting successful school leadership in Alberta*. (LB2831.926.C2 A333 2009). Edmonton, AB: Alberta Education. Retrieved from http://education.alberta.ca/admin/resources.aspx

Alberta Education. (2011). Alberta Education: Action Agenda 2011-2014 (p. 20). Edmonton, AB.

Alberta Education. (2012). *Accountability pillar fact sheet*. Edmonton, AB: Government of Alberta. Retrieved from http://education.alberta.ca/admin/funding/accountability.aspx

Aydin, A., Sarier, Y., & Usyal, S. (2013). The effect of school principals' leadership styles on teachers' organizational commitment and job satisfaction. *Educational Sciences: Theory & Practice, 13*(2), 806-811.

Bandura, A. (1993). Perceived Self-Efficacy in Cognitive Development and Functioning. *Educational Psychologist, 28*(2), 117.

Barnes, C., Camburn, E., Sanders, B., & Sebastion, J. (2010). Developing instructional leaders: Using mixed methods to explore the black box of planned change in principals' professional practice. *Educational Administration Quarterly, 46*(2), 242-252. doi: 10.1177/1094670510361748

Bedard, G., Mombourquette, C., & Aitken, A. (2013). Calgary Catholic School District. In J. Brandon, P. Hanna, & K. Rhyason (Eds.), *Vision in action: Seven approaches to school system success* (pp. 165-231). Edmonton, AB: College of Alberta School Superintendents.

Bennis, W., & Nanus, B. (1985). *Leaders: The strategies for taking charge*. New York, NY: Harper & Row.

Biyd, V. (1985). *School context: Bridge or barrier to change*. Austin, TX: Southwest Educational Development Laboratory.

Black, P., & Wiliam, D. (2010). Inside the black box: Raising standards through classroom assessment. *Phi Delta Kappan, 91*(9), 81-90.

Blank, M. J., Melaville, A., & Shah, B. P. (2003). *Making the difference: Research and practice in community schools*. Washington, DC: Coalition for Community Schools.

Blase, J., & Blase, J. (1998). *Handbook of instructional leadership: How really good principals promote teaching and learning*. Thousand Oaks, CA: Corwin Press.

Bloom, C. M., & Owens, E. W. (2013). Principals' perception of influence on factors affecting student achievement in low- and high-achieving urban high schools. *Education and Urban Society, 45*(2), 208-233. doi: 10.1177/0013124511406916

Bottoms, G., & Schmidt-Davis, J. (2010). *The three essentials: Improving schools requires district vision, district and state support, and principal leadership* (pp. 1-53). Southern Regional Education Board.

Bowers, A. J. (2009). Reconsidering grades as data for decision making: more than just academic knowledge. *Journal of Educational Administration, 47*(5), 609-629. doi: http://dx.doi.org/10.1108/09578230910981080

Boyd, V. (1992). *School context: Bridge or barrier to change?* Austin, TX: Southwest Educational Development Laboratory.

Breiter, A., & Light, D. (2006). Data for school improvement: Factors for designing effective information systems to support decision-making in schools. *Journal of Educational Technology & Society, 9*(3), 206-217.

Brown, A. A., & Green, R. L. (2014). Practices used by nationally Blue Ribbon award winning principals to improve student achievement in high-poverty schools. *National Forum of Applied Educational Research Journal, 27*(1 & 2), 1-18.

Brown, K. M., Anfara, V. A., & Roney, K. (2004). Student achievement in high performing, suburban middle schools and low performing, urban middle schools: Plausible explanations for the differences. *Education and Urban Society, 36*(4), 428-456. doi: 10.1177/0013124504263339

Brown, M., Boyle, B., & Boyle, T. (2000). The shared management role of the head of department in English secondary schools. *Research in Education* (63), 1-33.

Bryk, A., Sebring, P., Allensworth, E., Luppescu, S., & Easton, J. (2010). *Organizing schools for improvement: Lessons from Chicago*. Chicago, IL: University of Chicago Press.

Burnett, E. (2007). Applying an holistic decision-making model to priorities in school reform. *Catalyst for Change, 35*(1), 30-42.

Camburn, E., Rowan, B., & Taylor, J. E. (2003). Distributed leadership in schools: The case of elementary schools adopting comprehensive school reform models. *Educational Evaluation and Policy Analysis, 25*(4), 347-373. doi: 10.3102/01623737025004347

Capper, C. A., Frattura, E., & Keyes, M. W. (2000). *Meeting the needs of students of all abilities: How leaders go beyond inclusion*. Thousand Oaks, CA: Corwin.

Chappuis, S., Chappuis, J., & Stiggins, R. (2009). Supporting teacher learning teams. *Educational Leadership, 66*(5), 56-60.

Copland, M. A. (2003). Leadership of inquiry: Building and sustaining capacity for school improvement. *Educational Evaluation and Policy Analysis, 25*(4), 375-395. doi: 10.3102/01623737025004375

Darling-Hammond, L., Meyerson, D., La Pointe, M., & Orr, M. T. (2009). *Preparing principals for a changing world*. Boston, MA: Pearson.

Datnow, A., Park, V., & Wohlstetter, P. (2007). *Achieving with data* (pp. 1-84). Los Angeles, CA: Center on Educational Governance.

Deal, T. E., & Peterson, K. D. (2009). *Shaping school culture* (2nd ed.). San Francisco, CA: Jossey-Bass.

DeVito, P. J., & Thomas, B. F. I. (2010). *The oversight of state standards and assessment programs: Perspectives from a former state assessment director*. Thomas B. Fordham Institute.

Dewey, J. (1959). *Dewey on education*. New York, NY: Teachers College.

Doll, B., & Lyon, M. (1988). Risk and resilience: Implications for the delivery of educational and mental health services in schools. *School Psychology Review, 27*(1), 348-363.

Donaldson, M. L. (2013). Principals' approaches to cultivating teacher effectiveness: Constraints and opportunities in hiring, assigning, evaluating, and developing teachers. *Educational Administration Quarterly*. doi: 10.1177/0013161x13485961

DuFour, R., & Eaker, R. (1998). *Professional learning communities at work: Best practices for enhancing student achievement*. Bloomington, IN: NES.

Duncan, H. E., & Stock, M. J. (2010). Mentoring and coaching rural school leaders: What do they need? *Mentoring & Tutoring: Partnership in Learning, 18*(3), 293-311. doi: 10.1080/13611267.2010.492947

Education Act, Statutes of Alberta, 2012 Chapter E-0.3 Stat. 171 (2012 Retrieved April 29, 2013).

Elfers, A., & Stritikus, T. (2013). How school and district leaders support classroom teachers' work with English Language Learners. *Educational Administration Quarterly, 20*(10), 1-40. doi: 10.1177/0013161X13492797

Epstein, J. L., & Sanders, M. G. (2006). Prospects for change: Preparing educators for school, family, and community partnerships. *Peabody Journal of Education, 81*(2), 81-120. doi: 10.1207/S15327930pje8102_5

Frick, W. C., Faircloth, S. C., & Little, K. S. (2013). Responding to the collective and individual "Best Interests of Students": Revisiting the tension between administrative practice and ethical imperatives in special education leadership. *Educational Administration Quarterly, 49*(2), 207-242. doi: 10.1177/0013161x12463230

Friedkin, N. E., & Slater, M. R. (1994). School leadership and performance: A social network approach. *Sociology of Education, 67*, 139-157.

Fullan, M. (2010). The awesome power of the principal. *Principal, 89*(4), 10-14.

Goddard, R., Tschannen-Moran, M., & Hoy, W. K. (2001). A multilevel examination of the distribution and effects of teacher trust in students and parents in urban elementary schools. *Elementary School Journal, 102*(1), 3-17.

Goddard, R. D. (2003). Relational networks, social trust, and norms: A social capital perspective on students' chances of academic success. *Educational Evaluation and Policy Analysis, 25*(1), 59.

Goker, S. (2006). Leading for learning: Reflective management in EFL schools. *Theory Into Practice, 45*(2), 187-196.

Goldring, E., Huff, J., May, H., & Camburn, E. (2008). School context and individual characteristics: What influences principal practice? *Journal of Educational Administration, 46*(3), 332-352. doi: http://dx.doi.org/10.1108/09578230810869275

Goodley, D. (2010). *Disability studies: An interdisciplinary introduction.* London: Sage.

Gordon, M. F., & Seashore Louis, K. (2009). Linking parent and community involvement with student achievement: comparing principal and teacher perceptions of stakeholder influence. *American Journal of Education, 116*(1), 1-31.

Griffin, S. W., & Green, R. L. (2013). Transforming high poverty, underperforming schools: practices, processes, and procedures. *National Forum of Applied Educational Research Journal, 26*(1-2), 77-93.

Gronn, P. (2002). Distributed leadership as a unit of analysis. *The Leadership Quarterly, 13*(4), 423-451. doi: http://dx.doi.org/10.1016/S1048-9843(02)00120-0

Gumus, S. (2013). The effects of teacher- and school-level factors on teachers' participation in professional development activities: The role of principal leadership. *Journal of International Education Research, 9*(4), 371-380.

Guskey, T. R. (2007). Multiple sources of evidence: An analysis of stakeholders' perceptions of various indicators of student learning. *Educational Measurement: Issues & Practice, 26*(1), 19-27. doi: 10.1111/j.1745-3992.2007.00085.x

Hallinger, P. (2005). Instructional leadership and the school principal: A passing fancy that refuses to fade away. *Leadership and Policy in Schools, 4*(3), 221-239. doi: 10.1080/15700760500244793

Hallinger, P., & Heck, R. (1996). Reassessing the principal's role in school effectiveness: A review of empirical research, 1980-1995. *Educational Administration Quarterly, 32*(1), 5-44. doi: 10.1177/0013161x96032001002

Hallinger, P., & Heck, R. (1997). Exploring the principal's contribution to school effectiveness. *School Effectiveness and School Improvement, 8*(4), 1-35.

Hallinger, P., & Heck, R. (2010a). Collaborative leadership and school improvement: Understanding the impact on school capacity and student learning. *School Leadership & Management, 30*(2), 95-110. doi: 10.1080/13632431003663214

Hallinger, P., & Heck, R. (2010b). Leadership for learning: Does collaborative leadership make a difference in school improvement? *Educational Management Administration & Leadership, 38,* 654-678. doi: 10.1177/1741143210379060

Hallinger, P., & Murphy, J. (1986). *Instructional leadership in effective schools.* (ED309535). ERIC database.

Halverson, R. (2010). School formative feedback systems. *Peabody Journal of Education, 85*(2), 130-146. doi: 10.1080/01619561003685270

Hansford, B., & Ehrich, L. (2005). The principalship: How significant is mentoring? *Journal of Educational Administration, 44*(1), 36–52.

Harris, A. (2012). Distributed leadership: Implications for the role of the principal. *The Journal of Management Development, 31*(1), 7-17. doi: 10.1108/02621711211190961

Hatch, T. (1998). How community action contributes to achievement. *Educational Leadership, 55*(8), 16-19.

Hattie, J. (2003). *Teachers make a difference: What is the research evidence?* Camberwell, AU: Australian Council for Educational Research.

Hattie, J. (2009). *Visible learning: A synsthesis of over 800 meta-analyses relating to achievement.* Oxon, UK: Routledge.

Hattie, J. (2012). *Visible learning for teachers: Maximizing impact on learning.* Abingdon, Oxon: Routledge.

Hays, P. S. (2013). Narrowing the gap: Three key dimensions of site-based leadership in four Boston charter public schools. *Education and Urban Society, 45*(1), 37-87. doi: 10.1177/0013124511404065

Heck, R., & Hallinger, P. (2009). Assessing the contribution of distributed leadership to school improvement and growth in math achievement. *American Educational Research Journal, 46,* 659-689. doi: 10.3102/0002831209340042

Henderson, A. T., & Mapp, K. L. (2002). *A new wave of evidence: The impact of school, family, and community connections on student achievement.* Austin, TX: Southwest Educational Development Lab.

Higgins-Norman, J., Goldrick, M., & Harrison , K. (2009). Pedagogy for diversity: Mediating between tradition and equality in schools. *International Journal of Children's Spirituality, 14*(4), 323-337.

Honig, M. (2012). District central office leadership as teaching: How central office administrators support principals' development as instructional leaders. *Educational Administration Quarterly, 48,* 733-774. doi: 10.1177/0013161X12443258

Horvat, E. M., Curci, J. D., & Partlow, M. C. (2010). Parents, principals, and power: A historical case study of "managing" parental involvement. *Journal of School Leadership, 20*(1), 702-722.

Jacobson, S. (2011). Leadership effects on student achievement and sustained school success. *International Journal of Educational Management, 25*(1), 33-44.

Jacobson, S. L., Brooks, S., Giles, C., Johnson, L., & Ylimaki, R. (2007). Successful leadership in three high-poverty urban elementary schools. *Leadership & Policy in Schools, 6*(4), 291-317. doi: 10.1080/15700760701431553

Jasmin-Olga, S., & Chatziioannidis, G. (2013). Teacher participation in decision making and its impact on school and teachers. *The International Journal of Educational Management, 27*(2), 170-183. doi: http://dx.doi.org/10.1108/09513541311297586

Johnson, L. (2007). Rethinking successful school leadership in challenging U.S. schools: Culturally responsive practices in school-community relationships. *International Studies in Educational Administration (Commonwealth Council for Educational Administration & Management (CCEAM)), 35*(3), 49-57.

Joint Advisory Committee. (1993). *Principles for fair student assessment practices for education in Canada.* Edmonton, AB: Joint Advisory Committee.

Keith, N. (1996). Can urban school reform and community development be joined? The potential of community schools. *Education and Urban Society, 28*(1), 237-268.

Khalifa, M. (2012). A re-new-ed paradigm in successful urban school leadership: Principal as community leader. *Educational Administration Quarterly, 48*(3), 424-467. doi: 10.1177/0013161X11432922

Klar, H. W., & Brewer, C. A. (2013). Successful leadership in high-needs schools: An examination of core leadership practices enacted in challenging contexts. *Educational Administration Quarterly, 49*(5), 768-808. doi: 10.1177/0013161x13482577

Knapp, M. S., Copland, M., & Swinnerton, J. A. (2007). Understanding the promise and dynamics of data-informed leadership. In P. A. Moss (Ed.), *Evidence and decision making. 106th yearbook of the National Society for the Study of Education: Part I* (pp. 74-104). Malden, MA: Blackwell.

Knapp, M. S., Copland, M. A., Honig, M. I., Plecki, M. L., & Portin, B. S. (2010). Urban renewal: The urban school leader takes on a new role. *Journal of Staff Development, 31*(2), 24-29,58.

Kutsyuruba, B., Walker, K., & Noonan, B. (2011). Restoring broken trust in the work of school principals. *ISEA, 39*(2), 81-95.

Ladky, M., & Peterson, S. (2008). Successful practices for immigrant parent involvement: An Ontario perspective. *Multicultural Perspectives, 10*(2), 82-89. doi: 10.1080/15210960801997932

Lalas, J. W., & Morgan, R. D. (2006). Training school leaders who will promote educational justice. *Educational Leadership and Administration, 18*(1), 21-34.

Lambert, L. (2005). Leadership for lasting reform. *Educational Leadership, 62*(5), 62-65.

Lapointe, P., Poirel, E., & Brassard, A. (2013). Beliefs and responsibilities of educational stakeholders concerning student success and effective principal leadership. *Canadian Journal of Educational Administration and Policy, 1*(142), 33-49.

Leithwood, K. (2009). *Closing the achievement gap: What successful school leaders know and do.* Toronto, ON: Ontario Ministry of Education.

Leithwood, K., Day, C., Sammons, P., Hopkins, D., & Harris, A. (2006). *Successful school leadership: What it is and how it influences pupil learning* (pp. 1-132). London, England: U.K. Department for Education and Skills.

Leithwood, K., & Jantzi, D. (1990). Transformational leadership: How principals can help reform school culture. *School Effectiveness & School Improvement, 1*(4), 249-280.

Leithwood, K., & Jantzi, D. (2005). A review of transformational school leadership research 1996-2005. *Leadership & Policy in Schools, 4*(3), 177-199. doi: 10.1080/15700760500244769

Leithwood, K., & Jantzi, D. (2008). Linking leadership to student learning: The contributions of leader efficacy. *Educational Administration Quarterly, 44*(4), 496-528. doi: 10.1177/0013161x08321501

Leithwood, K., Jantzi, D., & Steinbach, R. (1999). *Changing leadership for changing times*. Buckingham: Open University Press.

Leithwood, K., & Mascall, B. (2008). Collective leadership effects on student achievement. *Educational Administration Quarterly, 44*(4), 529-561. doi: 10.1177/0013161x08321221

Leithwood, K., Mascall, B., & Strauss, T. (Eds.). (2009). *Distributed leadership according to the evidence*. New York, NY: Routledge.

Lewis, A. (2008). *Add it up: Using research to improve education and minority rights*. Washington, DC: Poverty and Race Research Action Council.

Luo, M. (2008). Structural equation modeling for high school principals' data-driven decision making: An analysis of information use environments. *Educational Administration Quarterly, 44*(5), 603-634.

Marynowski, R. (2013). *Formative Assessment in High School Mathematics Classrooms*. Edmonton, AB: Alberta Assessment Consortium.

Marzano, R., Waters, T., & McNulty, B. (2005). *School leadership that works: From research to results*. Alexandria, VA: Association for Supervision and Curriculum Development.

Mason, B., Mason, D., Mendez, M., Nelsen, G., & Orwig, R. (2005). Effects of top-down and bottom-up elementary school standards reform in an underperforming California district. *The Elementary School Journal, 105*(4), 353-376. doi: 10.1086/429947

May, H., & Supovitz, J. (2011). The scope of principal efforts to improve instruction. *Educational Administration Quarterly, 47*(2), 332-352. doi: 10.1177/0013161X10383411

Miller, T. (2013). Using large-scale assessment scores to determine student grades. *Canadian Journal of Education, 36*(3), 317-353.

Millican, J., & Bourner, T. (2011). Student-community engagement and the changing role and context of higher education. *Education + Training, 53*(2/3), 89-99.

Miron, L. F. (1997). *Resisting discrimination: Affirmative strategies for principals and teachers*. Thousand Oaks, CA: Corwin Press.

Mittler, P., & Mittler, P. J. (2000). *Working towards inclusive education: Social contexts*. New York, NY: Routledge.

Murphy, J. (2005). *Connecting teacher leadership and school improvement*. Thousand Oaks, CA: Corwin.

Murphy, J., Elliott, S. N., Goldring, E., & Porter, A. C. (2007). Leadership for learning: A research-based model and taxonomy of behaviors. *School Leadership & Management, 27*(2), 179-201. doi: 10.1080/13632430701237420

Murphy, J., Hallinger, P., & Heck, R. (2013). Leading via teacher evaluation: The case of the missing clothes. *Educational Researcher, 42*(6), 349-353. doi: 10.3102/0013189X13499625

Murphy, J., Smylie, M., Mayrowetz, D., & Seashore-Louis, K. (2009). The role of the principal in fostering the development of distributed leadership. *School Leadership & Management, 29*(2), 181-214. doi: 10.1080/13632430902775699

Naseer, A. S. (2011). Successful leadership practices of head teachers for school improvement. *Journal of Educational Administration, 49*(4), 414-432. doi: http://dx.doi.org/10.1108/09578231111146489

Nzinga-Johnson, S., Baker, J. A., & Aupperlee, J. (2009). Teacher-parent relationships and school involvement among racially and educationally diverse parents of kindergartners. *Elementary School Journal, 110*(1), 81-91.

Orr, M. T., & Orphanos, S. (2011). How graduate-level preparation influences the effectiveness of school leaders: A comparison of the outcomes of exemplary and conventional leadership preparation programs for principals. *Educational Administration Quarterly, 47*(1), 18-70. doi: 10.1177/0011000010378610

Parmigiani, D. (2012). Teachers and decision-making processes: An Italian exploratory study on individual and collaborative decisions. *Canadian Journal of Education, 35*(1), 171-186.

Pascopella, A. (2009). A superintendent's high expectations. *District Administration, 45*(5), 34-36.

Podsakoff, P. M., MacKenzie, S. B., Moorman, R. H., & Fetter, R. (1990). Transformational leader behaviors and their effects on followers' trust in leader, satisfaction, and organizational citizenship behaviors. *The Leadership Quarterly, 1*(2), 107-142. doi: http://dx.doi.org/10.1016/1048-9843(90)90009-7

Printy, S. M., & Marks, H. M. (2006). Shared leadership for teacher and student learning. *Theory Into Practice, 45*(2), 125-132. doi: 10.1207/s15430421tip4502_4

Reynolds, A. J. (1999). Educational success in high-risk settings: Contributions of the Chicago Longitudinal Study. *Journal of School Psychology, 37*(4), 345-354. doi: http://dx.doi.org/10.1016/S0022-4405(99)00025-4

Richmond, G., & Manokore, V. (2011). Identifying elements critical for functional and sustainable professional learning communities. *Science Education, 95*(3), 543-570. doi: 10.1002/sce.20430

Riehl, C. (2000). The principal's role in creating inclusive schools for diverse students: A review of normative, empirical, and clinical literature on the practice of educational administration. *Review of Educational Research, 70*(1), 55-81. doi: 10.3102/00346543070001055

Riehl, C. (2008). The principal's role in creating inclusive schools for diverse students: A review of normative, empirical, and critical literature on the practice of educational administration. *Journal of Education, 189*(1/2), 183-197.

Roth, J., Brooks-Gunn, J., Murray, L., & Foster, W. (1998). Promoting healthy adolescents: Synthesis of youth development program evaluations. *Journal of Research on Adolescence, 8*(1), 423-259.

Sabin, S. (2011). The relationship between instructional leadership style and school culture. *Educational Sciences: Theory & Practice, 11*(4), 1920-1927.

Sackney, L., & Walker, K. (2006). Canadian perspectives on beginning principals: Their role in building capacity for learning communities. *Journal of Educational Administration, 44*(4), 341-358. doi: 10.1108/09578230610676578

Salisbury, C. L. (2006). Principals' perspectives on inclusive elementary schools. *Research & Practice for Persons with Severe Disabilities, 31*(1), 70-82.

Salisbury, C. L., & McGregor, G. (2002). The administrative climate and context of inclusive elementary schools. *Exceptional Children, 68*(2), 259.

Sammons, P., Gu, Q., Day, C., & Ko, J. (2010). Exploring the impact of school leadership on pupil outcomes. *International Journal of Educational Management, 24*(1), 83-101. doi: 10.1108/09513541111100134

Sanders, M. G. (2008). How parent liaisons can help bridge the home-school gap. *Journal of Educational Research, 101*(5), 287-298.

Schrum, L., & Levin, B. (2013). Leadership for twenty-first-century schools and student achievement: Lessons learned from three exemplary cases. *International Journal of Leadership in Education: Theory and Practice, 16*(3), 379-398.

Seashore-Louis, K., Dretzke, B., & Wahlstrom, K. (2010). How does leadership affect student achievement? Results from a national US survey. *School Effectiveness & School Improvement, 21*(3), 315-336. doi: 10.1080/09243453.2010.486586

Seashore-Louis, K., Leithwood, K., Wahlstrom, K., & Anderson, S. (2010). Investigating the links to improved student learning, *Learning from leadership project* (pp. 1-338). Minneapolis, MN: University of Minnesota.

Seashore-Louis, K., & Wahlstrom, K. (2011). Principals as cultural leaders. *Phi Delta Kappan, 92*(5), 52-56.

Silins, H., & Mulford, B. (2002). Leadership and school results. In K. Leithwood & P. Hallinger (Eds.), *Second handbook of educational leadership and administration* (pp. 561-612). Norwell, MA: Kluwer Press.

Somech, A. (2010). Participative decision making in schools: A mediating-moderating analytical framework for understanding school and teacher outcomes. *Educational Administration Quarterly, 46*(2), 174-209. doi: 10.1177/1094670510361745

Sommerville, D., & McDonald, S. (2002). *Developing school and community partnerships to meet the needs of students with challenging behaviors.* Arlington, VA: Council Exceptional Children.

Southworth, G. (2002). Instructional leadership in schools: Reflections and empirical evidence. *School Leadership & Management, 22*(1), 73-91.

Spillane, J., Halverson, R., & Diamond, J. B. (2001). Investigating school leadership practice: A distributed perspective. *Educational Researcher, 30*(3), 23-28. doi: 10.3102/0013189x030003023

Taylor, D., Tucker, P., Pounder, D., Crow, G., Orr, M. T., Mawhinney, H., & Young, M. (2012). The research base supporting the ELCC standards: Grounding leadership preparation & the educational leadership constituent council standards in empirical research. Charlottesville, VA: University Council for Educational Administration.

Teaching Profession Act, RSA 2000 Stat. 32 (2000).

ten Bruggencate, G., Luyten, H., Scheerens, J., & Sleegers, P. (2012). Modeling the influence of school leaders on student achievement: How can school leaders make a difference? *Educational Administration Quarterly, 48*(4), 699-732. doi: 10.1177/0013161x11436272

Timperley, H. (2011a). Knowledge and the leadership of learning. *Leadership and Policy in Schools, 10*, 145-170. doi: 10.1080/15700763.2011.557519

Timperley, H. (2011b). *Realizing the power of professional learning.* Maidenhead, England: Open University Press.

Timperley, H., Wilson, A., Barrar, H., & Fung, I. (2007). *Teacher professional learning and development: Best evidence synthesis iteration.* Wellington: Ministry of Education. Retrieved from http://www.minedu.govt.nz/goto/bestevidencesynthesis

Timperley, H., Wilson, A., & Fung, I. (2008). *Teacher professional learning and development.* In J. Brophy (Ed.), *Educational practices (2-31).* Brussels: International Academy of Education.

Tschannen-Moran, M. (2003). Transformational leadership and trust. In W. K. Hoy & C. Miskel (Eds.), *Studies in leading and organizing schools*. Charlotte, NC: Information Age.

Tschannen-Moran, M. (2009). Fostering teacher professionalism in schools: The role of leadership orientation and trust. *Educational Administration Quarterly, 45*(2), 217-247. doi: 10.1177/0013161x08330501

Turan, S., & Bektas, F. (2013). The relationship between school culture and leadership practices. *Egitim Arastirmalari-Eurasian Journal of Educational Research, 52*, 155-168.

Urick, A., & Bowers, A. J. (2014). What are the different types of principals across the United States? A latent class analysis of principal perception of leadership. *Educational Administration Quarterly, 50*(1), 96-134.

Viachou, A. (2004). Education and inclusive policy-making: Implications for research and practice. *International Journal of Inclusive Education, 81*(1), 3-21.

Wahlstrom, K. L., & Seashore-Louis, K. (2008). How teachers experience principal leadership: The roles of professional community, trust, efficacy, and shared responsibility. *Educational Administration Quarterly, 44*(4), 458-495. doi: 10.1177/0013161x08321502

Walker, A., & Shuangye, C. (2007). Leader authenticity in intercultural school contexts. *Educational Management Administration & Leadership, 35*(2), 185-204. doi: 10.1177/1741143207075388

Waters, T., Marzano, R., & McNulty, B. (2003). *Balanced Leadership: What 30 years of research tells us about the effect of leadership on student achievement*. Mid-Continent Research for Education and Learning, Website: http://www.mcrel.org

Webber, C., Aitken, N., Lupert, J., & Scott, S. (2009). The Alberta student assessment study: Final report. Edmonton, AB: Alberta Education.

Westley, H., & Mintzberg, F. (1989). Visionary leadership and strategic management. *Strategic Management Journal, 10*, 17-32.

Ylimaki, R. M. (2006). Toward a new conceptualization of vision in the work of educational leaders: Cases of the visionary archetype. *Educational Administration Quarterly, 42*(4), 620-651. doi: 10.1177/0013161x06290642

Young, C. Y., Austin, S. M., & Growe, R. (2013). Defining parental involvement: Perception of school administrators. *Education, 133*(3), 291-297.

Youngs, P. (2007). How elementary principals' beliefs and actions influence new teachers' experiences. *Educational Administration Quarterly, 43*(1), 101-137. doi: 10.1177/0013161x06293629

Youngs, P., & King, M. B. (2002). Principal leadership for professional development to build school capacity. *Educational Administration Quarterly, 38*(5), 643-670. doi: 10.1177/0013161x02239642

Zaretsky, L. (2004). Advocacy and administration: From conflict to collaboration. *Journal of Educational Administration, 42*(2), 270-286.

CHAPTER 3:
Methodology

The ability to act within professional practice is based on knowledge of a repertoire of cases. These cases are based either on personal experience or are model cases established within the profession. Case studies contribute to the building of a professional repertoire.

—R. Johansson, (2003, p. (4)14)

For this study we employed a multiple-case orientation that featured 10 different principals' accounts of how they enacted the *Professional Practice Competencies for School Leaders in Alberta*. This process allows for each case to be read on its own merits. Together, the case studies offer readers a holistic understanding (Yin, 2012). Yin offers that "case study research is not merely a variant of . . . other social science methods . . . [It] follows its own complete method" (p. 4).

For our face-to-face interviews we prepared a semi-structured protocol that featured specific questions around the seven competencies. As we advanced through the interviews we found that mentorship played a large role in the preparation of most of our principals, and mentorship remains potent in their present-day practices. So we added a question at the beginning of our protocol. In total, we conducted 27 interviews with principals located in southern, central and northern Alberta (averaging 1 to 1 ½ hours each), and the 10 selected for this book represented a variety of school organizational types (K-12), all in publicly funded education. As the cases demonstrate, we supplemented the protocol with additional probing questions throughout the interview process in order to stimulate clarification and nuance. A professional transcribing company transcribed each interview and we downloaded each of the texts. Before editing, each interview ranged from 17-25 single-spaced pages.

The principals selected for the book represented schools from a variety of contexts: rural, small town, medium sized city, and large urban. They also represent schools from a variety of contexts—relatively stable, to relatively unstable with large English Language Learner (ELL) populations and lower socio-economic status. In order to put the empirical basis of this study in a theoretical framework, we developed a concise literature review that supports the validity of the competencies as grounded in current theory.

As Yin (2012) explains, "no such formula exists" (p. 9) to determine the number of case studies that are adequate for purposes of explanation. We chose 10 cases that allow both for organization type comparison (e.g., elementary with elementary, high school with high school), and for a holistic perspective (the 10 cases together). In the analysis section we address each case and the holistic perspective. Reading each case allows the reader to independently reach a conclusion as to whether or not our discussion of patterns is, in the main, accurate and correct.

This study employed a triangulation of data. This triangulation came from the choice of principals nominated by the district superintendent; from documents on school achievement data as presented by the Fraser Institute, the C.D. Howe Institute, and Alberta Education's Accountability Pillar; from school visits, and, of course, from the interview data. The 17 interviews not contained in this account did serve as confirmation of the lived experiences of the 10 principals on whom we do report. We also solicited, as supporting evidence, additional documentation from principals about competency-based instruments they used in their practices, particularly with staff.

Yin (2012) describes two types of questions that are pertinent for case study methodology: a *descriptive* question—"What is happening or has happened?"—or an *explanatory* question—"How or why did something happen?" (p. 12). We think our study is a *hybrid* of both orientations. We not only describe principal behaviours in the context of the competencies, but we also have them explain why they have used these competencies in their practices despite that, as of this writing, they possess only a *Guideline* status.

The main research question in this study is: "How do experienced and successful principals enact the seven *Professional Practice Competencies for School Leaders in Alberta?*

- Sub-questions include:

- What roles does mentorship play in the preparation and development of these principals?
- How do the strategies for enactment compare when juxtaposed among similar and dissimilar school organizational types?
- To what degree are the competencies formalized within their school districts?
- How do principals account for leadership practices before *and* after the introduction of the *Guidelines* in 2009?

Principals and Schools Included in the Study

To gather participants in this study we first turned to school superintendents (in the case of First Nation schools we turned to education directors) to nominate principals they believed exemplary. We wanted principals who had served a minimum of five years in their positions and who demonstrated knowledge, skills, and attributes consistent with the competencies found within the *Professional Practice Competencies for School Leaders in Alberta*. In total, 11 school superintendents recommended 45 principals as possible candidates for inclusion in the study.

Prior to interviewing we looked at publicly available data to ascertain that indeed the principals were providing service that produced student growth in their school communities. We also wanted to ensure their service was not just indicative of a school in a high socio-economic community. We looked at data available in Accountability Pillar result reports available to the public on the Alberta Education website.[13] We looked at information available at the Fraser Institute to gain insight into where selected schools ranked within the Province of Alberta.[14] Then we looked at the C.D. Howe Institute rankings of schools based on student performance, using a factor to compare schools of similar socio-economic standing.

The final step in the process was selecting principals for inclusion in this book. We wanted to highlight principal experiences from across the broad spectrum of education in the Province of Alberta. To that end, we included principals from elementary schools, middle/junior high schools, and high schools. We also ensured that rural communities

---

13   See http://education.alberta.ca/admin/funding/accountability.aspx for further information.

14   See http://www.compareschoolrankings.org/Index.aspx?jid=AB.

(less than 10,000 people), small cities (10,000 to 100,000 people), and large urban communities (population greater than 100,000) (Reimer, 2006) were in the sample. In addition, we recognized the need to include the experiences of a principal in a school operated by a First Nation. First Nation schools do not have the wealth of jurisdictional supports one typically finds in provincially funded schools.

The principals in this study, with one exception, shared the experience of earning a Master of Education degree. The specialization routes they followed varied. In some cases the focus was on leadership, in others it was curriculum. Some identified school improvement, and in one case the degree was centred on the Alberta Initiative for School Improvement. Time spent in the principalship also varied, with one principal having 4 years of experience and another over 30. The average length of time as principal in a current school was nine years.

The following descriptions highlight the reasons we selected the 10 principals (4 female, 6 male) in this study.

Donald – Elementary K to 5

Just over 600 students attend Donald's school in Kindergarten through Grade 5. The school is almost 30 years old. Donald's school is located in a public school division in a small city. Average household income in 2011 was $76,816, while median income was $62,298. Alberta's average income was $100,819, and median income $78,632 (Economic Development Lethbridge, 2014). The C.D. Howe Institute ranked the school in the top 50% of schools of its type in 2013 (Johnson, 2013)[15], with actual academic performance significantly higher than estimated based on parental income, parental education level, and various other economic factors.

Timothy – Elementary K to 6

---

15   Through the *Signposts of Success* series David Johnson and the C.D. Howe Institute developed a mechanism to rank schools after accounting for socio-economic circumstance. For a complete description of methodology used to rank schools please see: Johnson, David, 2013, Identifying Alberta's Best Schools, C.D. Howe Institute E-Brief 164, http://www.cdhowe.org/pdf/e-brief_164.pdf.

With a student population of roughly 250, this school is one of the smaller entities in our study. "Small in size but great in deed" could very well be the school's motto. Even though the C.D. Howe data indicated the school should be in the bottom third of elementary schools in the province, it is actually listed as one of Alberta's best schools. Students far exceed expected outcome levels on Provincial Achievement Tests. Located in an area of Alberta best described as rural, this school is also listed as one of the top elementary schools according to Fraser Institute data.

Steven – Elementary K to 6

Steven's school is also located in a rural part of Alberta. Like Timothy's school this one has a population of roughly 300 students in Kindergarten through Grade 6. However, unlike Timothy's, this school did not fare well on the Fraser Institute Report on Elementary Schools in Alberta. What allowed this school to be included in the book was the fact the C.D. Howe data indicated that the school should be in the bottom third of elementary schools, yet it had a ranking that far exceeded that estimate. In other words, it punched well above its weight. Through the efforts of the staff and leadership of the principal, students that socio-economic factors indicated might have poorer academic performance produced much better results on Provincial Achievement Tests.

Ellen – Elementary K to 6 (FNMI School)

In the Province of Alberta, First Nation school authorities get to choose whether to participate in Provincial Achievement Tests. In this school they do participate. However, their results are not factored into Alberta results, nor do groups like the Fraser Institute or the C.D. Howe Institute have access to them. First Nation schools don't participate in the Accountability Pillar process used by the Province of Alberta to provide feedback from various publics and provincial assessments of learning to schools on their performance. We selected this school for inclusion in the study because of our access to its Provincial Achievement Test results as well as various data we obtained related to items like student daily attendance, parent survey data, teacher feedback, and standardized test results when compared to other First Nation schools for which we also had data access. Even though this school exists in a First Nation still recovering from the legacy of residential schools, and suffering from social ills like gang activity, alcoholism, and low employment, the school exists as a beacon of welcome, support, and significant student achievement results.

Joan – Elementary K to 9

Joan's school has over 600 students enrolled in Kindergarten through Grade 9. School data indicate it has one of the highest ELL populations in the large urban community within which it is located. Roughly 47% of the school population speaks a language other than English as a first language of the home. In the Fraser Report ranking it is placed in the bottom third of Alberta's elementary schools. However, C.D. Howe rankings note that the academic performance of students far exceeds estimated levels based on language spoken at home, parent income, and parent educational background.

James – Middle School 6 to 9

Just celebrating its 10th anniversary, this small city middle school is one of the newer schools included in the study. Over 500 students attend Grades 6 through 9. The school offers a middle school experience enhanced with a number of athletic academies. As the Fraser Institute only ranks schools if they offer both Grade 3 and Grade 6 (based on the Provincial Achievement Tests) they did not rank this school. In the C.D. Howe Institute ranking it was estimated this school would have results well below the provincial norm. In reality, the students far exceeded expectations, and their results placed the school in the top 25% of schools in their category.

Katherine – Middle School 6 to 8

Katherine's school is located in rural Alberta, with 350 students enrolled in Grades 6, 7, and 8. Grade 6 Provincial Achievement Test results, at both the acceptable and the excellent levels, far exceed those of the Province of Alberta. The C.D. Howe Institute data indicate that the socio-economic standing of the school is low. However, the same data also indicate the school results are better than what could be expected. In this school's case, items like parent involvement, student citizenship, work preparation efforts, and stakeholder belief in the quality of education at the school are all rated as excellent in the Accountability Pillar data from the Province of Alberta.

We have included three high schools in the study: one from a rural area, one from a small city, and one from the largest urban area in Alberta. Like their elementary and middle school counterparts, these schools represent a cross-section of students with a disproportionate number of lower income and/or ELL students. They also have a parent population with a lower than average income level as compared to some of the surrounding areas. Of particular note for this study is that they also have better than average academic results, as evidenced by student performance on Provincial Diploma Exams and positive data associated with items taken from the Accountability Pillar data. Unfortunately, the C.D. Howe Institute does not rank high schools, so their comparative type data are not available for this category of school.

Thomas – High School 7 to 12

Two hundred and eighty students attend this school, with roughly half in Grades 7 through 9 and the other half in Grades 10 through 12. Accountability Pillar results for this school are almost all in the excellent category. Fraser Institute data indicates that average parent income is in the $50,000 range. This income level would ordinarily indicate a school ranking in the bottom 20%. However, the Fraser Report rank places the school in the top 25% of high schools in Alberta.

John – High School 9 to 12

This high school is the second largest in the study, with just over 1200 students attending Grades 9 through 12. The school is located in one of Alberta's small cities. The Fraser Institute rates school performance as average. Accountability data indicates healthy stakeholder support for the school and reasonable student achievement.

Mary – High School 10 to 12

Over 30% of the students at this school are ELL, 11% are listed as special education, and parental income is in the $50,000 range. Fraser Institute rankings indicate that students in this school would not come close to hitting provincial averages on Diploma Exams, based on the proportion who do not speak English as a first language, the number involved in some aspect of the special education program, and a low median income. At this school, however, students outperform expected results. Parents, students, and teachers rate the overall quality of education at the school to be high, and they are collectively pleased with school performance.

We believe that the modified case study methodology proposed by Yin (2012) provided an appropriate and useful methodology around which we organized our research, interviews, and data interpretations. We had school superintendents recommend high-achieving school principals for inclusion in the study. By looking at publicly available data through the Fraser Institute Report, C.D. Howe Report, and the Accountability Pillar we selected 10 schools for inclusion in our study. We hope with this study to provide the reader with insights into how the principals in the sample attended to the demands inherent in the *Professional Practice Competencies for School Leaders in Alberta*.

REFERENCES

Economic Development Lethbridge. (2014). ChooseLethbridge. Retrieved from http://chooselethbridge.ca/business/income.php

Johansson, R. (2003, September). Case study methodology. *Methodologies in housing research.* Symposium conducted at the meeting of the Royal Institute of Technology in cooperation with the International Association of People–Environment Studies. Stockholm, Sweden.

Johnson, D. (2013) Identifying Alberta's Best Schools. *Signposts of Success.* Toronto, ON: C.D. Howe Institute.

Reimer, W. (2006). The rural context of community development in Canada. *Journal of Rural and Community Development, 1,* 155-175.

Yin, R. K. (2012). *Applications of case study research* (3rd ed.). San Francisco: SAGE.

CHAPTER 4:

Interview:
Kindergarten to Grade 5
School Principal

Donald, an elementary school principal, has spent 29 years as a teacher and 13 as a school leader, nine in his present school. The school has 573 students and 28 teachers in Kindergarten through Grade 5. He completed his Master's in curriculum/leadership in 1996.

The interviewer (co-author) asks Donald about his mentorship and then proceeds to ask how he enacts each of the professional competencies.

Interviewer: What preparation did you receive prior to your first formal leadership position?

Donald: Actually very little. Our district has a leadership course that they offer on a biannual, every-second-year basis, and I was part of that. We had people from all employee groups as part of that course. It was a really good introduction to administration at the school level. I think the thing that really prepared me the most was my work with the ATA.[16] I was very involved on a local level with the EPC,[17] and with the negotiating subcommittee (NSC) and some of those sorts of things. But most specifically I was an ATA PD[18] facilitator. I was actually a PD consultant at first, and then they switched that role into a facilitator's role, and so we would literally be parachuted into different locals around the province and asked to guide teachers and administrators through different processes to achieve PD goals and work with specialist councils.

Interviewer: I am going to change tack just a little bit and ask about **mentorship**. What mentorship did you receive that you would say helped you in your journey of leadership?

Donald: Our district does have a somewhat informal mentorship program for administrators. When we have new administrators, they are paired up with a mentor at the same level, so if you're appointed as an assistant principal, then you would be assigned with another assistant principal, and that would be your go-to person for all those dumb questions that maybe you don't feel comfortable asking other people. But beyond that our district really has not done a lot in terms of the area of mentorship for administrators, and I think that that is something they are working towards.

I know that they've expanded the mentorship program for teachers, to not just one year or two years, but for the first five years of teaching, and I see that as a real positive thing. I mean I've been at this for many, many years, and there isn't a single day that goes by that I don't say to myself, "hmm, never had to deal with that one before," and so you know that continuous growth, the lifelong learning, it doesn't stop, it keeps on going, and so I see value in the mentorship, whether it's formal or informal.

Right now I've got my colleagues. We talk all the time and they are calling on me just as much as I'm calling them, and it's a good relationship. It's nice to have because there are many issues and things that we deal with on the administrators'

---

16   ATA – The Alberta Teachers Association. The ATA is the professional organization in which teachers and school principals are members.

17   EPC – Economic Policy Committee of the ATA. This group formulates the initial negotiating position of the ATA Local contract talks with the respective school division.

18   PD – Professional Development.

level I just can't share with everybody. But I feel confident in sharing it in confidence with my colleagues that are at the same sort of space that I'm at.

Interviewer: And when you say colleague, in this case, [do you mean] other elementary school principals?

Donald: Yes.

Interviewer: Within your district, or do you go more provincial than that?

Donald: No. Mostly in district. Those are the people that I know and trust the most.

Interviewer: Do you find that version of mentorship helpful? Or at this stage in a long career, would you have said I want something more?

Donald: Well, I wouldn't say helpful; I would say invaluable. The support that I get from colleagues is so important. Would I want something more? I think that that would be a real nice model of professional growth for administrators to have some more formalized structured approaches to the mentorship, so that we could examine societal issues, educational issues that are beyond the scope of what we live each and every day, but we're looking at things in Canada, US, globally. I would be very interested in something like that.

Interviewer: In your district, what, if any, use has been made of the **principal leadership competencies** in identifying potential leaders and preparing them for a leadership path?

Donald: Very interesting you ask that, because I'm not sure, in terms of the selection process, how much attention is paid towards the leadership competencies. I do know that I was just in a position where I have been given a second assistant principal for the fall, and so we just interviewed and shortlisted and all that kind of process . . . but at no time did we get together and talk about the competencies, so it may have been part of the process at the executive council level for example, I don't know. But certainly from my perspective, where I talk to my staff, we did develop a profile of someone, qualities of a leader that we felt we needed here. Maybe there's just an assumption that people that apply for a principalship or assistant principalship just come with those competencies, and I'm not sure that that's the right assumption to make.

Interviewer: But yet your district, if I am not mistaken, was either the first, or would have been within the first three, that moved towards the competencies as part of the supervision and evaluation process?

Donald: Absolutely.

Interviewer: Can you speak to what is involved there?

Donald: Well, certainly all administrators are aware of the principal competencies and what is involved when we are given perhaps a one-year appointment when we first start out, and then it becomes a three-year appointment or a five-year appointment. When we go through that process of evaluation, those competencies are front and centre, and that provides the structure for the observations, and the interviews that take place with the staff, and parents, and all the rest of it. So in the evaluation component I see that the competencies are front and centre, it's just . . . when I was responding earlier, in the hiring of people, I wasn't sure.

Interviewer: What about in your own supervision, as being a well-tenured principal with a very good reputation in the community? What evidence of competencies do you have to present now, or do you have to present that evidence to anyone?

Donald: I don't. There's no formal structure that says on an annual basis I need to provide evidence that I am meeting the competencies. Every school in our district is assigned an executive council liaison, and this year it happens to be the superintendent of schools that is working with me. He is here on a fairly regular basis, just touching base, looking at how are things going and that kind of thing. The visits, I guess, gets the central office staff out into the schools, and that's part of their supervision component. However, in terms of a formal process, once every five years is when I go through that process of evaluation and affirmation where they can say, Donald, you must be doing an okay job, things are going all right.

The only other piece that I might add is that every year we do meet with executive council. When I say we, I mean our admin team meets with our executive council to go over our annual plan, and that's the time where we get to celebrate some of the success of our school and share a little bit of our dream and some things that we are going to be doing in the future. And there is a document that goes with it, and so from that plan I guess they would get a little bit of a sense of how the school is progressing.

Interviewer: We will change tack again, and we will go to **vision**. In some respects, it is almost like presenting evidence of each of these competency areas. What is the vision of your school?

Donald: I think our vision is somewhat generic. If you were to go to any website of any school in town, you would see similar words. I think the important thing though is what does that vision mean to us as a staff? Our vision is that children need to do their best, they need to feel good about themselves, we need to get along, and we need to build a sense of community. So everybody has a part in a child's education. We have goal statements that support the vision, but again those are somewhat apple-pie type statements. The important thing for me as a leader of the school is to get to the why part—not necessarily the what part, but the why part—and to make sure that everybody is on the same page, and we have that common language, common vocabulary. One of my pet words these days is alignment, so that everything we do in our school aligns with what we believe in. Staff or parents may disagree with some of the decisions that are made in this school, but they can never say that they don't understand why decisions are made.

Interviewer: Tell us how this alignment was created, when, [and] why. Talk about it from a historical perspective and bring us up to today.

Donald: When I first came to this school it was very different than from what it is today. Quite cliquey. Staff had been together for a long time. I would walk down the hallway and teachers wouldn't make eye contact with me. I would say good morning and there would be no response. That is where I started. And so when I came here there was that aspect. Oh, what's the new guy like? And how's the new guy going to respond in various situations?

I believe everything that we do in schools is about trust, and I needed to earn their trust, and that became really apparent to me whenever I switched schools. Whether it's in a leadership role or one of a teacher I had to prove myself all over again, and so it was during that first year with me at this school. I didn't rush into it, but during that first year we did a lot of talking, a lot of dreaming, a lot of visioning. And we actually did go through a formal process of what is it that we believe in, and what could that look like at this school. Then we discussed what sort of practices would have to align with our beliefs, and so we did go through that process. I put on my ATA PD facilitator hat and worked through a visioning process, and we arrived at the common vision a number of years ago. But each and every year we revisit it, and ask, "Is this still what we believe?" Things are changing around us, and does it still work, does it still meet the needs? This is always the bottom line for us: does it still meet the needs of our students and their families?

Interviewer: How do you determine if the vision is still meeting your needs?

Donald: That's a tough one. I think much like teacher supervision: by collecting information from a variety of sources. So here I am trudging in from my car with two jugs of milk, and why? It's because this year—and I would never have believed based on past years—this year we started a breakfast program, because kids are coming to school not ready to learn. As a staff we talked about that. So what do we need to do? We needed something to give these guys energy, because it's not being done at home. We responded to the feedback that I'm certainly getting from staff, but also from parents, from students themselves. Some people would debate whether we should be listening to students at an elementary school level, but I think that they are quite often a forgotten voice in this. So we take all that information together and then blend it with a lot of reading, professional type reading, and paying attention to some of the things that are going on across the country, and make change. I think that we've done a really great job at our school of trying to keep ahead of things and being proactive as opposed to always being reactive. We do this by listening to parents, gathering information from various sources, and by paying attention to what the students have to say. We also the same process when reviewing our vision and making sure it is still meeting the needs of the students.

Interviewer: Tell us about a couple of actions you took to blend this vision into the practices of the school.

Donald: In the last couple of years we talked a lot about inclusive education, and we talked in our vision statement about wanting to meet the needs of all of our learners, not just some of our learners. So how is our Inclusive Ed model—or Special Ed model, or whatever you want to call that—how does that reflect our overall vision, and what can it look like? Of course that has staff implications. It has time tabling implications. It has lots of implications that impact the daily life of the school. So the Inclusive Ed model would be one example of blending vision and practices.

  We have an Inclusive Ed committee at our school. Each year we reinvestigate the whole model. I don't mean we scratch everything that we have done in the past, but we always ask ourselves the question, like any good teacher would: What can we do better? How can we better meet the needs of the kids? We involve lots of staff input, parental input—which sometimes is a little bit of a delicate matter—but trying to get as much input as we can to make things good for kids, but again aligning with our school vision. Another example is our AISI[19] cycle, we are just beginning a brand new cycle of AISI, and so we are talking a lot about student engagement and having the students become owners of their own learning, and how we can facilitate that. Does that mean that the role of the teacher and the role of parent, and the role of administrator, and all the support staff is changing? We think so. We see the change as having the student as the driver, as opposed to just the passenger in the car.

And so all of those things we're trying to align, all of those aspects of our school [we're trying] to fit with our vision, but involving lots of people. My main goal, though, is to be the conduit, to be the facilitator, to make sure that everybody is talking the same language.

Interviewer: Expand on that a little bit.

Donald: Well, I think that everybody needs to know exactly what that "vision" means. And they probably get tired of me saying this, but every decision that is made at this school is about kids, and what best meets the needs of kids. Sometimes there is a conflict there, because what is best for kids may not be the best for the staff members. It might mean they need to come in a little earlier, or they have to stay a little bit later, or something like that. And obviously there are rules that need to be adhered to. But people always need to be reminded what is best for kids. It is funny; I start talking that way and pretty soon I don't really have to say it because everybody else is saying it for me, and I think it's important that everybody is on that same philosophical base. Yes, so that is my role.

Interviewer: You alluded to the use of data already, but what role does data play in the accomplishment of the vision of the school? If you can, give us some concrete examples of the types of data that you and your staff would look at.

Donald: Well, certainly you know most schools would say the most common form of data they would use are the PAT[20] results. Schools would use them to analyze the achievement of their students. At our school, while we are an extremely

---

19   AISI – Alberta Initiative for School Improvement. AISI was a funded program of Alberta Education where school districts and schools could try out innovative student learning projects. AISI funding was cancelled in 2013.

20   PAT – Provincial Achievement Tests. The PATs are Alberta Education mandated student assessments written in Grades 3, 6, and 9. These tests are based on various Alberta Programs of Study.

high-achieving school, I don't think it has anything to do with PATs. I think it has everything to do with relationships built with kids.

Interviewer: But you do pay attention to the PAT result?

Donald: Oh, absolutely.

Interviewer: And then you would have committees that would analyze them?

Donald: Yes, we sure do. We have our Grade 3 teachers actually taking the lead there, but it's not just a Grade 3 issue; it's an entire school issue. And then we work through a process of looking at the data and asking: What is this telling us? And we are not looking at small things; we are looking at trends, themes, [and] things that jump out at us.

Our school district is now using a *Tell Them From Me* survey,[21] and so this year we are collecting data from our staff, and next year it will be from our students with this survey. Questions like, do you think your teacher is caring about you? Do you feel comfortable sharing things? Do you have enough access in the library? How is technology working in this school? Questions like these are asked in the survey. There are also parental surveys that we have conducted in the past. We also pay attention to our Accountability Pillar results that we have yearly. That kind of data is very important to us. And largely that is directed by admin, and we involve teachers.

What is really exciting about our next cycle of AISI is that we are really getting into action research, and I am excited about it because that was the project that I did in 1996 when I was doing my Master's. Our school district has an umbrella project, and it is talking about student engagement, as a staff we went through quite a process to align our school project with the district's. It took us maybe two or three months to take that overall question that the district was contemplating and say, "okay, now what is a question that we can apply specifically to our school?" So that was the next layer. Recently the last layer was grade level teams. Because of the size of our school—we have five Grade 1 teachers, for example, and four Grade 2s and four Grade 3s—we have grade level teams, and . . . we structure our school around the grade level teams a lot.

---

21   For more information on the *Tell Them From Me* survey see:

http://ideas.education.alberta.ca/hsc/current-projects/tell-them-from-me/

Each grade level is comprising a PLC[22]—I may be jumping ahead a little bit, but those PLCs are now developing their own research questions that will fall under the umbrella of our *school's* research question, that falls underneath the umbrella of *the school district's* research question. And so, it is an action research project where there is a little bit more formality to it, where we are developing smart goals and collecting data and then analyzing the data. We are also planning and implementing, revising, and going through that spiral—and so that's pretty exciting.

The key, though, is data. Data can be a kind of a dirty word to teachers, because it means something extra to classroom teachers who have 25 to 30 kids in front of them. Those teachers might say, "You want me to collect data?" However, my focus is on data that makes a difference . . . data are a really good thing because they actually affirm that what we are doing is making a difference, or what we're doing is not making a hill of beans difference. And if it's not, then we shouldn't be doing it. Why would we be wasting our time doing that? So the key though, from my standpoint, is to make the data collection and the analysis as simple as possible and as meaningful as possible, so that the teachers are actually feeling that there is value in it. If they don't soon see the value we're hooped.

Now, do I personally believe data are important? Absolutely. Many times—and you have probably had this situation as a principal—where a parent or a staff member will come in and say, "I think we have a problem," and then we say, "well, we can do this, or we can do that." We are very good at listing off a number of things that we can do to change it. And in the end maybe it wasn't that problem at all. Well, let's collect some data, so how many incidents have we had before classes start for example, or on the bus, or whatever the case . . . go to the data and the data might say, you know what? It may seem like it's a lot, but over the past year we have had just three incidences. Is that worth changing all these practices because of three incidences? So data can be a good thing. It can be kind of [a] freedom thing, I think.

Interviewer: I would like to go back to the vision. How do you communicate and celebrate school accomplishments so as to inspire people in your school?

Donald: I think that communicating and celebrating are items that I personally struggle with the most. I work very hard and I don't do it for accolades or the pat on

---

22   PLC – Professional Learning Community.

the back, and I have to remind myself that other people don't always see it that way, and I think that we do have to actually consciously carve out our time to celebrate, because we are very quick to add on, [but] we are not so quick to say "you are doing a great job here," and to affirm things. So when I think about celebrating successes, I think about including people, staff members in the dream. I think inclusion is really important, and to do whatever I can to encourage people to be as reflective as possible.

I am now surrounded by a group of teachers and staff members that are so reflective that they are always looking for better ways of doing things. If something goes wrong they become problem solvers rather than being complainers. I think that the key for me is to lead by example in that respect, and so enforce the belief that this is their school. It's not my school—it's their school. I say the same thing to my students, this is your school, you know you are a big part of what we do at this school. I think that that is really important. It should be front and centre in everything we do. What we have learned lately is to provide opportunities for our staff members to share at conferences, professional development opportunities they have been a part of, so they can share their excitement and their passion and all the rest.

Interviewer: And how do you do that?

Donald: Staff meetings, PD days. Quite often teachers will be using the email system to share articles and things like that, and our staff now has a book club. But they talk about professional practice, and isn't that cool that they're doing that outside of class? Certainly, the professional learning communities and getting dialogue started in these groups was important. People feel comfortable saying, you know, "we had an epic failure today in the classroom." We use this term a lot at our school. People are comfortable sharing these failures because we can learn. That is what we say to kids when they come into my office. You know, "do you think I'm a smart guy?" And if the kids say yes, I say that's because I have made so many mistakes, but I have learned from them, so you can learn from those too.

Creating that atmosphere of trust and risk taking, I think that's a big part of it too. I think also teachers by nature are not blow-horn type people. Creating that atmosphere where the trusting and the risk taking is important. Important for people to feel they can share the neat things that are happening in their classrooms, without feeling that they're blowing their horn, and they are being boastful about things; but instead, it is not that I am doing something better, it is just I am all fired up about this, and that enthusiasm is contagious. That is the environment that we are building.

Interviewer: Perfect. Let's move on to **fostering effective relationships**. So tell us about how you went about developing a positive working environment in the school. You alluded to a school culture as you took over as principal, which is not the school culture now. Can you work us through that evolution, please?

Donald: Yes. I started even before I came here as the principal. When I was hired, I worked with the superintendent at the board office, just as his assistant for a year, kind of as a district principalship role. And he called me into his office and he says, "I need to give you some advice before you start your role as principal at this school." He says, "I know you are a go-for-it type of guy, and you want changes, and you want changes now." That's just me—he had me pegged totally right. He then said, "So my advice is to not take things too quickly." I took that to heart, and when I got to the school I listened a lot. I had my assistant principal run the [first] staff meeting. I sat back and I just watched the dynamics. And from then on it was heavy relationship building, one on one, identifying those key staff members to kind of sow seeds.

I still sow seeds now, and I get people thinking about ideas in a very non-obtrusive way. And it's about trust, all about those relationships, and that takes time; time and consistency, and integrity, and knowing exactly why we made certain decisions. I think early on I made a real conscious, concerted effort to tell the "whys." I don't have to as much now because people know, but I think that that was a big part of it. I think valuing people, and saying, you know, you are amazing at what you do, and so I did a lot of that, and I still do a lot of that because that is important. People are doing great work. Can they do things better? Differently? Sure. But so can everybody—that is what continuing growth is all about.

Interviewer: Go a little deeper into that "why" business, because I think this is about the third or fourth time [you've] referred to it. I think there is a really important learning [point] if we can get at it. So, if we were in a meeting with a group of teachers, right now, and you were talking about the "why," what would that sound like? How do you bring a practical face to the "why" and make it real for the people in this building?

Donald: I always bring it back to the kids, and to me I describe the people in this school in terms of the importance. I always use an archery target, and I say, okay that bull's eye, that's where the kids are, and the next circle out, those are the classroom teachers, because they are the ones who really have an impact on the kids. And the third circle is where I put the caretakers, and the principal, and the secretaries, and all the support staff, and everyone to support the teachers who support the kids. And of course there is some direct support as well.

Interviewer: But along the way conflict would have happened?

Donald: Yes.

Interviewer: Could you relate for us, then, a story about [a] serious conflict that occurred during your leadership, and how you resolved it?

Donald: Sure. So early in my principalship I believed very strongly in sharing candidly with parents in terms of student achievement, and I had a teacher that believed very strongly that a mark was all he needed on a report card—no anecdotal comments at all. We only have a three-point scale, so when a child achieves a two, does that mean meeting grade level expectations? That's all that that document says. It doesn't really indicate how well the teacher knows my child, or the strengths that my child has, or areas that they need to improve in. So we talked a lot about that. Eventually, it went to the superintendent. The superintendent came in and we met, and you know, to this day, that teacher and I—he's now retired—are very close friends. And we talked about that all the time, on how that process was done with integrity, and right up front, and honestly, and he believed one thing and I believed another thing, and I think we did meet in the middle, and I'm okay with that.

Interviewer: What did that middle look like?

Donald: The middle looked like it wasn't certainly as in-depth as I would have liked, but it was a lot more than he would have liked.

Interviewer: He had anecdotal comments that ended up on the report card?

Donald: Yes, he sure did. But again, I'm a shoot from the hip, fairly direct type person, because that is the way I like people to treat me, and I think staff appreciate that. They know exactly where I stand on things, and so if conflict does arise, you know it surfaces at times, but we deal with it head on. But it always comes back to what is in the best interest of students at this school. And can we make it work for you? Absolutely. But I am not apologetic to say we need to make it work for those kids.

Interviewer: How do you demonstrate responsibility for all students and act in their best interest?

Donald: Well, I think that being really involved in the school and knowing what is going on—I think that is really important. I mentioned already I am in every classroom every day, and that takes time, but it pays off in spades.

Interviewer: We are probably going to get to this later, Donald, but describe for us what it looks like when you are in every classroom every day.

Donald: It might look different. Sometimes I will actually talk to the teacher, most of the time I won't—I am talking to students.

Interviewer: What are you looking for when you are talking to students?

Donald: It is more of a relationship thing. I ask students about their lives. So how was soccer, or hockey? That kind of thing. But it is also very much about them and their learning. How is your social studies, what are you learning, why do you think you're learning that? I'm very interested in that because I am a big believer in objectives for a lesson, and that everything we do has to have purpose, and I'm a big believer that the kids need to know what that purpose is, even when they are in Grades 1 and 2. As a staff we talked about posting objectives and making sure students know what they are going to learn. We have talked about "I can" statements, and so at the end of the lesson, an exit slip, or in an informal conversation, students should be able to say I can do this, so it's a relevancy for learning and things like that. So I guess the answer would be "it depends."

I have attended a number of sessions on what to look for to see if students are learning. I have also used walk-throughs as a means to record what I am seeing when I go through the classrooms. I have learned some interesting things when I went through the walk-through process. Last year I actually kind of picked on my Grade 2 team with a more formal process. I went in once a day for about three weeks. During the visits I gathered a variety of data, different categories and things like that. Themes emerged, and then I met with them as a group—didn't talk to them individually, met them as a group—and we had a great dialogue, just about teaching and some of the things that I have noticed. It might have been about relationships, it might have been in the curriculum area, the GLOs and the SLOs[23], and all that kind of thing. It might have been in the delivery of the lesson. So I guess

---

23   GLO – General learner objectives from the Alberta Program of Studies.

SLO – Specific learner objectives from the Alberta Program of Studies.

it really varies. I love teaching, and I am very interested in the practice of teaching and in the art of teaching, and I love those dialogues with teachers about teaching.

Interviewer: This is another aside but it still fits within the building relationship section—one of the criticisms of the whole classroom walk-through process is that it actually interferes with the relationship of principal and teacher, because of the checklist perception. There is even a language used in some schools where the walk-through is referred to as a drive-by shooting. So . . . for you, and it sounded like with meeting just with the Grade 2 teachers, it has turned into a positive aspect of relationship building?

Donald: Yes.

Interviewer: So how did you take something like a checklist and turn it into healthy relationship building?

Donald: Well, I think first of all, before I undertook a project like that, I had to have that good rapport with my staff, and that trusting, and , , , being able to take risks. I think I have that with my teachers. Before I visited their classrooms we talked about, "okay this is what I am going to do, so it might be a little daunting. I'm in there with my little clipboard with my sheet and all the rest, but this is the purpose of it. It is not to go in there and make judgements, it is to go in there and bring things to your attention." You know, as a teacher I would have very much welcomed you to come into my classroom and sit at the back, and say, you know, "can you just sort of just jot down if I am missing anybody in the questioning," or just [have] that extra set [of] eyes and ears in there to help me with my teaching. And in that situation that I described people were not bothered by it. They were curious.

I guess it is the competitive nature of people. In some cases I wondered if people were wanting me to compare them with others. But I wasn't there to do that. The bottom line was I just wanted to sow seeds around getting people to be reflective about their own practice. I have people that are reflective, because I hired most of them now, and they really do care about their practice, and they know that things change and they want to be changing with them.

Interviewer: So let's go to **leading a learning community**. Outline the process you follow to increase the level of student learning in your school.

Donald: Well, again, it is very much grade-level focused—based on terms of what grade level needs are, and what individual classroom needs are. PD is a funny thing, you know. If I was to say as a school we are going to work on assessment of learning, well, I have got eight teachers, then some will be here and some that are there, and everything in between, and it is hard to meet everybody's needs, and hence the grade level groupings. Kind of somewhat subversive on my part, because I want them to be cohesive at a grade level too, and it is also team building, but there are certain things that are somewhat grade specific, and that is the context for the team building to take place. And so encouraging them to look at their practice and say what can they do better, and to collaborate and get into each other's classrooms—I think that is really important.

Interviewer: How often would that occur, getting into each other's classrooms?

Donald: I would say it would depend on the grade level, but I will pick on my Grade 5 team. We have three teachers. I bet they are in each other's classrooms every day.

Interviewer: Just for a five-minute snippet, or to sit through an observation of how they are teaching a concept?

Donald: Not so much sitting in for an entire lesson, but they talk about their kids and they do some switching and so on. So they do a lot of talking about their kids. What they are starting to do though is access ATA funds for subs, which is a huge underutilized resource, to get in other classrooms to watch.

Interviewer: Other people within your school, within the district, or the province?

Donald: Within the school and within the district. They haven't gone outside of our school district, but the Grade 5 teachers have taken upon themselves to create a PLC, not only among themselves, but with the other Grade 5 teams in the other schools. So all three of those schools are now collaborating, and they have common activity days where they meet at another city school. They are really starting to get into the mode of collaboration, getting into people's classrooms. But the most important thing for me is just to have that great professional dialogue about teaching—not specific instances, or dealing with some minor discipline issue, or that kind of thing—it's more about teaching and what they can do differently, and trusting each other, that they are just there to support each other.

Interviewer: Do they meet during the day, or do they meet at four o'clock in the afternoon when all the kids are gone?

Donald: Yes, both.

Interviewer: Where do they get the time to do that?

Donald: We built in time with our AISI project to allow each of our grade levels to meet during the school day, once every three weeks, so they have some embedded

PLC time. A lot of it happens outside of school, though. Our Grade 2 group, for example, went to Whitefish [Montana] on the weekend together. Being from a family of teachers myself, I know that when you get people together and you start talking, I know what they're talking about. So there is a lot of professional growth going on in those sessions too. It happens both in school and out of school. One thing that we do struggle with is providing more time for teachers for that professional dialogue, within the school day, and having it more job-embedded. We know that to do it will obviously cost money. Next year we are changing a little bit in that every grade level will have six afternoons throughout the year that they can book subs and meet. They have six sessions throughout the year where they can determine when those might be, to work towards their research project, so we are trying our darnedest to free people up to collaborate. It gets a little more interesting when we get teams of five or six at a grade level because of the number of subs involved. The other thing that we are doing is with our learning support teachers. We have one and [a] half learning support teachers, and those teachers are involved in the teams as well, so they are working with every one of our grade level groupings around how to meet the needs of these kids.

Interviewer: So . . . and you've sort of answered this, but I will ask you again, see if you will take a different tack—How involved are teachers in the school in setting the professional development goals and sessions? Explain how this is done at the school.

Donald: We have five teachers on our AISI committee and they are our leaders in our school.

Interviewer: One per grade?

Donald: They represent different grade levels, yes, and we also have our PD committee. The AISI committee looks after the AISI project. For the overall professional development goals, the PD committee [looks] at topics and the areas that we are going to focus on in different school-based PD sessions, [and] the PD committee itself is going to look after the nuts and bolts of those days. And there is some crossover there between those two committees.

We also have support staff involved in our PD committee. Typically, PD for support staff is very minimal. In terms of the time that they're here and the things that we're asking these folks to do, it is really hard to provide PD for them because they are working with kids on the whole spectrum. In many cases little or no training is included, so we try to include them as much as possible.

My belief with professional development is that it won't work unless it is ongoing, unless there is buy-in, unless staff are directly involved, unless staff are providing input in terms of what they need. PD needs to meet a need. If I am sitting in here, in my office, with my door closed, saying this is what I think you guys all need, well I am sorry but that's not going to work. When it comes to the actual PD days and various sessions I am there, I am part of it. There are lots of things that can draw me away from participating in PD sessions, because there are lots of things to be done, but that is something I believe very strongly in. The vice-principal and I need to be part of those PD sessions, so that it is not do as I say, not as I do type thing. And we need to lead by example.

Interviewer: You have answered the question about professional community, but how would you facilitate meaningful parent involvement in the school community, and ensure that parents are informed about their child's learning and development?

Donald: Yes, the informing part is the easy part. We send newsletters home. We have our school council. Part of our school council is we have classroom reps. Our school council is very involved in our school. We have about 26 to 30 people each month who come to our school council meeting, and yes, trying to keep it within the two-hour limit is a challenge at times. But part of that structure at our school council is we have a class rep from the school council, for each classroom, and it is one of their roles to keep parents involved in terms of things that are going on at the school. Not only keeping them informed but also soliciting feedback. So that is a mechanism that we use to get parental input. I will be really honest, though: that is one of the things that we struggle with, and I am sure we are not alone, but certainly we struggle with engaging parents in a meaningful way with their children's education, without allowing them to call all the shots. In this day and age it is amazing how everybody is an expert, everybody knows how to run a school better than me, without necessarily keeping the best interest of all the students in mind, as opposed to their child's class. It is a little bit of [a] balancing act.

That is certainly something we have talked a lot about as staff in terms of student engagement, and the roles of all of the stakeholders. One thing that we are going to have next year as part of our AISI project is information/educational sessions for partners on how they can support their children. Some parents think supporting their child is to do the homework for them, then send it with their child or make the phone call and excuse their child from doing that homework. To me that is not the way it should be done, and so the question is how can we engage those parents? I haven't got the answer yet, [but] we are working towards that.

Interviewer: I am curious about you having classroom reps sitting on parent council and using it as a two-way communication mechanism. Has there been a change that has evolved in the school as a direct result of the feedback that a class rep received from parents and presented at school council?

Donald: It has been more like collecting the information, and if it pertains to the school council on fundraising or whatever the case is, they may take it and run with it. If it is more of an issue that is dealt with better by the staff, then I take it, and then I work with it. Have there been changes as a result of that, in our practice? Absolutely. Have they always been great changes? I'm not sure, but we certainly try to value that input and work with it.

Interviewer: **Providing instructional leadership,** tell us about how you see your role as the instructional leader of this school. What does that mean to you?

Donald: Everything that I have just talked about, I think that that is the role that I relish, that is the candy in my job. I love to do that. I love working with student teachers, and interns, young teachers, veteran teachers. I think a highlight for me is watching the veteran teachers take young teachers under their wing and share their expertise, and yet also are willing to learn alongside with them, and to have that open mind. I think that my role as the instructional leader is the most important role that I know. All that managerial stuff, it is something that needs to be done for sure, and it contributes to the instructional leadership in many respects. I do know that there are a lot of things that tend to pull me away from my role as an instructional leader, just because of time. There is only a fixed amount of time, and sometimes things that are right in front of my face, I need to deal with them, and take that time. I do that.

My instructional leadership is so important as I am the director of this school. Quite often the Grade 1s will ask me down to interview me for their social studies about what do I do in the school. I use the director of an orchestra as an example, or maybe Phil Jackson as the coach of the Chicago Bulls, back in the day. I look at our team and I see the strengths that they have, and say okay, I've got a Denis Rodman there, that's a little bit rough around the edges, but boy, can that guy rebound, and say okay, I've got a job for you. I look at how do I fit all those roles together to be successful for kids. I see that is my biggest role when it comes to instructional leadership—determining how can I put people in spots where they can be successful with kids. I need to be out there, I need to be visible, I need to be initiating conversations, and good conversations that encourage reflection, that encourage what is good teaching. And then I need to put the tools in people's hands, and so technology would be a prime example of that. I am maybe like any other guy. I like lots of technology and gizmos and things like that, but not because they are gizmos, but because they are good for kids, and it is another way, another tool that teachers can use to help kids. So yes. Support, support, support, but always-focused support. Not just support. Focused support on what is best for kids and for their learning.

Interviewer: And it carries over directly into the next question: How do you ensure that your teachers are actually following current pedagogy? How do you know?

Donald: That is a really good question, and I haven't done it this year, but I have in the past . . . actually taken the teacher quality standards—you know, the KSAs—and we've focused on one or two per staff meeting. And throughout the whole year we can get to all 16 or 17 of them, and what each might look like. We did this by breaking people up into groups, and so every staff meeting we have group discussions on the KSAs. I'm not a big meeting person, but I see value in that type of extended conversations. I would rather spend most of [the] time in a staff meeting talking about what we can do better for kids, as opposed to talking about the Christmas concert. Those items can be handled in different ways.

And so I think that keeping it on the agenda, keeping good teaching on the agenda, and what might that look like, is really good. I think that exposing our teachers to our supervision model and evaluation model of our school district, and this is what is required, it is not that I think any of you aren't accomplishing that, but let's be proactive and let's think about this, and you just need to know this is a professional responsibility of teachers. So I think the information piece is important, but the bigger piece is creating an environment, a culture, where people talk about what they do.

Interviewer: How do you ensure that student assessment and evaluation practices throughout the school are fair, appropriate, and balanced?

Donald: Same thing. Initiating the appropriate conversations. It always comes up in November, March, and June when we're doing report cards. I read every single report card that is issued at this school, every single time, so those report cards are due to me. I read through them, and not that I am not trusting, but because I want to know what is going on. I think assessment needs to be front and centre, and we talk a lot about consistency of assessment, particularly at the grade level. If we have a set of twins, and one is in one class, and one is in a different class, you know parents will come to me and ask, "How come they got a particular grade in one class and the twin got something different in the other?" So we talk a lot about grade level expectations at our school. We try to maintain that consistency. We have also talked a lot about articulation between grades, [which] gets a little bit harder, but for sure we want some consistency within a grade level and between grades when possible. Again, it is my role to just say, "Okay, it is that time of the year. We need to start talking about this. And by the way, if you are finding that in November you are struggling to come up with something to put on a report card, and you don't have any data to support your judgement on this child, something is wrong." So we talk about assessment for learning, and the need for ongoing assessment, and the need for these kids to be part of their assessment so students can be reflective learners.

Interviewer: Have your teachers within their grade level PLCs moved towards a common assessment scheme? For example, when they finish a social studies unit, all the Grade 5 teachers may give the same assessment instrument, whatever that might look like?

Donald: Yes, they sure have. I can't ask them to work harder, but I can ask them to work smarter. And so I get them to start divvying up the workload a little bit. They have been doing that. They have been developing the "I can" statements and informal authentic measures to collect information from students. They have been busy doing little things, like as a grade level buying those little individual whiteboards, so you can tell that they are thinking about assessment. Earlier this year we actually tackled this whole understanding by design [UbD] concept, and the result has been looking at things a little bit differently. Subtle changes, where we start with the program of studies and then we get to where we ask what is this going to look like in the end, and what is the assessment part, and then how are we going to get there? As opposed to, this is what the program of studies is, let's find a bunch of strategies and then at the end we might want to think about how we are going to assess this whole darn thing. So we have talked a lot about the understanding by design concept, backward design concept.

Interviewer: How far has that progressed? Would you say that your teachers holistically from Grade 1 to Grade 5 are using that as a design methodology, or is it sporadic?

Donald: I would say that our school as a whole is on-board with UbD, I think in terms philosophically, and I think that they are trying their best to work towards it. Are some teachers further along than others? Absolutely. But I think that with assessment, we have done a lot of work in our district AISI project over the last three years with differentiated instruction and assessment and learning in 21st century classrooms, and so those things are not foreign to our teachers. I think that we are well on the way in terms of how things are done, and that it is assessment that is driving much of our instructional program. The way teachers have tackled assessment tells me they know where we [are] going and that everything has a purpose, and that we are not doing things for something just for fun. I'm like anyone else, I like fun, but let's have some learning along the way. I will actually say things like that to our staff. I say, "I have no problem with having fun, but if you say why you did a particular lesson, well I thought it would be fun, well that is not good enough." Everybody should know why it was done and how it connects to student learning.

Interviewer: You are in the classroom often enough to pick up on that?

Donald: Absolutely.

Interviewer: How often do you see just the fun stuff on your breeze through the rooms?

Donald: I see it on a daily basis, but I also see kids that are engaged, and I see value in what they are doing. So, yes, when you say fun, fun just with no purpose—no. They are engaged and enjoying the learning. Seldom do I see fun with no purpose, but do I see kids very engaged, and I define "engagement" as different than "on task." "On task" is when the teacher is in the room and the kids are compliant; "engaged" is when the teacher can leave the room and the kids are still working, because they are so into the task, and they are wanting to do it because they are engaged. I see a lot of that.

Interviewer: We will go to the legal side again. What does supervision and evaluation look like in this school?

Donald: Absolutely. Well you know, as with any group of people, it doesn't matter about the organization. You have people that are here, and you have people that are there, and our job is to support everyone. Some folks down at one end of the continuum may need a little bit more direct support, and that is there. We might even see that there are certain standards that an individual is not meeting, and it's not that I want to, but it is my role to point those out. And we will support them, but I need to see some evidence of change. And so have I gone down that path before? Yes, I have. Am I undergoing that today? Yes, I am. Actually, I am having a real tough meeting with one of my teachers this afternoon, about that very thing. Is this the time of the year to do that? I have my doubts, but on the other hand it gives this teacher six weeks of this school year and all summer to kind of plan for the fall. Why am I doing that? Simple: to give this person an opportunity to succeed. The supervision and evaluation policy is in place in our school. It is different for each person though, and my role is to make everybody aware of it, and to come at it from a very supportive stance, as opposed to a punitive stance. I would never do that. I care too much about the people that are here.

Interviewer: But if a teacher doesn't meet the standard?

Donald: Then we will go down that formal process that our district has in place where there is a plan of remediation; there are very specific timelines, there are very specific expectations, and ultimately, if those expectations are not met, then that person will be terminated, I guess. I mean, worst-case scenario.

Interviewer: It is good to hear it is there, but hopefully you don't have to use it.

Donald: Yes.

Interviewer: **Developing and facilitating leadership** within this building—How do you as school leader identify and promote different types of leadership in the school, particularly teacher leadership?

Donald: Well, I gave you some examples of our AISI team and our Inclusive Ed team and so on. I'm all about building capacity, and I will be really honest, some of it is self-preservation. I can't do it all. I mean, I just have to get other people involved. I have had many opportunities in my teaching career to assume leadership roles at the school level, and I ran with those, and my administrators were—God bless them—they were so good about letting me have those opportunities, so building capacity is big for me, and trusting is big for me. I think though, that it is my role to sort of set the parameters of any group, or any initiative, to say that certainly anything within these parameters is great. If you are kind of getting near the edge you need to bring me in the loop and make sure it is okay, because there may be other things that are influenced by it. But yes, we have all kinds of teachers at our school doing all kinds of really cool things.

Interviewer: Internal to the grade level PLCs, who appoints the PLC leader?

Donald: They do, I don't. It is funny how that works, as the leaders just seem to emerge, and sometimes this is done by committee and sometimes we can see that there is a definite leader involved. I don't . . . I stay away from that. In my mind that might set that person up for a little bit of a tough time, knowing the person might be perceived as the "chosen one," because whenever there is a chosen one, there are also some people that are not the chosen ones. I am going to let them worry about that.

Interviewer: Besides you, who are the leaders in this building? Can you identify the roles that they play?

Donald: I have always treated my fellow administrator as a team member.

Interviewer: Give us some of the names of some of the long-term committees, and what would be some of these short-term committees?

Donald: Sure. A long term committee might be the social committee, the technology committee, fine arts committee; we need our ATA reps, we have our staff development committee, we have our learning support committee, spirit committee, people that are in charge of the art supplies and that kind of thing, the phys. ed., school promotions. The short term committee could be the PAT analysis committee, Remembrance Day assembly committee, the Christmas concert, education week. So more event-coordinated. Coordination of Arts Alive in the schools. We had an artist in residency program this year, [the] farewell and year-end assembly, the sports days that we have at the end of the year. So that kind of gives you a flavour as to some of them.

Interviewer: **Managing school operations**, key question: how does the budget for your school reflect the goals of your school?

Donald: Everything comes down to money, doesn't it? This year I am balancing a $3.8 million budget for our school; 96% of our budget goes towards staffing, so the 4% that remains is our operating budget. The biggest bill that we have in our operating budget is photocopy. Even with SMART Boards in every classroom, teachers are still photocopying a fair amount. The next largest budget line would be grade level budgets, and so it kind of goes back to what I was talking about before, we do a lot at the grade level. The Grade 1s, they know how much money they have, and it is based on a per student figure. I can't remember the exact dollar amount, but they might have $2,000/$3,000 to spend at their grade level. And in that amount would be any curriculum materials that they need, unless there is a major shift in curriculum and we all need textbooks. We have another budget line for textbooks, but curriculum materials, if they are going to go on any fieldtrips, if they need to have any bussing or anything like that. So basically, whatever they need at a grade level they decide. The decisions are made by consensus at the grade level to spend that money.

Interviewer: No carry-overs?

Donald: No carry-overs, unless there is a specific reason for it. Sometimes they need to pool their money for consecutive years. Then there is a carry-over. The intent of the money is to meet the needs of the children that we have in our grades now. So why would we wait until May to buy all our materials, when we only have a month of school left?

Interviewer: Larger society context—How do you advocate for the needs and interests of children and youth, generally speaking?

Donald: Well, that is a really hard one. Sometimes I think it helps when you are dealing with individual conflict, or situations that occur in a school, to realize that this isn't unique to this school. It is a societal thing, and some of the practices, policy, and practice that we have put in place at our school may be determined by what goes on in other schools. I mean, I guess the biggest example of that would be this whole lockdown thing. We didn't really know much about that until Columbine, and it has really changed our practice. That would be just one example of how something that happened a long ways away has influenced our practice. So I think that that is one of my roles, is to bring in that perspective, because I think a lot of times teachers will come at it from a classroom perspective. I will come at it from a school perspective, the superintendent comes at it from more of a district perspective, and I think that it is very helpful to have all those perspectives at the table to contribute to the overall mission and goals of our school. That is important.

CHAPTER 5:

Interview:
Kindergarten to Grade 6 School Principal

Timothy has a 34-year teaching career, with 31 of them as a school leader in various settings. He has been principal at his current small-town school for 22 years, with 240 students and 15 teachers. He completed his Master's in 1998.

The interviewer asked Timothy about what mentorship he received and proceeds to ask him how he enacts the competencies.

Interviewer: When you first became a principal, was there anyone who fulfilled the role in a formal way of **mentor**?

Timothy: Not really. The fellow that I was an assistant principal with was like a mentor, and he is actually a really good friend of mine. But it was a different era, it was a different time, and it was more of a top-down kind of a hierarchy that really did not mesh with my philosophy or my personality. So no, there really wasn't at that point in time.

Timothy: I have been asked to be a mentor more than once. Sometimes it has been a good experience, as long as the person whom I was mentoring was with it, wants to be part of it. I have had the experience where a new principal to the district has come, and it was a different superintendent, but was told by the superintendent that I was going to be his mentor.

That didn't work out too good. We didn't get to know each other. He didn't know me from anything. So that probably wasn't a good experience. A recent mentee was excellent. He was open to the things that I had to share, and I certainly was open to learning about things from a younger perspective as well. So it was more of a partnership, which is what I like to look at.

Interviewer: Would you consider that like a generational thing? Is the younger generation a little more receptive to the notion of mentorship? Or would you say it comes down to human qualities and attributes—or some combination thereof?

Timothy: The latter. I would say the latter.

Interviewer: Did you have to do anything from a structural sense to help make it a neat mentee-mentor relationship?

Timothy: Yes. Basically try to make it as relaxed and informal as possible, and so that we can just share with each other whatever our problems are. I guess that is the way I approach things.

Interviewer: Was there anything formal, say, from the school division where you would have to meet twice a month or—

Timothy: Yes.

Interviewer: What kind of guidelines did you have?

Timothy: So the guidelines were that we were given so many days—I think we were given three days—to actually have release time to meet with each other wherever we felt we wanted to. But as long as we followed the leadership competencies, and we related to what we were doing with the competencies, that was basically the only guideline. So we were pretty much free to approach it how we wanted to.

Interviewer: Of course that is an interesting comment as well—as long as it related to the competencies. So did the superintendent give you some guidelines to pay attention to in addition to the requirements of the competencies? How did that work?

Timothy: That is right. Each of us as principals sit down with the superintendent and go over what we want to work on for the year. And so we choose a dimension[24] and explain why we chose the dimension. The person who was my mentee would also meet with the superintendent, as he is also a principal. The superintendent would

---

24   Dimension – The word dimension is used interchangeably with the word competency.

then know which dimension the person was working on, and I would share what the mentee was working on with me.

The conversations that we had with the superintendent around the dimensions were very fascinating. These conversations around the competency document were led by the ATA.

Interviewer: So we will go into the competencies then. Timothy, tell me, what's the **vision** of your school?

Timothy: The vision of our school is based on the community school concept. We were designated as a community school when that program was in place, and we felt that it did so much for what we were trying to accomplish, we kept community in our name without the funding.

Basically what that has done for us, and our vision for our school, is that we want to make education as relevant as possible for students, and so we take the basic curriculum and we try and give it that practical aspect by involving the local community, whether it be the water for the sewer system for the Grade 4 science water unit. So that's part of it.

As far as our vision for our school is, it's basically—apart from the community school concept—ensuring that the students get the help that they need in a timely fashion, effective in a timely fashion. That would be our vision.

Interviewer: How was it created? When was it created? Why was that created?

Timothy: Basically just through discussions. When we have our meetings, we are always talking about kids and what they need, especially kids with special needs. The conversations drive what our professional development is to be. Really, that whole idea of getting the help for the kids in a timely and effective fashion came from our teacher assistants more than anything in those discussions, because they were working with some very challenging cases. So yes, special education I guess drove that vision.

Interviewer: And you feel that that aspect of the program has actually carried over right into what we might say would be the regular part of the program. Is the same focus there for kids who were not even coded in some way as special education?

Timothy: Oh, absolutely. It is the whole area of, you know, the pyramid of interventions thing that is so popular right now—we have been into that for quite a while. That drives our professional development meetings, our staff meetings. We re-examine our pyramid every meeting. We examine the kids on the pyramid every meeting.

Interviewer: How do you make it all fit? You have 250 kids in the school. How do you get to each kid when you have 250?

Timothy: We have a very talented teaching staff. Probably if there is one message that I want to share with you today is this whole area of distributed leadership has been a passion of mine for quite some time. What I mean by that is each of the people that work in this building is a leader. I am the official one. But we have just an amazing group of people that have different passions about different things. When they show that they have that, we let them run with it and they become the leaders, I become the follower. And that whole distributed leadership thing—I think I'm pretty safe to say is the staff really has responded well to it. We didn't have an assistant principal for quite a few years and suggested we needed an assistant principal to build the capacity.

We have sat through, I don't know, several interviews for that position. When it was all said and done, I just felt that the people not in this building, the people we interviewed were great people, but they did not mesh with the direction that we were going with. And so the school division gave us the permission to do a distributed leadership model instead of an AP [assistant principal], where we have group leaders. So we have a learning support teacher who becomes a leader in that area. We have an effective behaviour support person who has a passion for that area, became the leader in that. So we distributed the leadership within the school.

It was received really well in the school. People really felt that their opinion meant a lot, and I guess in a roundabout way that's kind of the answer to your question.

Interviewer: I want to pick up on that just a little bit as well and deal with some dollars that would be connected. So the division gave you permission then to use the money internally. If there was $20,000 attached to an AP position, how did you actually use the money with these various informal leadership positions?

Timothy: Right. Contractually, we had to use the AP stipend for the various leaders. So we just divided that up and they got a small stipend reflecting the time that they put into it.

Interviewer: Did they get release time to do their job as well as part of a stipend?

Timothy: Stipend and release time.

Interviewer: Neat. I don't know any other school that is doing it that way. Do you know of any others?

Timothy: No. I actually put the plan in place as part of my professional growth plan, and so I did research into that area. It is really difficult to find a lot of research in that whole area. New Zealand has done a little bit. I made a contact there. But it's not a model that you'll see very much.

Interviewer: What kind of an impact has it had on the **relationships** in the building? Because that's the competency I want to go to next.

Timothy: Yes. That area of trust is huge in this building. That area of caring and support is huge. I think you could go talk to any of the people that work in the building and they would affirm that. People feel safe in sharing challenges, and we get together and we brainstorm. It is a pretty ideal situation.

Interviewer: I want to push you a little bit further on that, Timothy. But think of the brass tacks—how did you develop the environment where you can say that your teachers trust you, trust other informal leaders in the building? How did you develop that?

Timothy: PLCs were something that interested me long before it became mandated. I went and took a course at McGill in the summertime and the instructor was Dufour. So in the middle nineties I became familiar with some of the ideas in professional learning communities and I thought, hmmm—well, a couple things came from that.

Because I was at that course—there were people from all over Canada and the States—I discovered in Alberta we have a pretty good thing going. We actually have a curriculum where all the teachers know what they are teaching, whereas these are the challenges in the rest of this continent.

So that was a positive thing, to see that there was a lot of good things going on in Alberta. But developing the whole respect thing and collaboration—here was a really good model that we could use. So we started in the mid-nineties. Many of the staff in the school are still here from that time.

Interviewer: Did you find that when you first set up PLCs, even before there would have been a lot of models in the local area to follow, did you have to lead all of the PLCs? Or even then, were you assigning off leadership roles to other people?

Timothy: At first I took the leadership role, in fact in the district as well. I came back, I was quite excited about it, I shared it with our own district through a couple of sessions. But as I lived it, I got to understand it better, and distributing was seeded then.

Interviewer: Perfect. Did any of the teachers at the time not buy into what you wanted to do? Did you have to transfer any teachers out of the building?

Timothy: No, no, never had that. No.

Interviewer: They followed.

Interviewer: Supportive. Good. In **leading a learning community**, of course, as competency number four, what do those PLCs look like today? No doubt they would have evolved from when you originally brought them in.

Timothy: Yes.

Interviewer: Could you talk us through what a meeting maybe at one of the PLCs looks like today? And maybe also interject some of the pyramid of interventions actions?

Timothy: Previous to that time, we were pretty much an island unto ourselves. Like each classroom was an island. We met and we had our staff meetings and we discussed the playground or the Christmas concert. But each teacher was most responsible for his or her own class, and that's where the learning happened. I'd say the biggest change is now people working together in teams, even sharing teaching. It's opened up teacher collaboration. We are much more team-oriented than we were previously.

Interviewer: Would you have teachers actually observing each other?

Timothy: That's a tough one. We set it up so each teacher had that opportunity. You know, "I'll cover your class if you want me to." That was pretty tough for people to take actually sign up to visit another teacher's class. But if I gave them a project—so say they're going to work on writing rubrics—that seemed to be the catalyst. They would then say things like, "We're both working on writing rubrics. This is what I'm working on, do you want to see it?" And then all of a sudden that changed the orientation—rather than just going in to see how another teacher was doing something, they would visit and observe how another teacher was actually using the rubric that they came up with together.

Interviewer: If they were working on a writing rubric together, and they came up with a template of something they would like to try, would some of those division teachers start to go in and watch each other actually use the rubric?

Timothy: Yes. And not only that, all of a sudden at our staff meetings people were bringing samples and passing them around, and were using the rubrics to mark each other's papers to see if they had similar ways of looking at it.

Interviewer: Say in Grades 4 to 6, Division 2, and if they solidified on a particular rubric that they might use for some aspect of the writing, is there still the lone holdout that perhaps gives lip service to the rubric but doesn't really implement it?

Timothy: You know, there's not. Sometimes we need to remind ourselves that we have them, you know, from year to year to year. Or we need to look at things and [ask] is this still appropriate or do we need to amend things, and stuff like that. But once we've agreed on a course of action, everybody's on board.

Interviewer: What's the next project? What do you see your teachers are going to have to take on and solve in PLC format?

Timothy: Inclusive education in the sense that we are a little nervous in terms of the budget coming down, and we are getting more and more children with exceptional needs and less and less financial resources to meet those needs. We are already starting to work on that, pyramid of interventions. What can we do in the building to support each other while we can? Hire teacher assistants.

Interviewer: Would this school continue to run what I used to call a resource room? Or are the inclusive education students all fully integrated into the regular classroom?

Timothy: We still believe in that. We still believe in pull-out time. Certain kids need to be away from the distractions. And we still believe that is important, that we have opportunities for 20-minute sessions to perhaps work on decoding in a quiet environment by somebody who specializes in the area. So we have two or three people who are reading specialists. So what better use of time is there than to get those people working with more than just their class? We have a master teacher. She has her own classroom, but we have managed to free her from the classroom so that she can help out with other kids.

Interviewer: How do you judge if that is being successful or not? What kind of data would you look at to say that teacher's involvement with this other group of children is making a difference in their lives?

Timothy: We believe in informal reading inventories, and those kids that we have targeted we test in the fall. We do two or three other reading inventories throughout the year to ensure that their reading is improving.

Interviewer: And what is the fodder for those informal reading inventories? Is it a take-off with something like a Gates-MacGinitie, or is it something that has been developed in-house by your teachers?

Timothy: We don't really subscribe to standardized testing in that sense. We think there is a whole lot that gets missed in just sitting down and doing a test like Gates-MacGinitie. Or achievement tests—same thing. We find that when students can read levelled material, we can get a whole lot of information pretty quickly in terms of comprehension, in terms of decoding difficulties, and that kind of stuff.

Interviewer: Okay. Many schools have gone with levelled reading. Many schools have gone where they—whether they call it a balanced literacy approach or if they are using reading groups—but where they will blend their Grade 1s, 2s, and 3s together with similar reading levels, and kids who need some intensive work might get a specialized or master teacher. Students who are okay might get somebody else. Have you followed that approach in this school as well?

Timothy: No, we have a caution there, and the caution being that maybe the eight- or nine-year-old doesn't want to be working with a six-year-old. So we have a little bit of a concern with that approach.

Interviewer: With the **instruction leadership,** competency four, and for providing instruction leadership to the staff, how do you ensure yourself that every one of these professionals in this building is actually doing what they need to be doing and making maximum impact on kids in their classrooms? How do you go about your job of instructional leadership?

Timothy: Probably the biggest thing is reporting periods. I analyze every report card and look for trends, and then I use that as a discussion point when I go back to the classroom teacher and say, "I see you have these four or five kids that are performing fairly low in reading and whatnot, and do you need some help with that?" I don't prescribe what we are going to do with them, but certainly I know the staff appreciates having those discussions in terms of "okay, I've done everything I can, Johnny's not improving, are there any other ideas out there?"

Interviewer: How would you bring those other ideas into the conversation with the teacher? Is that something that you are starting to lead, or do you start actually pulling some of your specialist people into the conversation?

Timothy: We do grade level meetings. They have an 80-minute slot every week where they do grade level meetings, and that's where we have those discussions. That master teacher will sometimes attend them. It may have to do with our AISI project, but first of all it has to do with any learning challenges. That's where we start.

Interviewer: How did you work out that you are freeing up your two Grade 2 teachers for 80 minutes a week?

Timothy: That's a challenge. We do it through the health curriculum. So this year we were able to actually hire somebody .25 to work with the health program. We include our counsellor, she likes to take groups and do different themes in the whole health area. We also assign a TA, and that's how we do it.

Interviewer: You must blend a lot of kids together for that same time frame.

Timothy: Yes, that's right.

Interviewer: All of the Grade 2s for health would go together?

Interviewer: At times. And then when they go together, their homeroom teacher is freed to work in PLC format?

Timothy: That's right. So the homeroom teachers—and we actually combine the Grade 1s and 2s—and so they meet down in this area, someplace away from the kids, and we have the kids covered. I bet you the staff would say that is probably the most valuable bit of time that they get in that sense.

Interviewer: Of course, then, I assume, you are following a pyramid of interventions format inside of that meeting. So when you just said you also blend the Grade 1s— so with that 80-minute time frame, would it be the two Grade 2 teachers meeting, or would it be the Grade 1 and Grade 2 teachers meeting in that 80 minutes?

Timothy: Yes, so both Grade 1 and Grade 2 teachers.

Interviewer: Are you in that meeting?

Timothy: Not always. Sometimes. Sometimes I'm covering kids. I'm there if I feel I need to be. Certainly our learning support teachers are in that meeting. The teachers themselves, however, run the meetings, though. They identify the areas that they need help with and they run with that. They do the research. If there needs to be some research, they'll go online and find different websites that they may find advantageous or they may find it's crap. So they have time to actually sit down and look at different strategies and whatnot. They establish their own agenda. They keep records, so we have a yearly record of the kinds of things that they worked on.

Interviewer: Do they submit something back to you formally after each meeting? Or is it semi-annually? Or is that at the end of the year?

Timothy: No. They post the minutes so I can look at them if I need to. Or if I have to write a little report for somebody at central office, I just run it from the minutes.

Interviewer: How do you pick the person who's going to be the lead teacher internal to that meeting? Or is there one?

Timothy: There's not. They're pretty collegial and they don't need a lot of direction in that sense. They're a pretty tight group.

Interviewer: But as principal, I'm getting the sense from you that you are also very confident that the work of improving education is what's driving that meeting.

Timothy: Absolutely. They appreciate that little bit of time that they get to do that and they use that time wisely. I'm absolutely positive about that.

Interviewer: Do they have some prep time over and above that 80-minute collaborative time?

Timothy: Yes. So they have two 40-minute prep periods.

Interviewer: The kids are doing all right in this school. So that competency about **developing and facilitating leadership**—without putting words in your mouth, I want to start with the fact that I get the sense that leadership is being developed in this school through these PLC teams.

Timothy: Teams. Yes.

Interviewer: Have you developed a capacity internal to this building for somebody to simply take over your job, if you were to retire soon?

Timothy: Yes. So I was out for four months and we didn't have an assistant principal. The school just went on. I don't think it missed a beat that I wasn't here. It's a pretty special place.

Interviewer: But somebody must have been designated—

Timothy: Yes.

Interviewer: I assume it was the master teacher.

Timothy: Yes, that's right.

Interviewer: She gets the designation. What about discipline, which is always a thing for principals to deal with? If you're not here, who deals with that?

Timothy: I'm really glad you brought that up, because that's an area that's dear to my heart and that's the whole area of effective behaviour supports—the EBS program that was run in this province for a few years, maybe about 10 years ago.

Interviewer: So talk us through that. Pretend I don't know a thing about it.

Timothy: Okay. This could take a long time.

Interviewer: That's okay.

Timothy: So I attended a meeting—the superintendent couldn't make a meeting, I was in Edmonton on behalf of the superintendent. Previously to that, I was having one of those weeks where I had a lot of discipline problems, and it was the old thing where the students get sent down to the principal's office. In my mind, I didn't feel that this was the most effective way. There had to be a better way.

So I went on the computer and I was looking for ways of dealing with poor student behaviour. I had some really interesting links pop up. But anyways, one of them was about this whole positive behaviour supports out of the States. I went to this meeting, and Alberta Ed at that time was going to start an initiative called EBS based on positive behaviour supports [PBS]. I had heard about it and read about it, and they wanted each jurisdiction to have a school to volunteer to participate in a project where EBS was implemented. Because I was at that meeting, I volunteered to do that.

So I went up to Edmonton and I spent a week learning about this effective behaviour supports program, and I've been sold on it ever since. I now have a team within the building that's an EBS team, and we've in-serviced every school in this district as well as several other schools in the province.

Basically, what you're looking at is a positive way of looking at the whole area of discipline. So you want to set it up so that you try and prevent a lot of the stuff that's happening from happening. So when you're looking at the whole concept of EBS it is important to develop an environment where you have what is called a 4 to 1—four positives for every referral.

So you look at your building, and you look at every part of your building. You have the teachers develop expectations for every aspect that you can imagine, whether it be in the assemblies, whether it be on the playground, whether it be in the classroom, whether it be in the library. The staff sits down—and this takes a while—you develop these expectations for the children that everybody can live with, and so we all have the same expectations.

Then we teach them to the kids. We have the kids teaching them to other kids. So there's a whole teaching aspect of it. And so you go through this, and you spend a lot of time looking at virtues and what good student behaviour entails. Takes a lot of time to set this up. Now we take the first 20 minutes of each day and we actually teach the virtues or positive behaviour we expect students to exhibit. We also spend time in these sessions making sure students know about items like the sliding hill being very slippery and what that means for their actions when they out to the playground. So we'll deal with specifics or more generalities to give them—I don't know, we feel that they need good, strong role models and understanding of that whole aspect of it. So we put a lot into teaching the whole area of virtues.

Then, if indeed a child still has a problem, we have a program set up where we call it a learning room, and they go and spend time getting extra lessons in terms of whatever behaviour they need assistance with. As a result of that, I don't have a parade of kids coming to the office anymore. I get called in on maybe the odd exceptional case. So the whole school runs the effective behaviour support program. I would never be in another school if we didn't have an EBS program.

Interviewer: So how many kids would you have to deal with as principal in a week? Discipline kids?

Timothy: Sometimes never. What I do is I like to keep an eye on what's happening in the learning room. If things are getting busy in the learning room, I'll go in and lend a hand. But I very seldom get referrals to the principal's office. It's a very exceptional kind of thing. We had a critical incident where a kid brought a knife and he pulled it on a kid and I was very involved.

Interviewer: As well you should be.

Timothy: But the day-to-day kinds of things, very little.

Interviewer: So who runs the learning support room? A teacher? Teacher assistant?

Timothy: Yes, teachers. We have two teachers and a teacher assistant.

Interviewer: And they must do more than if kids are not complying in some way with behaviour. There must be other stuff going on there as well.

Timothy: That's right. One of the things we do is we document. We have run data on everything on behaviour. So we look for data—is there an area of the school that's a hot spot? We examine this data every month. This team examines this data every month, brings it to the staff planning session and say, "Well, look, we've had quite a few problems in the gym." Then we'll discuss it as a group—is there something we could do about that?

So they take the lead role, they run data, they do graphs for us. We have all sorts of graphs for just about everything—even which day is the most popular day for incidents and that kind of stuff. They also are very positive people in terms of helping the kids. So a kid comes in there and he's been just a hellion on the playground and is pushing kids down and is generally miserable. They dig away [at] it and push away at it and usually there's an underlying reason for that. What's going on at home? We work closely with our counsellor. It just depends on what we need to do. We may need to call in parents and say, "What's going on?"

So anyways, they develop that. They look at strategies for helping kids—10 different things to do instead of hitting one thing.

Interviewer: So the folks who are manning this learning resource centre, do they find they get a lot of repeat customers?

Timothy: Yes. And so the repeat customers are part of our staff meetings as well. So if we have a repeat customer—usually it's more than one—and the nice thing about running data is it's not just one person dealing with that. Usually that student has had run-ins with multiple adults. So then we look at, okay, what can we do to help this kid?

Often, one of our strategies is to recognize that it takes 21 days to change a behaviour. So somebody will volunteer, that's not the student's teacher, but a trusted adult in the building, and will make contact with that kid 21 days in a row and just check in. [Check] how things are going and befriend that kid. We find that just makes an amazing difference in that person's attitude towards life.

Interviewer: I bet. Changing [the] subject to **managing school operations**—how do you **run the budget** in the school? How do you go from when the superintendent says, "all right, here's everybody's budget for next year"—how do you take that all the way through to involving your staff, to actually spending the money? Can you talk us through that process?

Timothy: Right. Our biggest priority is making sure we have a reasonable number of kids with teachers. So we look at our teaching staff first, and class sizes first. Then when we subtract that from whatever our budget is, we have that little bit that is left to figure out what to work with. We take that to our staff planning session. We have a number of categories within the building, whether it be art supplies, science supplies, phys. ed., the different areas that typically make up the school, and we just allot that money out.

This year's an ever-greening year for technology, for computers, so we are going to add a little extra money to whatever ever-greening money we get so that we can get what we need. So different priorities for different years.

Interviewer: Do you have different teachers in charge of different budget areas or does that all flow back to you?

Timothy: So it all flows back to me. They know how much money they have to spend and then they keep an eye on that.

Interviewer: But they're responsible for the spending.

Timothy: Right. Yes.

Interviewer: Do you work from a premise of school goals that tie directly into district goals, which might be impacted some way by provincial priorities for education?

Timothy: Yes, we do. Basically we run on three school goals. We feel any more than that and then all of a sudden you don't have priorities at all. Too many priorities and then you don't have a priority. We've done that whole thing. We've had a binder of things we wanted to achieve and didn't have a whole lot of success in meeting some of those needs.

So we look at our AISI project, which also ties in with the district. So that's our first goal, whether it be reading comprehension, whether it be writing, whether it be math, whether it be inclusive education. Those are recent ones that we've done. That's our first goal. We've got strategies set out to meet that goal.

Our second one is an effective behaviour support, so we make that a goal every year. We look at revising that, if revisions need to happen. We look at going to conferences, different ways of looking at that whole area. Our third one is a community goal, and so we look at how we maintain our partnership with the community. So we say in our model that we are a home and school community partner, so how are we doing that?

Interviewer: How did you go about tying dollars from your budget to implementing the various aspects of EBS and virtues education? What process did you follow?

Timothy: Okay. So there again, just like everything else, everything else comes up at our staff planning meeting. These are on the table. Each team—to continue with the EBS example—the EBS team will come and say, "Look, there's this conference in March. This person is known to be a guru in that area. Are you interested? If you are, we need to set so much money aside for that. There's a whole bunch of videos coming out on character education for this and this. Are you interested? Okay." So we build a budget that way.

Timothy: Each of the teams? So basically we have the EBS team, we have our learning support team, we're doing math problem solving so we have a whole team set aside for that. So those are our major teams—

Interviewer: Three big ones.

Timothy: Three big ones within the school. Then we have team leaders of different squads. So we have a passionate music teacher who obviously leads the cultural group, so there's a number of people [who] volunteer to be on the cultural. Within each year plan we have an artist in residence, where we have a two-week program where we bring in an artist. So they look after that.

We have a teacher who's passionate about sports, and he has two or three other people that have joined his team in terms of what do we need for supplies in the gym? They have awards all year, so they organize games in the gym to celebrate good behaviour. So we have that team.

We have a passionate art teacher who also has two or three people who sit in, and they look at the kinds of supplies we need for art and the different projects we can do for art. We have a cultural committee where we try and look at—perhaps it's a handicap or some type of empathy kind of project.

So each team comes up with a plan. This year we are going do this, this, and this, rather than, you know, how you get inundated all year by worthy groups wanting you to do the read-a-thon and the skip-a-thon and all of that. So they come up with a plan. Okay, does this plan work for you? It's probably getting there.

Interviewer: For a staff with about 15 teachers, that's a lot of leadership.

Timothy: Yes, it is. It really is.

Interviewer: And then in addition to that, you have your Grade 1s and 2s meeting together 80 minutes a week. Are Grade 3–4s meeting together?

Timothy: And after that, it's Grade 3s together, Grade 4s together, until the end of the year and then we try and join them, so we do the transition kinds of meetings. So the 4s will meet with the 3s and the 3s will share the challenges as they see them.

Interviewer: And they'll do that in those 80-minute blocks.

Timothy: That's right.

Interviewer: That's a great structure in place. So with your community school, how are you responding to the **larger societal context**? The types of things that might appear in your newsletters that go out into the community, what you would write for the local newspaper—what types of things do you tend to focus on when you are bringing this school out into the community?

Timothy: We've always had a newsletter. We have a person on staff who actually was a journalist and was excited to start a journalism club. So the children write all the articles in this school newsletter, like a newspaper, and they take it to the doctor's office, they take it throughout the community. We also have a huge email list beyond just parents, and it gets shot out to those people.

The types of things in there of course are whatever's happening in the school that particular month of interest. There's always a "From the Principal" message in there. I'll often talk about character education or trying to explain that we have the similar challenges in a school that you would have in your family at home, except our family is way bigger. So we will look at different ways that we can explain life in school in relationship to the life of the typical family.

Interviewer: If you are focused in on three core goals, would one of those goals tend to be the message inlaid in there somewhere?

Timothy: Yes. Absolutely. We look at—so we have math as our goal. So my last one was on math and what you could do at home with the children in terms of practical day-to-day kinds of things.

CHAPTER 6:

Interview:
Kindergarten to Grade 6
School Principal

Steven is the principal of a small-town school with 15 years' teaching experience combined with eight years as vice-principal and principal. The school has 300 students in K to Grade 6. He has a Master's degree in educational leadership.

The interviewer (co-author) asks Steven about his journey to leadership, how he was mentored, and how he enacts the professional competencies.

Interviewer: As you entered into leadership describe your journey for us. You are literally a three- or a four-year teacher, and all of a sudden you are a leader, and then you are a leader of another school, and then you are a leader of another school. Describe that process, please.

Steven: So initially, my going into leadership was maybe just by good luck, or maybe unlucky circumstances. The division that I was in was a northern school division that was having trouble recruiting leaders, and they knew that they had a number of people retiring. So they began a leadership program where they identified schools that had experienced principals in them, even though they were smaller schools that demographically didn't have the numbers to support an assistant principal or a vice-principal. They put four or five vice-principals into the division with experienced principals. The school I was at was one of the schools that was putting it in place, and really it was a 0.1 admin designation to start off with. Like very, very minimal. But my principal approached me and said I should put my name in for this. This was my second year of teaching. He said he'd love to work with me, thought I had potential. So [I] applied and I got it. The idea was that over three years I would get a sense of what school leadership was all about. I would work with the principal and get a sense of what does the budgeting process look like, what does the hiring process look like? I would have a chance to dip my toes into all of these things, but I was still primarily teaching at that point. After three years of doing that—so it would have been in my fifth year—I got offered a K to 9 school as principal. That was another community school in the same northern school division. The school had about 135 kids, K to 9. I spent three years there. It went well, and then it was time to move the family down south.

Interviewer: So describe the value or the usefulness of that early **mentoring** with this experienced principal. And in hindsight, was that a good thing?

Steven: Some of the circumstances just lent itself to it. First off, [he was] a fantastic person with just a ton of experience, lots of advice to pass along. Like in every mentee/mentor relationship, I weeded out what was valuable to me and what were things that I may not replicate in my own practices.

After that, there was still some version of mentoring. Through the whole time I was doing that they also had an aspiring leaders' program which met once a month—maybe once every two months, I can't remember now—where you come in and go through research pieces. They actually had a consultant that was coming from BC and providing that course, I guess for us. But at the same time I started my Master's. I was at a point I wouldn't have started it as early as I did, but they were paying. They were willing to pay up to $2,800 for people to pursue their Master's, and it would be ridiculous to turn down that offer.

Interviewer: Do almost a comparison thing for me right now. The value of the mentoring and the school division-based instruction in how to be a leader versus what you received throughout your Master's degree. What was the more valuable experience?

Steven: Probably the Master's. The other was nice, just to see it in context, but the Master's gave me a completely different look at how I did things, and a research base that I didn't have for how to set up some of the structures that I would later put into place in the principalship pieces. By the time I had started my principalship with that K to 9 school, I think I was in my last year of my Master's, so I pretty much finished it.

Interviewer: Why did you choose to go into leadership? What excites you about this profession?

Steven: For me at the time it was a challenge. Try something new. Sure, it'd be great to get that experience. But for me now it is all about having a greater impact. I found when I was a full-time classroom teacher I was very isolated. I'd have an impact on 20 kids and 20 families, but that was it. But as a principal I can have—even though trying to have an impact makes me want to pull out my hair sometimes—it was still a chance to have a greater impact and, you know, reach a greater number of kids. Not as directly as a classroom teacher, but it just felt like I was doing more. And for me now it is just feeling like my efforts are having a greater impact than just that smaller cohort of kids.

Interviewer: In your present district what, if any, use has been made of the principal leadership competencies in identifying potential leaders, and also preparing leaders for the next generation?

Steven: In this district, none. So if the identification of future leaders is happening, it is a central office level discussion. It has never been pushed down. However, in saying that, they have a Master's cohort that exists right now, but I wouldn't say that the purpose of that is to grow leaders. It wasn't set up with that purpose. Now as far as the leadership competencies, they have redesigned their entire evaluation around those seven competencies. So they're evaluating people completely on that, and the assistant principals are being evaluated on that as well. But as far as a mentorship program, or a grow-your-own, or identifying people, no, it's not there.

Interviewer: Would the same comment also apply to the principal?

Steven: Yes.

Interviewer: Very rarely do the principals go under formal evaluation. Were you having to present evidence of meeting the various competencies?

Steven: Yes.

Interviewer: And what would that look like?

Steven: Okay, so it was all through the superintendent. The superintendent would handle all administrative evaluations. And so I went through that process. Administrators in that school division were hired on three-year contracts. That's the max. One year for the first year, and then three years. So I went through my one-year, and then I also went through a three-year during that time. So the last three-year one that I had, it basically was a sit down, and through a conversation identifying what areas I wanted to work towards. And so in that document identifying pieces that I felt I needed to work towards. And then it was developing a portfolio to present.

Interviewer: As evidence of meeting competencies?

Steven: Yes. So I would identify which competencies I was looking at. I was actually just looking at this a couple nights ago, the binder that I had—if I was looking at [a] visionary leader piece, I'd have artifacts such as my mission and vision for the school that we established. I had a meeting agenda for meeting with the School Council to develop that. And all those pieces. Now the superintendent still came out and observed a staff meeting. They do a school review with every school, so that was part of the evaluation processes. But no, it was mainly creating those artifacts.

Interviewer: And from what I know of, and from what I have heard, Steven—and you are also a very modest man, so you will probably downplay what I am going to say next, but I want to set the context for this—my understanding of your school. I am going to use the term remarkable change in the way in which **instruction leadership** has been carried out, and the way in which teachers are teaching. And a focus on kids and learning. I would say, if anything, what you have brought to that school is nothing less than a remarkable change. I might be overstating it somewhat, however, I doubt that. That is the light in which I am thinking about your school. Am I in the ballpark?

Steven: I think I just put some structures in place to help people.

Interviewer: Okay. Then the structures that you put in place to help people get there is the story we are looking for.

Interviewer: In the first part let's talk about **vision**. So what is the vision of your school?

Steven: During that time we reached a place where the vision was very simple—and again, the school started as a K to 3 and we morphed into a K to 6 through a consolidation, and modernization, which is another story entirely. But from the start we made our vision very, very clear and simplistic. It was, "Every kid has to be a reader by the end of Grade 3, and every kid has to enjoy school." That's it. So, I mean, the wording, we would also have our smart goals and whatnot established through that.

But the vision was just those two things, and we are going to work our tails off to get ready for that.

Interviewer: What was the process you followed?

Steven: Initially, when we began, we just looked at all of our data pieces. And at that time we didn't have great data pieces to get it started, but there was enough there to start looking and engage in a conversation. We had our School Council doing the same thing, and then just some conversations around staff tables to reach where we needed to get to. To boil that down. But then once we started building some structures it just further clarified that in everyone's mind. Now as we looked at the other thread that was running through all of this, which was what happened to the community as it went through a consolidation process of reducing from three schools down to two. So there was an elementary, a middle, and a high school. And there right now, there's an elementary and a junior/senior high. We decided that it was silly for each school to go and develop their own mission. So we developed a K to 12 mission, which was one of those exercises where we are bringing every voice around the table possible. But then we had a steering committee that would boil it down to the exact wording of "creating success."

Interviewer: And did the district direct you in any way to engage in that process or is this something that was strictly homegrown?

Steven: Between the high school person and myself we knew what we were both going to end up doing anyway. So we started talking, but as we started those conversations, and we started to involve central office, they provided support. So I'd say the genesis started with us.

And the way I framed it was: "Each one of you is working your butts off for kids, but the school doesn't have support structures to support your network. So you are doing it all on your own, but we are not supporting you as a school. So we are going to develop some of those school supports so you can do your job even better. I am not saying it is going to be less work. I am just going to say to you if this gets to where we want it to get to, you are going to see more effective results from our school. You are going to see higher levels of student learning come out of that same work."

Interviewer: How did you make it learning focused?

Steven: We talked about some of the principles, but there's a few things that I just stated, "This is how it will be in the school."

Interviewer: Like what?

Steven: By the second year each grade level team was having—we were facilitating them—a chance to look at their student data as a team. Their outgoing data [included questions such as] how did the students perform while they were in Grade 3 for instance, plus what do the Grade 2 students look like coming in? So we examined that data together in August, and each grade level then was responsible for setting a priority for their year. And it had to fit within that frame of every child becoming a reader. So they would say, "Our priority is working on strategies for vocabulary development for kids." So we would drill down to the specifics and I'd work with each one of those teams to develop that priority. But a lot of the things that I did was just setting some templates, and that the expectation was you will use the template and I will be there to help, so it is not additional paperwork that you are doing but just something to kind of frame what they were doing. So each grade level had to develop a priority, and I would help them through that based on data, and then that would become their professional development focus during the year. I eventually also set up my schedule so I was available during every grade level meeting time, and I set up the schedule so that each was happening at a different time. So once a week I was available, and at certain times during the year I would set it out. So the second week of September I would come into that meeting and we would talk about year priorities. "So what have the data told you? What's your priority going to be for the year?" And we would do some of those initial things. I would come back in November just to say how are we doing so far? And then, formally, back in February for a mid-year review. And then I think just the end of the year, or it was May. I can't remember now.

Steven: And then we also started collaborative team meetings every five to six weeks and we set it up in the annual schedule. We would have a collaborative team meeting, let's use Grade 2 as an example, where we would bring out the board of 50 kids on a tri-fold board, all the Grade 2 kids. And every five to six weeks we'd have a conversation. And again it was a structured conversation. We had what the agenda looked like at every one of these meetings. But we would talk about which kids were struggling, which ones do we need to focus on? And then that led into our pyramid of interventions in the school. But in those collaborative meetings, myself, the learning support teacher, and the teaching assistants at that grade level would flood the room and we would just talk about kids. So that they knew every five to six weeks it was purely student-based. But I found that the offshoot of that is quite often during the other weeks that student focus just started to permeate more and more through the school.

But during their other weeks, the other thing that I had the administrative team do—and again, this always sounds so dictatorial, when you're stating it like this, but it was always through conversations with staff and whatnot—we said we needed common assessments at grade levels. When I first came into the building the staff was really collegial. But they were not collaborative. So we had two Grade 2 teachers working side by side who had no clue—one person's expectations were here and the other was there. So we said we have to have common assessments established at every grade level, and we will keep working on it, and we are going to develop curriculum maps at each grade level. And our expectations will be common, but how you teach to get there is totally up to you. So we respected and honoured what was going on in the classrooms.

Interviewer: In all subject areas or language arts only?

Steven: Language arts, specifically reading to start.

Steven: And the other thing that I said is if that is our focus area we will take all the other stuff and set it aside. So even though a new math curriculum was coming in—we had divisional meetings around that, so it was still there, but it wasn't school focused. We will make, and keep, reading as our focus.

Interviewer: If you want to change the culture you have to change the structures.

Steven: Yes.

Interviewer: And change the structures and change the agendas of what goes on in structures. And then you will start to impact on the wider culture.

Steven: And that was it exactly. We had to change the behaviours, because when I first started again we had a critical mass that saw this was great, and I worked on that critical mass. But we had a fairly decent population of experienced teachers that didn't see value in this right off the bat. But because they were collegial, they said we'll try it. Like it was not aggressive opposition but questioning. But we put some things in place and slowly that belief structure changed completely.

Interviewer: You mentioned that data led the way. And the next part of the question leads into what role does data play in the accomplishment of the vision of this school? Tie those two pieces together. First of all, explain what data looked like in your school.

Steven: Right. I would set up tri-fold boards, myself and the assistant principal, when we first started this. Later on it actually became teachers pulling this stuff together. But we would have a board with our PAT results. And we would have a board with our attendance. And when we first started, that was basically all we had—it was pretty minimal, the things that we had. But we would go around and do the post-it notes of what are our strengths and what are areas to work on. And we'd pull it all together. But then, and I knew it already, but having the staff do that the first thing that came up was we don't have the right data to tell us what we need to do. Which in my head goes bingo, thank you. And so, at that point we started looking for some standardized pieces that we could use to start having those conversations, which eventually fed into teacher-created assessments, which is where we always wanted to get to. But you know how long it takes to create those things. So we just said let's start somewhere, and that became a huge learning for me in a leadership role, is start with something, even if it's not where you want to be eventually, but the start is there. And we started building a culture of learning, and this became our slogan: that assessments flag kids for conversation, that's it. All the data that we get in on kids doesn't make or break them. We are not going to take standardized assessment data and say a kid is failing because of this test and how they scored. But it always became this data set is showing that students are struggling. So what do we say? Is that true? So it always became the vehicle that would start the discussions off. Flag kids for conversation.

Interviewer: And Steven, with that, and I'm curious to know that after two, three, four years of doing this, what happened with your PAT results?

Steven: Went up.

Interviewer: Up substantially, or up—

Steven: No, not substantially because that was one of the barriers that this school had. They had one way to measure success and that was the PATs and the PATs were good, they were high 80s, 90s. But then, and I've spent lots of time talking with other schools about what we did there. Basically, we had 10% of kids not making it and we had no structure to ensure what do we do for the 10%. And the tell-tale sign of that was when our kindergarten teacher would look at the Grade 3 list to see which kids weren't making it and say, "Oh, yeah, I knew that." And so then the obvious question was if we knew that collectively in kindergarten, what have we done since? And the answer was we passed them into Grade 1 and let the Grade 1 teacher try and solve it. And then we passed them to Grade 2 and let the Grade 2 teacher do it—there was no school structure to do it.

Interviewer: So with that 10% of the kids after three years of doing this, what happened then?

Steven: Our PATs stayed consistent, maybe improved a little bit, but I wouldn't say the PATs shot up. Our other pieces shot up a ton. I don't think our PATs showed the kind of improvement, because the gap was pretty small to show improvement anyway, and we had phenomenal Grade 3 teachers who knew how to get kids to score well on that test.

Interviewer: Talking about that 10% who historically don't make a passing grade on a PAT, what evidence could you show that they became more effective readers?

Steven: Our other data pieces showed improvement. We had library circulation data that showed that we had established steady improvement, reading interest surveys that showed that these kids were now actually picking up books. And our collaborative team meetings, they would always start with celebrations, and the kids that in the past that would have nothing to do with books were checking things out of the library. So in some of those other pieces we saw great growth. But some of that you just don't see in a PAT, which our staff, once we started doing those examinations, were the first ones to say, "But this doesn't tell us everything."

Interviewer: You say the word celebration and that is where I am going next. How do you communicate and celebrate school accomplishments and inspire continuous growth?

Steven: Big piece for us. And just to preface this a bit, we definitely moved the culture of the school away from overall percentages to show success. So we moved away from we are at 88% on whatever, let's move to 90 over the next three years. Like they meant nothing. But instead we made it to individual students, right down to we have 24 kids entering Grade 3 as non-readers. At the end of the year, now there [are] 15. Wow. We hit on nine kids. One of the ways that I would celebrate is that in June we would have our regular end-of-year staff meeting, but I would have a PowerPoint where I would flash up the pictures of the kids who entered their current grade level below where they should be, and then show the growth they made through the year. We had established, just for the purpose of conversation in those collaborative team meetings, red, yellow, green, and blue to indicate where students were at coming in. Red if they were more than a year below grade level, and again when we first started it was based on one reading assessment that we used, not the PAT, but an assessment from an instrument from Pearson. But we eventually made it so that it was a student profile where red was [a] student significantly below, and we had criteria of what that meant. And it became more of a teacher professional judgement of saying, "based on everything I know about this student." So I would project up on a PowerPoint here are 30 kids across the school who went from green to yellow. Or, wow, here are five kids who went from red to green over the course of the year. Or, blues were our high-end kids. So these ones that went from green to blue. So we'd show that.

Steven: But it took us a while to get to the point where we could celebrate in this way. When we first started it was all about the kids' score from the teacher side of things, but we kind of had to let that evolve and grow.

Steven: But we just kept moving forward. We would ask, "What are we going to do?" We would note that we have identified what the problem is, then we had to ask, "What are we going to do?" Once we had our intervention set up we could then ask, "So okay, well what about this, this, this?"

The whole process was very holistic in nature. The best example I have of this was a kid in Grade 2 who had just gone into a new foster home. The kid was a wreck, and he was our weakest reader in Grade 2. We had him in probably five different support intervention programs, some classroom support, but also some pull out. And in that meeting we went around the table and just said, "Take him out of everything right now, and our job with that kid is now just hug him when he comes in the door. You see him in the hallway, you high-five him. Somebody watch him at recess time. Just love this kid for the next five weeks, and then we will see where we are at." So that was the nice part. It wasn't that he scored this on a test so he goes into this program.

Interviewer: And I bet he learned to read.

Steven: He's in Grade 6 now, and he is getting there. I mean, it's—

Interviewer: A work in progress.

Steven: Yes, it always is a work in progress.

Interviewer: So then we move to **relationships** and it is a huge component of what you did. So tell us about how you went about developing a positive working environment in this school?

Steven: First thing I did is I learned every kid's name in the school. And I did that my first three days. When I went in I didn't see my office for three days. I did all my paperwork stuff at night. It meant for some late nights that first week. But I spent all day in classrooms and told everyone I just want a class list. Help me. And the reason I did that is it got me close with kids off the bat, but probably more importantly it modelled for the staff that I care about the kids. That was my primary focus. And then I could very quickly, when a staff member came and would have a concern about Jacob, I could picture who it was. I never had to say, "So which one is he again; can you show me in the directory who he is?" So that one was huge. But then the first step for the positive working environment for me was just being visible. Getting into classrooms and at first I had some veterans—when I started at that school I was the second youngest person in the building. There was one TA younger than I was. So people were pretty apprehensive, and I had no experience, credibility, in some of their eyes, right? I spent all my time going into classrooms, smiling, not talking about instructional practices. Sending lots of notes of encouragement of wow, I loved what was happening today. But I didn't critique a thing off the bat. The message that I was here for kids helped a ton as I moved forward into some of those instruction conversations and whatnot. But it always focused around kids. But through everything that we did we wanted to honour professional judgement, so with everything that we said, you know, we are bringing in data to support your professional judgement, not to eliminate it or not to de-value it. We are building common assessments to encourage the conversation and the practices, but never to question what instructional approaches you are using in the classroom. Although the funny thing is that they did that on their own. Like, a lot of that movement came from the teachers rather than dictatorially from me.

Interviewer: What was the atmosphere like in the school before you took it over?

Steven: Caring, loving, kid centred, collegial.

Interviewer: Focused on kid learning?

Steven: No, no. Focused on kids.

Interviewer: How do you demonstrate that you are responsible for all students and that you are going to act in their best interest?

Steven: First off, again, knowing all of those kids and making them the focus of the meetings, and just further modelling that and promoting it in the school, but making tough decisions and going down tough roads. In one case, we could have turned it very differently to protect an abusive teacher at the expense of the child. So some of those situations just further show that it's kids who come first.

Interviewer: **Leading a learning community**. Outline the process you followed to increase the level of student learning in your school.

Steven: Individual. That focus from the overall to the individual. Because the way the staff had gone before—and in all honesty, what I had done in my previous school, too, [was] improvements in learning [that] came from whole-staff PD. So it was, okay, we are going to look at guided reading this year and we will do that all together. Or differentiated instruction, we're going to do all of that together. But we moved it down to individual kids and what do individual kids need? Which once we started that examination it just led into the Grade 2 teachers looking at guided reading structures in their classroom, while the Grade 4 teachers are looking at vocabulary instruction and how do you build word walls to support kids, to the kindergarten teacher looking at how to bring in some wraparound services through speech and OT. So I think we increased the level of student learning by focusing on individuals and letting staff work, still coordinated around that central vision and our goals, but working in the different areas that they felt they needed to rather than whole-staff directed things. And by looking at that data regularly we set up progress monitoring assessments as well, so that our assessments before were the annual standardized things, but for our at-risk kids in the area of reading, every two weeks those kids were getting [their] progress monitored. Just real quick assessment with them just to keep that right at the forefront to know, okay, how are they doing? Are they getting to where they need to go? To whom do we need to talk? Yes, just moving right down to that individual level.

Interviewer: So with teachers it became differentiated professional development and professional learning? How involved were the teachers in the school in helping to set what these professional development goals were, or how involved [were they] with what the actual sessions would look like?

Steven: Completely on them, with me again providing support—sorry, when I say me I mean the administrative team, myself, and the vice-principal—providing support to help coordinate some of the pieces, but it comes again to the priorities. We would ask, "So what is your team's priority for this year? How are you going to address that priority?" We had some that would go to a conference together. That was at the grade level. But we also set up action planning teams. So for instance our overall goal of enjoyment in school and reading, we had three sub-strategies under that in the first three years. One of the sub-strategies was developing common assessments in reading. So we had an action planning team that would work at that one and coordinate some PD around that for our staff. We had a second group that was looking at building a pyramid of intervention, so what does that look like? They went to some DuFour conferences and whatnot together. And we had another group that had looked at student reading interests in building up the library and whatnot. So again all those team structures that were happening.

Interviewer: And who was coordinating all of this?

Steven: I was coordinating it but each team would have a leader, and then we had a staff steering committee. This team had a person from each of the strategy teams who then would come together and say things like, "We are really hoping that the next PD day we could share what we have been doing with this and lead people through a two-hour workshop. Okay, let's do that." So it kind of became a much more focused PD committee. Like lots of schools have PD committees, but this one became really focused. And then in my last year we ended up getting to a spot where rather than each team selecting, or me helping select, the leader of the teams—and in my first year, it was teachers who expressed which team they'd like to be a part of, but then I assembled the teams and set who was the leader in each one. In the last year that we were there, as we got kind of further along in our distributed leadership model, the James Spillane stuff permeated through. Teams would send a different person each time. So we would have those every couple of months, and now this teacher would come and participate and then take back to the strategy team what was discussed. I don't think we could have started at that level because not everyone was at that place where they could take that kind of leadership.

Interviewer: Inside out, I mean, really inside out conception of professional development.

Steven: Yes.

Interviewer: And the inside part starts and ends with student needs.

Steven: Yes. So it was all data driven pieces. Data informed, not data driven. We moved away from that term of data driven.

Interviewer: And on top of all of this would you have what we would refer to simply as PLC groups as well? Or embedded within this elaborate team system lay your PLCs?

Steven: Embedded in.

Interviewer: Embedded in.

Steven: With the PLC structures I, we, had two layers to it. One was the action planning teams. Every teacher had to be on one of the teams, and that was more the overall school improvement goals. But then every teacher was also part of the grade level team. And all of them were infused with the DuFour stuff. So each one of those teams was creating their team's norms. They were keeping a record. We have SharePoint established where they would keep a record from each one of their meetings, but it was not intense. Like lots of times at Grade 4, on their weekly meeting record, and again I had the template developed on the sites for them, it would just say, "worked on geometry unit common assessment." That's it. That's all it would say for that week, which was perfect. So then I could observe through that and help—and again it wasn't [like] lord[ing] over what was going on. But it was just to keep me informed, because then I could talk to the Grade 2s and say, you know, the Grade 4s are looking at that. So again, coordinate support rather than controlling it all.

Interviewer: But your non-negotiable expectations were also out there.

Steven: It was very much about setting the banks of the river and then letting the water flow. So I set the banks. Every staff, every team is going to develop team norms, and I'll help you. I'll sit there with you and coordinate that. But we will have team norms. You will have a priority, and I never stated it like that but it was pretty clear. If they weren't completing the notes each time I'd talk to them. But after our second year, in their first meeting where we developed the priority, I also had a template that had every one of their meeting dates through the year, and they'd say who was going to record the minutes at each one of these. And they'd take turns. Like having some of those support things.

Interviewer: So this was a version of accountability.

Steven: Yes.

Interviewer: They did it because they knew everybody else knew they were supposed to do it.

Steven: Yes. But eventually it reached a place where we did this because it just helps us do our work better.

Interviewer: How do you facilitate **meaningful parental involvement** in the school community and ensure that they are informed about their child's learning and development?

Steven: So when we started off that was one area that the school was weaker in just because the technology expertise wasn't quite there. We spent a lot of time worrying about and improving our one-way communication. Our newsletter became enhanced. I started sending out a weekly principal's update which just highlighted what was going on in the school. We revamped the website completely. We helped teachers to provide monthly newsletter type things. So we enhanced our one-way communication. But over time in the school I really tried to move it towards two-way, and made quite a bit of traction, quite a bit of growth that way. Nowhere near what I wanted to get to eventually. But in two-way I am meaning utilizing social media. So we set up our Facebook page for the school, where parents could go on and start discussions and ask questions and whatnot there. I started using Twitter to communicate out things. We started using some text messaging and email to get things back and forth. I had a blog where I would share directions that we were going in and invite comments back on it. And always set up so that I could monitor what was coming in so that somebody couldn't go on it anonymously.

Interviewer: Steven, what percentage of parents [that] have access to computers actually use them for this purpose—do you know?

Steven: We reached a spot where I had an email address for every parent in the school, that we would send a note [to] and we went paperless in my last year. Where we didn't send home paper anymore unless the parents requested it. And some did because they preferred that. But I quickly found that a lot of the parents weren't using the email, even though they'd given us an email address. We got our most parents when we went to Facebook.

Actually, no—onto Twitter, which connected to Facebook. The other thing I started doing was rather than me spending an hour on a Sunday night making a one-page principal update and formatting it and getting it all the way I wanted, I started making videos. So we called them the "principal podcast." And I'd sit down Monday morning when I got into the office with my post-it note of things I need to remind some of them about, would start the webcam, post it up on YouTube—say my little four-minute deal, post it up on YouTube—send it out and then embed it on the school website.

Steven: It ended up saving paper. And then we started to hear from parents.

Interviewer: Well more than that, you're making contact.

Steven: Yes. But trying to get it to two-way so it's not just us. We will tell you what is going on at the school—but like in my last year when we started the budget conversation, I started a budget blog and asked for parents to tell us what is important about learning. We would ask questions like, "What is more important to you, that the child has TA [teaching assistant] support in the classroom with a larger class size, or smaller class sizes?" And so we would use Survey Monkey to get feedback on that.

Interviewer: And what was the answer there, by the way?

Steven: Smaller class sizes.

Interviewer: Is that right?

Interviewer: And the danger is many would recognize that the TAs are only for a certain proportion of kids.

Steven: Yes, but we had reached a place in our school where our TAs were everyone's TAs in a sense. We didn't have high, high medical need kids. We had behaviour kids that sometimes were doing just great and the TA could venture off to other places. I think after a year, though, the staff and families would say more adults in the building is better, even if they are not teaching adults.

Interviewer: We are going to change and go into **instructional leadership**, but yet it's a continuation of the previous one. Tell us about how you see your role as the instructional leader of this school.

Steven: Build the structures and supports. Just build the structures and then let people who have the expertise in the classroom take over. I'd say that was one thing that when we share what we did in that school we get some teachers kind of going like this and it's an affront to what I'm doing as a professional. But once you further explain and then they have a chance to talk to the teachers at the school it's no, this is all about honouring what's going on in the classroom, and giving you support and validation and the opportunity to risk-take and the opportunity to say, "I've done that for 20 years. It wasn't good practice so I'm going to change." So for me, my role was just [to] build all the structures and supports for that collaboration and conversation to happen. And then support teams. And whether that support meant that I was going to sit in on a meeting and help them build their common assessment while they just talked about it, great. If it meant that I had to go online and find a certain resource from another school that somebody thought they heard about at a convention, then I'd go do that. If it meant just sitting in a meeting while they were talking about what they were going to do for a field trip they were designing around these outcomes, I'd do that. Just support.

Interviewer: Support.

Steven: Yes.

Interviewer: How did you ensure that your teachers were actually following current pedagogy in teaching practice?

Steven: You know what? I would go to where Marzano and DuFour—in their new book, *Leaders of Learning*,[25] it's the blue and yellow one—[where] they talk about how our practice of evaluating and supervising individual teachers isn't efficient. That we should be supervising teams. I'd back that 100% 'cause that is where I ended up going to.

Interviewer: Give us an example of how you supervised teams.

Steven: So I'd sit in those meetings and I'd hear the practices that people were talking about. And I would reach a spot, and again different teams were at different places in their trust cycle, but I would reach a spot where I would ask, "Say, have you tried? What I hear from [what] you are saying is that you are round robin reading with the kids. Have you tried looking at this a little more deeply? I know that Susan does this in her room." So kind of making some of those bridges and questioning some pieces without being critical—do you know what I mean? Or providing articles for a team where I knew they needed to go in this type of direction. And then still being out in the classrooms to see some of that piece. But in my last year I was not in the classrooms as often as I was in my first year, and I would say I knew more about the pedagogy that was happening than I did in my first year by trying to be in rooms all the time, 'cause I can't get to 17 rooms effectively. But I could sure sit in six team meetings.

Interviewer: It's akin to the notion of leverage isn't it.

Steven: Yes.

---

25   For more information on this book please see: http://www.solution-tree.com/leaders-of-learning.html.

Interviewer: That's what you are doing. You are leveraging your learning through the teams to get a much clearer idea of where things are at.

Steven: But then it also gave me in my mind the freedom to say the Grade 2 team is doing awesome, I'm not even going to worry about them. But the Grade 5s, I'm worried, I'm going to make sure I'm in those classrooms, make a stop in every day this week just to see what that looks like. Where before it was equal. I would try and get to every classroom, you know, once a week for a meaningful block of time.

Interviewer: It's like your development was structured. You wanted it to be purposeful—and individualized. That's fascinating, Steven. How do you ensure student assessment and evaluation practices throughout the school are fair, appropriate, and balanced?

Steven: By expecting common assessments to get built and then supporting them. Then again being available for those meetings, being able to, most of the time invited, but sometimes I'd be, "Hey, do you guys mind if I sit in with you?" When I asked, I would always get, "Yeah, sure, come on in." But in doing that I could— for example, if they were building a common assessment that didn't quite have the rigour that we were trying to get to—[be] able to question that. So building the common assessments was huge. And I found that teachers pushed themselves to a higher level of rigour than any of them were doing on their own.

Interviewer: Because their colleagues were watching . . . Was it the responsibility piece or was it because the conversation led to something more?

Steven: I think so. I think that and also when you put three Grade 3 teachers in a room nobody wants to be the weak link. So everyone rises up to it. But then the other thing we did in the school is we moved to outcome-based reporting. And as soon as we went to that it turned over a rock of some poor assessment practices that had been in place when we were trying to figure out how to assign a percentage to spelling lists and that kind of thing. But as soon as we went to outcomes-based it made everyone re-examine everything we were doing, and a ton of stuff went by the wayside in time.

Interviewer: I am also curious—was another rock that you turned over the fact that a lot of teachers [who] said they were paying particular attention to the program of studies were not?

Steven: Yes, exactly. We had people who went, "I didn't even know that was in the program of studies." Or someone who—and I'm making this up just for the purposes of illustration—but maybe 20% of their language arts mark was based on the spelling list. When they actually got in and went there with two outcomes that kind of relate to spelling it just opened up their eyes. "So why do we do this? Because the person who taught Grade 2 before us, that's how they did it. It just made sense for us to keep doing it." People became really knowledgeable by looking deep into the program and when we did some curriculum mapping activities.

Interviewer: Did you use a particular format for the curriculum mapping?

Steven: We made our own. We would take the curriculum outcomes and developed "I can" statements for each one, or for clusters where appropriate. And then grouped them into overarching items, and sometimes the curriculum had the overarching already. If not, they created that piece. But then we set it up that if that's your outcome, how will you assess that in November—assess it in November, March, and June? And then teachers would say we are not assessing this in November or March because we are not covering it until June. Or we are only going to assess it in November, not in March and June. So then it just kind of helped. It got all of us to be more efficient.

But it took us a long time to develop those. And when I left last year we still had some gaps in some of the maps.

Interviewer: Let me ask you this question, Steven. Over the past several years from K right through 12 we have seen social studies curriculum change, we have seen mathematics change, and now the focus is on inclusive education. How did you address the challenges posed by understanding and implementing curriculum changes in those areas?

Steven: So our division was really strong in getting teachers to work together and map curriculum. And so our expectation was that we would always be involved working with the curriculum areas you identified. To dig deeper we brought in subs. I told the staff, "I will worry about all that stuff. You guys need to go to work." And so luckily our division was doing some of the curriculum mapping. It helped that one of our teachers got hired to do some of the work. So, yes, it was advantageous for us. But they did a lot of that curriculum mapping as they went through. So teachers were having dedicated amounts of time, for instance in math, to do the things that we were already doing in the school. So it just fit perfectly. Nowhere in the division was the reading focus the same way we were doing it. But when we first started, what we said was, "Everyone work on your reading maps. That's where we are going to start. Reading is going to be our focus." And looking back I almost wish we would have gone a bit broader and looked at it more as literacy than just reading. It made people really get intentional about the curriculum, because they went through the curriculum and said, "That's a reading outcome, that's a reading outcome." And so they then pulled all that out to make a reading map. And then they made a writing map, and then they made another literacy skills map. And then last year we started the process of bringing that together.

Interviewer: What does **teacher supervision and evaluation** look like in your school?

Steven: So now, if I went back in, but definitely in my last year, it would all be about supervising teams. But our divisional policy was still, "New teachers, this is what your evaluation process looks like." The divisional policy identified how many formal observations were required, pre-conference observation, and post-. So I still had that in place, but what I also did is I had it as my personal mandate to go into every classroom every day for just a minute, you know. And I usually tried to do it right at the start of the day if I could, or right after recess or something. But [it was] basically just a chance for me to cruise in.

But as people got used to it, it was just to wander in and say things like, "Hey, how you doing? Great to see you." And then wander out. It eventually got to a place where it didn't impact anything that was going on. But it was more for visibility. But it gave me just a sense of the school. But I definitely moved away from the, "I'm going to spend 30 minutes in your classroom and try and get here every two weeks."

Interviewer: Provide feedback on your teaching.

Steven: Yes. It all became notes and quick emails. "This looks great." Or, if I saw things that weren't going as well, then making sure I'm in the next team meeting and help direct that a bit.

Interviewer: We will move over to **facilitating leadership**. How do you as school leader either identify, promote, or develop leadership within the school?

Steven: All of Spillane's distributive leadership stuff. And we started initially in this evolution of our school by identifying team leaders. In the beginning we identified the leaders, but eventually getting to that distributive model where, depending on the situation, different leaders would percolate up and through in each of those team structures. So we started deliberately naming those people, but then reached a point where everyone was a leader, but depending on the circumstance would go in different ways. So for instance, we would have a staff steering meeting and

I'd say, "Okay, this one is going to be looking at our upcoming three-way conferences. What do three-way conferences look at our school?" And so this Grade 2 teacher had a passion for three-way conferences, this Grade 5 teacher had a concern about the process—they both volunteered to work with the process, and so the right people were at the table for that conversation. And then our next staff steering meeting might be something different, and so someone else would show from those teams. Where when we first started it was, "You are the Grade 2 leader, you are the Grade 4 leader this year."

Interviewer: Is that also the way you get maximum input into the running of the school?

Steven: Yes. Everything that needed attention would get put out to people, and if they had any concerns they would bring them up. But I found that most of the time—then again, this was just something that I learned as we went through—for most things, most staff members don't care about things. "Just decide what it is and tell me what I need to know," was the attitude. So we would decide that together and put it out. But before I would always think, "Well, we have got to have a staff conversation about it." And so there are still some things that we did. But there is other stuff where [we] let that team decide, throw it out, if I don't hear anything back, great, that is what it is. And again it is just that efficiency piece too and recognizing that teachers are busy.

Interviewer: And the SharePoint where most of the committee work flows into, is it also visible to all other staff?

Steven: Yes. So one thing that we did, this was in my second year, is we took a computer, one of our older ones that sat in the staff room and was turned on all the time with SharePoint and that was its only role. It's not a staff computer, it's not a work computer, it's a communication computer only. And that's what we use it for. And so then on the front page I would post announcements like, "Remember to let me know who the kids are to recognize in assembly this Friday." But we would also post up the schedule for what's going on in the week, and whatnot. But then every team could access the Grade 1 SharePoint, the other SharePoints.

Interviewer: You alluded to **budget (management competency)** earlier in our conversation, so how does the budget for your school reflect the goals of the school? Talk us through that.

Steven: One hundred percent. If our focus is around reading, our resources go towards reading. Which means physical resources of building classroom libraries, and developing guided reading sets and whatnot. But human resources, too. So we are going to hire, and this is one thing that I know the school has moved away from this year—but while I was there it was our K to 3 is critical so we are going to direct staff that way. So even though there's a TA at Grade 6 for this student and there's a good reason why they're in this classroom during period 3 they're going to move into our elementary. So plan your class knowing you're not going to have that support. So we would set that up. But our budget was 97% staffing. And that was so key that I made it as a pie chart and made a really simplified budget and expenditures page that we would publicize on our website and put out to parents and talk about at council meetings. Because we got the school spending so much money on technology and all on textbooks that, you know, like you get those kind of offhand things. But as soon as we said 97% of the money we get into this building goes into adults in the building it changed a ton of conversations.

Interviewer: So what about the 3% discretion, who would have a say?

Steven: We all would. But I would use those staff steering meetings again, that "we are going to look at the budget this time." I would throw it out to parents as, "What is most important to you?" So I would hear that back. And then typically when it came down to staffing I would show a few different scenarios to people and we would get feedback and whatnot. But usually when it came to budget development I ran all of those things as feedback. "Tell me everything that you know." And then I would build a budget and put it out. "Give me some more feedback." Take it back, revamp, and put it out. But it was never, "Let's have six people run the numbers." Just because it was too time consuming. I tried that one year and it was just frustrating.

Interviewer: So with that total focus on reading and enjoying school—if we looked at your budget the year prior to those becoming the two focus areas of the school and look at the budget the year after, would we have seen a significant difference in the way in which funds were allocated?

Steven: Probably not significant. But you would see so much money put towards furniture, and we said, "Our desks are fine, we're not going to worry about the furniture piece. Let's direct that to resources." Like you'd just see some movement pieces in there. And we would have the idea [that] a teacher assistant is there to support the teacher, and we shifted that to, no, they're there to support the kids. So you'd definitely see a funnelling of support towards K to 3 staff.

Interviewer: Steven, I just want more clarification that refers to this in the other dimensions that you have addressed. And that is you are talking about a large investment in communication, collaboration, teams, crosstalk, learning from each other, etc. This all adds up to time well spent. Where did the time well spent come from?

Steven: The time that people would use making bulletin boards.

Steven: Just some of the things that we did as a school that was just inefficient. Yes, it put a lot on me, like because I saw my role as I got to build a schedule so that people can do this work which took time to build.

Interviewer: Did you have to build in extra prep time or embedded PD time?

Steven: When I first started I took prep time away. Let's say five staff had five prep periods in a week. The first year, and again just for simplicity of what I'm saying, we moved to four preps and a collaborative period instead of five preps. So it ended up being more teacher time than what they had previously, but even if it was a little more they didn't have as much individual time even though their overall time was increased. And then we started finding ways to combine classes for art or combine classes for library or some things like that. Or we got rid of computer classes. We got rid of those and tried to embed those pieces into the rest of the program. So it ended up that I was able to find ways to create more teacher time, but with that—the teacher time—anything that we added to it became collaborative time. So we actually reached a place where, when I left, the teachers only had three prep periods in a week, but I think overall they had gained almost an hour from when we first started.

Steven: When I present at other schools now one of the first things I hear is, "Well we can't do that because all of our kids are bussed and they have to . . ." I hear excuses as to why some things can't be done. So I would say, "Well our teachers actually said if you can get us out of classroom supervision we will use that as our collaborative time and eat together because that time is valuable. We can have a sandwich and work together." Like the teachers, once they see the value of it, [they] will figure out all the different ways to make that work. But it took me pushing it off the start. The first time I suggested a change to the schedule to do that, you would have thought that I was proposing—

Interviewer: Heresy.

Steven: Yes, exactly. And then we reached a spot where I can remember in the one meeting teachers going, "Well, we could just change the schedule. Why don't we change the schedule and we'll do this, this, and this." And so my outward appearance was, "Yes, that sounds great, let's do that." And inwardly I'm going, "Oh, shoot, there's three evenings away trying to revamp the whole schedule again." But it got to a spot where they would say, "Let's do this and this and this," and they knew that they could. We went one year where we changed our master schedule three different times as we adjusted, which, for some schools, would send people into early retirement. But for our people it was just, yes, done.

Interviewer: There's a huge story there.

Steven: The culture has shifted.

Interviewer: How do you go about assessing and responding to the unique and diverse community needs in the **societal context** of the school's vision and mission?

Steven: I think that was just being visible, like being at the front of the school every morning. I made it my practice. We set it up so that myself and the vice-principal were at buses every morning and at buses at the end of the day, too—and we both committed that if one's at the buses the other's in the entryway or vice versa. So just being visible all the time, welcoming, greeting, and then being totally approachable. People knew that they could email me, they could phone almost to my detriment in some cases. It wasn't odd for me to get a 10 o'clock phone call. If I had to go back through it again I would set some parameters around that. And I would also set some parameters [because] it wasn't unusual for people to send me an email at 7 o'clock and I'd get back to them by 8. So people started to expect that, but then the negative offshoot of that is you get an email at 9 and then one at midnight asking why haven't you gotten back, and then one the next morning. So I would set my own personal boundaries very differently, but it was one of those things where it's hard to draw the line.

Steven: My vice-principal and I joked about it behind closed doors that this was our brand, like you have to keep selling the brand. The idea was that our leadership has to be larger than just this school, but it's got to be out there, too. So we got to a spot where we were presenting at conferences, working with other schools—in the last three years I was at the school there wasn't a cycle of those collaborative team meetings [that went] by where we didn't have some school coming to watch the process. And so that whole thing about success begets success, our teachers started to swell up with pride knowing that a school out of our district was coming down to hear about our programs. But I did a big job of selling those pieces out there.

Interviewer: But that's advocating for education.

Steven: It turned to that, yes. So it got to a point where yes, we could, on my blog I could write a bigger piece on education or I could have that conversation with the newspaper editor. But initially it started off just what's happening in Grade 1 this week.

Interviewer: Steven, is there any aspect of your leadership, leadership preparation, you'd like to talk about that perhaps we didn't cover?

Steven: No, I don't think so. The Master's for me was huge. I think I had an understanding of what school should or could look like, but that gave me a credibility—I don't know if it's even a credibility—a justification or verification of what was going on. And to be able to, yes, I know we wanted teams to have leaders, but to be able to attach some of Spillane's work to that, or the DuFour piece, or Marzano, really make it special. It just gave me an appreciation for research. And I think if I was to go into my next administrative position I would definitely adopt the belief that our role is not only to this school but to education in general. So I'm going to be out at conferences. When I am there I am going to have a chance to go and see other schools, and sell us to other schools.

CHAPTER 7:

Interview:
Kindergarten to Grade 6
First Nations School Principal

Ellen is a First Nations principal with 11 years teaching experience, and nine years after that as a school leader, all in this school. There are 638 students and 33 teachers in Kindergarten to Grade 6. She has a Master's in Leadership and School Improvement.

The interviewer (co-author) asks her about mentorship and then addresses how she enacts the professional competencies.

Interviewer: When you entered into the role of being principal was there anybody that was assigned to you, or somebody that you sought out, in a role of **mentor**?

Ellen: No.

Interviewer: None?

Ellen: I had a four-minute debriefing with the past principal. Like here is the budget, here is this, here is that, and that was it.

Interviewer: If no mentorship experience, I am going to ask you about the competencies. And the first competency deals with **vision**. So I'd like to ask you, not the one that is printed on your wall, but your own—what is your vision for your school?

Ellen: It has always been about doing what is best for kids. So for me, it is making decisions based entirely on the needs of our kids and doing what was best for them. I think for me as a school leader, especially in a First Nations school, it was always keeping in mind the First Nations perspective and always making sure that our school sounded like a First Nations school, felt like a First Nations school, and looked like a First Nations school. And that it was important to deal with being identified with identity. Identity, I think, is really part and parcel of the whole system in what I do. Keeping those two areas in mind was always part of my vision.

Interviewer: And then for about 11 years you were teaching and then moved into the principal position.

Ellen: Yes, when I first got my assignment. So to make change was really easy because my whole goal was just to build culture in the school to bring a sense of unity. I think having my Master's really helped with my understanding of those important relationships, and understanding the whole idea of trust. Understanding how to have those conversations with teachers and validate them and focus on their strengths, it was really easy to do.

But the other thing I learned really early on was I had to get rid of some of the negativity, and that meant letting go of some key people in the organization at that time. I went in with a deep desire to make a difference—and I think the other people expected it; the staff, then, who did get to stay realized that I had a really good idea of what we needed to do. So I had a lot of support in the beginning. The change was really easy in those first few years. It made me look like I knew what I was doing, because I made some really positive changes early on. To sustain that change in the last three years I've struggled. The struggle is due in some ways because of the school system. At the school we did some really extraordinary work, but I don't always feel like the system has caught up to the changes that we have been making at the elementary school.

Interviewer: Give me an example. What do you mean?

Ellen: I have been fighting for the professional learning time, weekly collaboration time with my teachers, since my first year. And I had a lot of resistance. It was always tied to the calendar, and I just felt like this is not the way it should be. We needed to look at what our teachers needed and what our students needed and then build from there. So sometimes I felt frustrated, more so recently than in the past.

Interviewer: My understanding is the collaborative time you get is referred to as PLC days.

Ellen: These PLC days have been fantastic, and I mean it's certainly a step in the right direction—but what is happening with the way it is set up is that the teachers are still having to plan for a sub. The students are not really gaining the full benefit of these days because they are having subs in the classroom. To some degree the teachers are benefiting for sure, and I guess if you look at it that way, but the kids are with a sub so the learning is not prime during those times. What I would like to see is an adjustment in our calendar. We need to look at dismissal times where we end school early on certain days. These days and times would lead to some really solid planning time. Might be good to have early dismissal every other week or every week. I think they are moving towards that. We are. I know our next calendar will look different. However, I still feel we were dictated by the calendar and I am not getting just that critical time with my staff. I don't have that time and it's very frustrating because I am constantly feeling like people are just not in the loop as much.

Interviewer: Okay, let's pick up that thread again here. So when you first took over the school the whole emphasis was in building culture. Only roughly 300 kids in the building. What had happened to the school; where were the kids? The Reserve population then was still the same as it is today.

Ellen: They were going to town schools, a lot of them. I don't think the emphasis with the Band was on getting these kids in school. Over the years we have seen more effort being put into getting those kids into school by the Band. But the other thing was we had a lot of kids going outside, and that has changed.

Interviewer: You left as a teacher. When you came back into the system you came back as principal?

Ellen: Yes.

Interviewer: Nine years. So if the vision is really getting kids to be successful and keeping that whole focus on the culture, great vision, then a **whole relationship piece** has to be developed. Relationships with parents, relationships with kids, relationships with staff. What did you do to build those relationships with those three groups?

Ellen: Well, it was first building the trust. How do you build trust? For me, it was by keeping my word. Speaking the truth, even if sometimes those are really hard things to do. I was really completely honest with staff. I would go into staff meetings and I would just be very honest about what I saw. "This is what I see, I see people not pulling their weight." So I really kind of did that, but I did it coming from a perspective of, "We are here for the kids, you guys. Like you guys can't be screwing around and doing what you are doing. Like if you sit there and you honestly tell me you are here for the kids, that's saying one thing, but your actions are speaking something different." It was just having a lot of those really honest conversations, and also I think it was just that I was very direct. I came in as somebody who had knowledge.

I was somebody who came into the system, and when I did people believed in me because I was doing my Master's, and I was kind of in the know—I knew of some of the new trends in education and what was working with kids in other schools and things like that. I would talk about what was working in other schools and what research was saying, so I shared a lot of things that I had been learning as well in terms of leadership and education. I would throw articles and things their way and just ask them, "What do you think of this or that?" In my weekly newsletter I would put out there First Nation issues or instructional issues, whatever the case was, and then ask, "What do you guys think of this?" So I think that built trust as well because they thought, "Oh, she actually knows what she's doing." And I don't think all of the ideas I put out there were always used.

I also think I became much more rigid with parents. I backed up my teachers more. I reinforced the idea and told the parents, "This is a school. You will not be going into the classrooms to interrupt instruction and learning." I was very firm with parents in terms of what was acceptable and not acceptable. We also really worked on procedures and aligning things. I have assistant principals who have worked really hard doing a lot of that with me.

Interviewer: Give me an example.

Ellen: Things like, how we were going to deal with lates? We would sit down as a team and we would ask, "Okay, this is an issue. What can we do?" We would have clear steps that would then be communicated to parents. We would align them with our staff handbook as well as our parent handbook. Really looking at some of the policies we had in place and how do support them. We actually took all of the policies that affect our school, and this has been the course over nine years, which ones don't have policies or procedures to support them. So we really focused on that to ensure that we had procedures that supported the policies that were in place. We always had something to say when a parent came in. We need to continue this work, so there will be no surprises.

It is actually a lot a work in progress too. I have noticed there are still things that aren't aligned and we are constantly revising because again the policies change so then they don't always support the procedures. We really tried to do a better job of that.

I think one of the other really big things in the beginning was that people didn't think our school was safe. When I first came here I did a parent survey just to see what they felt. And one of the big things I learned was the parents worry about student safety. Another thing that really stood out was that school culture and staff morale were really low. We lost 11 teachers that year, nine or 11, it was really significant.

So school safety meant that—I can remember my first month or two after coming, the honeymoon stage of my first year in admin, and I literally had about 15 kids every day lined up outside my office for me as principal to do something with them. I said to the assistant principal, "What do I do? I don't understand this. Like what am I supposed to do?" She goes, "Well you deal with them one by one." I said, "This is just such a waste of my time." The only way that I was going to get to the bottom of this was by building a better system with the kids. So I spent a lot of time in classrooms and just reviewing what my expectations were. I told students, "You are here to learn and that is your job as a student. My job is to make sure this school is safe, and I need you to be on board with me and I will not tolerate the things that have been going on." And I kind of came in with the attitude with staff and students, "I am here to support you, but you need to meet me halfway." So it was very pointed conversations I had with all the kids.

I had 14-year-olds in Grade 5. That was something that was truly wrong. No wonder we had issues. We did too. So we changed that policy. That came like that first year. It was like, you know, this is ridiculous. Like there should not be teenagers in our school. So we changed that. So that helped. But changes really happened by building the trust with the kids, and the rapport, and spending time and getting out in the hallways and getting to the playground and reinforcing the good things we saw. Literally within no time at all, I mean, there are days we don't have kids in our office. Even now there are days and days. I don't want to say we have no discipline issues, because we do. We have bullying issues, and I would be crazy to sit here and indicate we don't have any. We are still far from where I want to see it. But I'm not dealing with full out Grade 2 and 3 brawls outside on the playground. I still can't believe some of the things I saw in my first year. I was like, "How does this happen?"

In time it became really clear that those kinds of discipline things were really easy to deal with. Sustaining them and going really deep has been harder.

Interviewer: What do you think you have to be doing?

Ellen: Next? I absolutely have to build. It is not so much now all about convincing the kids. The kids trust the staff, even the parents trust the staff, and those relationships I think are really good. But it is building the relationships between kids and kids— that is where I see our breakdown now. The government gave out $1 million to help communities. Our school was selected as one. So we got $65,000 to implement the *Leader In Me*, and we're going to do that. When we implement it we want to bring in the Native component as much as possible to support it. So we have started that, and that will hopefully build the student-student relationship, because that is where I think we are still having trouble. It is not the teacher-student so much. It's not even administrators. Like they all know us, yes.

Interviewer: Next I want to ask about **leading a learning community**. How do you set up a process of continuous teacher learning?

Ellen: It's been a work in progress and probably an area that I know, for me, I need to work better at. I think with the coordinators and their help we have made some progress. But even with us doing our evaluations I think we are really strong in terms of providing the guidance and support and the ongoing conversations. All three of us, my two assistant principals and I, do supervision really well. We take the time when we do our observations. We often meet with teachers and talk about what great teaching looks like. And there are usually questions that we ask the teachers and a process we follow. Leading learning with our teachers also requires being open to the PD supports that are available.

We spend a lot of money on PD and I think we support it as much as we can, like we allocate quite a bit of money. But it is the collaboration conversations, having a lot of those. That is making a big difference. We haven't always been successful, though, with book clubs or things like that. We are going to do another one, and try it, but again teachers don't always want to embrace it. So my question is, "How can we entice them or make them want to participate in a book study?"

This year I have sat with every single teacher, reviewed their PGP,[26] and talked specifically on how the teacher was going to lead their own learning. We also discussed what kinds of things the teachers could do if they saw certain areas of growth, and what they would need to do and how could I support them? So, you know, one teacher will say, "I really want to get better at technology." So then I said, "You know what I will do? I will forward an email to the vice-principal and see what we can come up with, and we will provide something." So much of helping to lead learning was by just asking them questions about what they wanted to do.

Interviewer: Asking what they need?

Ellen: "What do you need? What can we do to support you?" Because that's really our role.

Interviewer: Do you have something that could be defined as a school plan which lays out some of the areas of growth you want to see happen and some benchmarks, and some measures as to what you're going to judge it against?

Ellen: We have our school plan. The whole school plan thing has been really hazy, and I think that is part of my biggest frustration. At one point we went through this whole thing. Like I have my own personal plan of what I want to see for the school, but it's not actually a school improvement plan because we were kind of given direction, like this is what we need to do. So all of our planning kind of just went sideways in the last couple years.

Interviewer: But the full focus is on literacy, numeracy—is it not?

Ellen: Yes.

Interviewer: And in improving those school retention rates.

Ellen: School retention, yes.

Interviewer: So literacy, numeracy, and school retention, which are not bad areas to focus on—and your school is seeing some success in the literacy and the numeracy areas.

Ellen: Yes.

Interviewer: What about the school retention areas? The stats I looked at I would say you are keeping more kids in school from year to year.

Ellen: Yes.

---

26   PGP – Professional growth plan.

Interviewer: So let's talk about each one a little bit. What do you see as having been done in your school to improve literacy, improve numeracy, improve school retention? What have you focused on?

Ellen: Literacy?

Interviewer: Yes. We're going to address each one, but we will address them separately.

Ellen: What we do in terms of literacy—we have done a number of things. We have aligned some of the programs in Grade 1 and 2 so all teachers are expected to teach Smart Start, and Writing Essentials. So they have implemented both those programs. Now the Writing Essentials has kind of taken a back burner. I don't think it's been used as consistently this year, but it's because I have a lot of new teachers. So we are just trying to play catch-up, too. But definitely the Smart Start is something that we have implemented for literacy. We have implemented a process for grade group meetings. The teachers in their grade groups have been aligning a lot of their practices and teaching some of the same lessons, and talking about best practices and sharing resources. Literacy, we recently trained all our EAs in Precision Reading so that they can do a pull-out program for all kids in Grades 1 to 6. So they all received that training so they are able to do that, and lots of them are using it and we are seeing a lot of really good success with that.

Interviewer: So as principal, how do you know the program is working?

Ellen: I think when we look at their benchmarks in literacy we see a year's growth. We see improvement. We are also seeing more and more kids at grade level.

Interviewer: On the benchmark?

Ellen: When I look at when I started nine years ago I had three classrooms in Grade 2, four classrooms in Grade 3. I would say we had completely two modified classrooms per grade. Now we are lucky to even have a full class. We don't even have enough students to make a whole class anymore. And I think if you look at the long term, that's how I kind of see it. We are having just more regular classrooms. We still have some kids in those classrooms. Their work is kind of adapted for them by the teachers. But more and more kids are just at grade level, like meeting the curriculum at that grade level.

Interviewer: That's a good measure of success.

Ellen: So that would be probably one of my biggest successes.

Interviewer: What do you see in the numeracy area? What are you doing to make kids more successful there?

Ellen: I think we have provided a lot of training.

Interviewer: Training in what?

Ellen: Prime is what the teachers received training in, and I think they really found it beneficial, but that's just been this year.

Interviewer: What is Prime? I don't know what that is.

Ellen: It's a way of teaching like base 10.

Interviewer: Oh, okay.

Ellen: And just learning how to count. Just numbers, because that is where our kids really need to have that solid basis. One teacher has helped the other teachers find resources and just really sending them things that they need. She's been coaching the others, doing specific math lessons if they struggle with say, skip counting or whatever the case is, she'll go in that classroom and help them. What else? We have had ongoing PD that is offered throughout the year, so we stagger it so if they wish to go they can go.

Ellen: An issue we face is that we don't keep teachers for the long term. I think why we don't keep teachers after three and four years [is] because of salary. I lose some of my best teachers, I think, after they get their permanent teaching certificates, and once they get that little bit of experience the local urban districts will take a look at them and they are gone. And they are some of our best teachers that we will lose.

Interviewer: So, if you paid on par with the provincial school system would you keep people, or do you think they would still leave?

Ellen: We would keep more if we could pay the same as the provincial schools.

Interviewer: And why not the others?

Ellen: Work ethic, their inability to plan, their inability to discipline. They just let the kids do what they want.

Interviewer: Which is what you inherited nine years ago.

Interviewer: I'm going to go on to the actual formal part of your job, which deals with **instructional leadership.** Instructional leadership includes supervision and evaluation of teachers. How do you conduct that? What does it look like, taste like, feel like inside of your school?

Ellen: Well, early in the year I talk just generally with all the staff. We have a professional growth plan meeting and we just talk about what my vision for the year is and these are the things I'd like to look at. Then I kind of share what a growth plan is. I encourage the staff to look at their growth for the year. I really talk about strengths and areas of growth and how we can do that and how I can support them. Really, it has to be about them. They are going to know what they need to work on first and foremost. So we do that, and they come up with their PGP. I meet with every teacher. My assistant principals are supposed to meet with every EA. The APs work with the EAs because we have so many in our school. I do all the teachers.

In terms of evaluation, at the beginning of the year I sit down with the assistant principals and we break it down, who's going to be evaluating whom. I still oversee what's happening, but I get them to share in the process of teacher evaluations. We have the pre-conference. We sit down together and this is what it's going to look like. We do several observations over a few weeks. Sometimes we try to look at a few different courses—math, of course, and literacy are always a priority—and usually one option or one other that they want. We select those times, we go in, we do the observations. We just have a very informal observation format—I always just leave a little note on their desk with something great that I saw, and then I'll meet with you after school or whatever. And then we write up the evaluation. We do have a formal evaluation form we are supposed to use from the Board, but it doesn't really align with what we are doing in the school right now, so we want to change it.

Interviewer: Good idea to change it.

Ellen: And then we meet with them of course, and we have that conversation and we share everything we did and that's pretty much it. We usually followed this process in the fall and again in the spring.

Interviewer: For all teachers?

Ellen: Not all teachers.

Interviewer: New teachers?

Ellen: Just the new teachers and those who are going to be applying for a permanent certificate. Usually an outside person comes in to do the evaluation for the permanent certificate, but we also do our own evaluation.

Interviewer: What about the rest of your teachers? How do you know that they are doing what they need to be doing?

Ellen: That has been a struggle for us this year. It has also been one of those items that has been difficult for us over the last little while. I have had struggles with teachers so we do walk-throughs with every single teacher.

Interviewer: Is that the five-minute walk-through with the little checklist you have to fill out?

Ellen: Yes, and we fill it out and we sit down with them and we meet. This is what I saw—and then I usually say these are some things you may really want to consider working on for the year, or we might just have a conversation. We usually don't just say there is something we don't like. We try to address by working with the teacher to identify something they could continue to work on. In that case, we will visit again in a few weeks.

Interviewer: How often do you think you have to do that?

Ellen: With each teacher?

Interviewer: Or just teachers generally. Would that be a conversation you are experiencing once a month, or once every six months?

Ellen: Oh, once a month.

Interviewer: Yes?

Ellen: There's a few. This is one of the areas that I struggle with. What do I need to say to teachers who might not be doing all the things they need to do? Perhaps teachers who are a little inadequate.

Interviewer: I always used to say "average at best."

Ellen: Yes, okay. So how do you support those teachers and not totally deflate them where they are just so resentful of you? I don't know how to do that. And I haven't figured it out yet. And that's the God's honest truth. And I don't know if I'm missing a big piece. Because I've had those conversations. Last year I had a teacher who hadn't planned. There was nothing. That really bothered me, so I pulled her in, and she says she's having personal issues.

But at the end of the day I still have concerns, so we're going to come up with a work plan and this is what I want to see. So we would set targets and then I would go in and meet with her, and last year it got better. But this year I still want to evaluate her. So in writing it will be, I just haven't done it yet, but I'm going to say last year we had these concerns and yes, they were corrected. However, I want to ensure the best interests of the kids and I would like to complete a full evaluation on her this year. I don't know how else to do it.

Interviewer: There is no other way.

Ellen: That's the only way?

Interviewer: Yes.

Ellen: I don't know what to do with these teachers.

Interviewer: You just said it. That's exactly what you do. Your job is first of all to observe, you have to come to know. And to know, it means more than just watching their daily practice. The best way to know of course is take a look and see what the children are doing. That's how you know if they know it. It only matters if children know it. Then you start questioning and you start having conversations. When the teacher is not planning for the whole year, that is a pretty obvious one. Rarely, though, are they that obvious; it's more subtle.

Ellen: But I have a number of teachers like that. I hate to say that it's not just the First Nations teachers. Like I have some non-Native teachers too who are just kind of winging it. And it's attitude. Or I don't know if it's just that or work ethic. I have a few, I don't have very many but I have, you know, three for sure that I can think of off the top of my head that are just winging it. Maybe not all the time, and I've called them all on it. And I just had a conversation with one teacher and I said, "I'm really concerned about a lot of things that I'm seeing." And I said, "You need to step it up. You need to be the teacher I expect you to be." I had that conversation and she cried, and she was like, you know, "You're right." Like it's not good enough that you're just nice to the kids, it's not.

Interviewer: Next area I want to ask you about is **developing leadership in others**. What do you do to help develop leadership in others?

Ellen: I think I've actually gotten a lot better with that, with the *Leader in Me*, having that training, but also just understanding that I can't do it all. And that to me doesn't mean delegating. I think I have learned that as well, although you have to be a good delegator. That doesn't mean you are really building leadership just because you delegate. So it is just providing leadership opportunities. So having leadership teams where they take control.

Ellen: We have a Social Studies Lead and we also have a Science Lead. So we have our literacy and our numeracy coordinators who basically provide a lot of that support, but we also have our supports for social studies. These people do things like newsletters, and you will see them on our website quarterly. They also provide information, notes about curriculum changes, we go through it together, and then they send it out.

Interviewer: It goes out to parents or the teachers?

Ellen: To teachers. In the newsletters the lead teachers usually write about curriculum changes, upcoming PD, new resources, usually some teaching strategies or just different things, theory-based stuff, usually funny jokes, whatever, and some of the successes some of the teachers are having in their classes. I didn't mention that before, but I know for me, that has been one of my biggest goals this year. [It's] important to really just focus on the success of teachers in their classrooms.

Interviewer: Tell me about **school management and budgets**.

Ellen: We use past budgets as our guide. A lot of it is just seeing how the money was spent. So one important thing we have done, and it doesn't always look good on paper, but we sometimes take something out of one budget area even if we are going into the red in that area, and make it up from another area. I find it really important that we are seeing exactly where the money is being spent. Then I sit down with the assistant principals and the administrative assistant, because they are a big part of budget. Probably more so in a lot of ways because the administrative assistant does a lot of the purchase requests. She does all the kind of manager stuff with the budget. But the three of us sit down and we just look at how the money has been spent in the past; we look at what we need to know, like we kind of list the stuff that is coming up for the following year, and then we look at that. And we basically do it together. It has always been done together.

Interviewer: You and your two vice-principals?

Ellen: Yes. Because they are really instrumental in terms of how they just catch so many things that I don't. I really depend on them in that sense. They are so knowledgeable. We do it together.

CHAPTER 8:

Interview:
Kindergarten to Grade 9
School Principal

Joan is principal of an economically and socially challenged urban elementary school. She has 22 years of teaching experience and 12 years in various leadership positions in different contexts. She has served as principal for six years—three of them in her present school with 600 students, 20 teachers, and 22 support staff in K to Grade 9. She has a Master's degree.

The interviewer (co-author) asks her about mentorship and then proceeds to ask her how she enacts the competencies.

Interviewer: As you moved from being a vice-principal to being a principal, what kind of **mentorship** did you get as you went into that leadership role?

Joan: Well, both formal and informal mentorships. I had a group of principals that I valued and admired so I really took my leadership style from them. And then formal mentorship came from my involvement with a first-year principal mentorship program that our district runs, as well as our leadership academy program. And those are more formal opportunities to build my leadership skills.

Interviewer: Dig a little deeper into the formal one, please. If we knew nothing about the mentorship program run by your district, how would you describe it?

Joan: There is a lot involved in the program. Some of it is process and protocol, and other parts of it are philosophical. The process and protocol, like any school district, we have very specific things that we need to do, very specific ways that we do things, from staffing to discipline to safety standards, and all of those kinds of things. Budgeting is a big one for new principals, and all of those things you wouldn't necessarily know as a vice-principal, depending on how much support your principal allowed you to give. So those are all processes that are put into place by our district for a new principal. We have sessions on each of those areas at different times, sessions on boundary issues, how to have difficult conversations with employees, and then the more philosophical ones are based on the idea of how do we lead? And for us it's all about leadership, so we've done a lot of work on the philosophical idea of service and leadership, and how we demonstrate them as leaders.

Interviewer: Would these be one-on-one sessions with your mentor, or would they be large groups of new principals meeting with various school division staff?

Joan: Both . . . each new principal is assigned a mentor principal, and that principal has typically been a principal for a number of years. Typically, the assigned mentor comes from the same vicinity as that of [the] new principal. There are opportunities for them to get together, time for a principal to go and visit another. It does not work out all the time, but that's really the philosophy behind the mentorship—principals meeting each other in a school and sharing ideas. Then, of course, there are larger group meetings. We have very interesting ways to meet in our district. We have what are called families of schools. In these groupings we have schools that meet in the same demographic area. Coming from the same area is very important because our schools have very similar issues, so we have those kinds of meetings. We have district leadership meetings where it is all of the principals all together, and then there is of course our high school principal meetings and our junior high and elementary principals' meetings. So there are lots of opportunities to ask questions, throw ideas out to other principals, and see what other people are doing.

Interviewer: I want to go back to the mentorship you receive from your mentor, the person assigned to you by your district. How often would you have visited the mentor's building? How often did the mentor come into your building? Did it make a difference with you?

Joan: Well, I have to say that I was in a kind of unique situation with my mentor. My mentor was fabulous and we did meet. But, the position I had previous to becoming a principal was a brand new position in our district, and it was a district leadership vice-principal position. The role of district vice-principal was really along the lines of a principal. There were a lot of things I learnt in that position that held me in good stead as I moved into a school-based principalship. So there were things that I knew, and [I] had background knowledge that a normal first-year principal would not have had. So even though I know many other mentor principal teams met a lot with mentee and mentors, I didn't meet so much with mine because a lot of the things I already had knowledge of. That said, my mentor principal and I had very similar philosophical beliefs, and so we met a lot about those kinds of things and to discuss and to share. We also happened to meet again in our family of schools, so we talked a lot about the families and the things that we shared. So it wasn't necessarily about that process and protocol that I talked about before, but more of the philosophical mentorship.

Interviewer: As you moved into the principalship it sounds like you understood that the competencies play a role within the job. What role did you understand that the competencies actually play in your district?

Joan: I think it is our founding document, and it certainly sits in the documents that we use to start that conversation, but we don't end with that document. One can see the document in a lot of things that we do, like our boundary presentations, like our OH&S safety and security. Even with our budget meetings you can see that, you know, that budget accounting, about being responsible, those kinds of things, are built on the competencies.

I will give you two examples, an example of staff and an example of students. One of the things that we always have is turnover of staff: staff going on sick leave, staff having issues, and how you deal with that staff member, or how do you deal with that staff member who is not doing a good job and needs to go on evaluation? We have established processes and protocols that are very black and white, but that humanity that we bring to that particular situation I think is what makes us different. So we have EFAP, the Employment Family Assistance Program, that we bring to bear to support those teachers, so it's not necessarily that we want to discipline a teacher, it's that we take it the other way, [as] in how can we bring that person up? How can we help them to achieve the standards that they need to achieve? And that is the same with a student. A student gets suspended; we don't expel a student.

Typically, what we do is we work with that student, work with that family, to see if we can meet the needs of that particular student.

Interviewer: Thank you, that was a good example. In getting into the competencies themselves, the first one I am going to ask you about is a **vision**. Please tell us what is the **vision** for your school? How was it developed? What sorts of processes do you put in place to deliver it?

Joan: Our school is a high needs school in a demographic area where 50 plus percent of our population cannot pay school fees. It is not that they don't want to; they physically cannot pay. We have a significant population of ELLs [English language learners] and immigrant families in our school. So when I came to this school, there were some programs involved to nurture students, but from my perspective they were not developed enough. The vision for me developed when I walked into the building. When I watched and listened, I saw our students were coming to school hungry, and every single day we had behaviour problems and 90% of those problems happened because kids were starving. So we instituted "an eat anywhere eat any time" program for the school. So we had a breakfast program, we had a snack program, we had a lunch program, and we had an after school program that kids could come to and get food to take home.

So the discipline program evolved from that. When students were sent to the office because they had "blown up" in a class or something happened, before we even talked to them about what was going on, we offered them something to eat, and our discipline issues plummeted. Kids knew that if they were hungry—and it was all about self-identification, so if students self-identified that they were hungry—we would feed them, no questions asked. And that was a real change for our staff. Prior to this many of our support staff who lived in the neighbourhood believed they knew who had money and who could afford food and who couldn't. They passed judgements on students and decided who could have food and who could not. We stopped that. We stopped making value judgements and we just made sure hungry kids could have food.

For this program we got some funding from the Boys and Girls Club and Brown Bag. We also had a private funder donate money every year for food, who didn't care how we spent it but it had to be spent on food, and we also wrote grants to get money to fill in the rest of the gaps.

We had to work really hard to make sure we were consistent, and that was the toughest piece, to be consistent with the kids. To get them to believe that if they came to the office that they would not be scolded or put down or questioned about being hungry. And so that took a lot of work, a lot of convincing. And that was just my philosophy, and that was a hill that I was prepared to die on, and the support staff were basically given an option to support this or look elsewhere for work.

Interviewer: Fascinating story about the role of treating all students equally and giving to each person what he/she needs. What about the academic aspect of your school? What about things like PAT results? Reading inventories? Is there a before and after story there?

Joan: Yes, well I think so. So that [nutrition] piece, that was the social emotional piece for me. The other piece of course was the academic piece, and there was a philosophy among many of the teachers that went, "Well, we are teaching in a challenging demographic area so no one really cares," and so poor pedagogy was kind of allowed and that just sent me over the edge. We really worked hard on increasing the skill of our teachers by building capacity. Two books, *Making a Difference* and *Lost at School* became very important to what we did. We went through a book study together, as a staff. And we really pulled apart the important things in the program of the school. From the book study we learned that no one wants to fail, and it is all about building skills. We talked a lot about failure and skill building as a staff. We asked questions about how to help our students build those necessary skills. Our teachers would always go back to the important role scores played on a Grade 6 PAT and the Grade 9 PAT. My philosophy was let's put those aside, or not pay as much attention to them. The fact is, our kids can't access the curriculum in Grade 9 because they're reading at a Grade 3 level, so it doesn't matter what the Grade 9 curriculum is. They're not accessing it anyways.

I believed it was important to take care of those skills that we change and to shrink the gap between ability and curriculum. Our students, I maintained, will do better by virtue of them being able to access that curriculum. That was really a mind shift for our junior high teachers, especially because they were all about "we need to deliver the curriculum," and it just wasn't working. I mean we had years of poor results. It didn't take a brain surgeon to figure out that we needed to change something, so we really took a look at differentiation and literacy in our school, and how we could support both. Didn't take long to figure out that it was tough slugging.

We got to a point that it was no longer the English teachers' responsibility to teach reading and writing. It was everyone's responsibility. We had word walls in science, we had all sorts of differentiation going on, we had life-size Jenga games with words on it. As a leadership team we supported ideas that teachers came up with. We supported them to really build that capacity. Through capacity [building] we shoved off from the pier. We filmed teachers and showed to their colleagues the strategies that were working. We highlighted them in our staff meetings. We brought in all sorts of consultants, we did all sorts of work with the ATA, and we did see improvement in PAT results. However, the PAT results didn't really matter to me as much as our students being able to access more and more of the curriculum. Many of our students weren't university bound, so we needed to build skills in these students so that they could move on to high school and get a high school diploma.

We worked backwards. We took a look at what do our students need to get a high school diploma? What do they need in Grade 11? What do they need in Grade 10? What do they need in Grade 9? And all the way down to Grade 1, Kindergarten. This is what we needed to work on, so that when we passed those students on, they would have a chance at being successful. We built learning profiles for our students, so every student had a learner profile. Our teachers did all sorts of learning assessments. Our students came to understand what they learnt best in. So the philosophy was that in any given week teachers needed to teach to students' learning styles at least once. It was important to us that students could access curriculum in a kinesthetic way, in a visual way, in an auditory way. That was a big challenge for our teachers. However, in the end we wanted to make sure that we married the academic piece with the social and emotional piece.

Interviewer: What did you do in order to build capacity? What did you do to build an almost familial **relationship** with the teachers? How did you bring the support staff into active participation with the academic and social emotional program of the school—especially in light of the fact that they seemed to be working in opposition to where you wanted to move the school.

Joan: Yes, very much so.

Interviewer: So what was your tack with relationship building?

Joan: Well, let's start with support staff first. All female, all lived in the community, and all had been at the school for a long period of time. So they really felt ownership of the school, but they also felt like they were underrepresented, and had no power within the school. So one of the things we did was to start providing professional development for our support staff. We would identify two or three kids along with their specific needs, and we would then go to our support staff and say, "Okay let's do some PD on how to work one-on-one with a student and teach them literacy skills." So we built that process. We also asked them what they needed. We wanted support staff to tell us what they would like to learn to help students to learn in a more effective way. The other piece was giving support staff ownership. We had support staff in charge of noon-hour supervision, the concession, and then they also did some work in the classroom.

With the teachers it was important to show them what I was really passionate about. My beliefs and demonstrating my passion came through in the amount that I cooked. I cooked all the time when I was at that school: I made pancake breakfasts, I cooked something good with celebrations. I was there, not organizing it, not running it, but saying "give me a job. I will do the grunt jobs; I will do whatever you want me to do if you are going to run the program." This process showed to my teachers that I will do what is necessary to support them in their efforts to increase student learning. I think that demonstration of leadership showed I am willing to roll up my sleeves alongside of teachers while also recognizing how hard the work of school is. [It] also showed I am willing to do what it takes to help teachers, and that my message to the teachers was, "I will try never to say no."

That "if you have an idea that you can't do something, let's figure out a way how we can do it, and maybe it's not exactly the way you envisioned, but it meets a bunch of different needs, and it's a yes." And that was really how we moved forward. Did I have some people who were not happy? Absolutely I did. When I walked into that building they were $26,000 in debt, and in the first year we had that debt down to $9,000. Photocopying was out of control. It was learn by worksheet. It was just a disaster. People were spending money like it was water, and I said, "We're not doing that anymore, we're doing it this way. You don't get a budget, zero-based budget, you have to come to me to ask, and then we will see if it works." So there were some people who weren't very happy about that, but there were other people who really believed in that vision and so they outweighed the non-believers.

Interviewer: What did you have to do to get the non-believers to become believers?

Joan: Well, part of it was taking a look at the TQS [Alberta Teacher Quality Standard]. I asked teachers questions like: What is your professional responsibility? What other things are you supposed to do as a teacher? It says right there [in the TQS document] all sorts of different ways to make connections to students, different modalities. What are you doing for professional development? How are you becoming a better teacher? What are your skill sets? Are you in the wrong classroom, would you like to do something different? Let's work together, let's support each other. These are my expectations. The expectations never change and they knew exactly what I expected all the time. Kids always came first, and helping them learn always came first. And were there discipline issues? Absolutely we had discipline issues. Were there kids that I actually had to expel? There were, unfortunately. They were a safety risk to our community, but when parents saw that and kids saw that and teachers saw that—that we were willing to take a stand and this is our community and we're going to protect it—they appreciated it. There was much more buying in that way. Did we have teachers on evaluation? Absolutely we did. Did a couple of teachers decide to go different places? For sure.

Interviewer: How did you know what these teachers were doing inside of their classrooms once you finished your professional work?

Joan: Because I was in the classrooms all the time.

Interviewer: What did it look like when you were inside of the classroom? Did you have a checklist that you were working from as to what the pedagogy looked like, or what student learning looked like?

Joan: Sometimes. What the deal was is that we would take a skill, one skill, and we wanted to make it simple for teachers. We didn't want it to be we have got to change all of our practices right away, because that is just too overwhelming. So we broke it down into steps. So we decided we were going to focus on one thing, and so we would in-service the teachers on just one thing, so for instance [how to build] a word wall. So we in-serviced the teachers on a word wall, how it would look, how you could do it in different subject areas, and then I invited teachers. I said, "You know, I would really like you to try this, invite me in, invite me to see how it is going. I would love to help. I would love to help you do the word wall."

We also had the support of the DLT, Diverse Learning Team, to support teachers as well. DLT members would go in to help with individual and small groups of teachers. It would be almost like a team effort. Teachers would sign up with the Diverse Learning Teacher and invite them to come into [the] classroom to observe a certain teaching practice. Teachers would indicate that they would like to try something in a particular class, and then they would also invite me. So there would be three or four of us in that classroom working with that teacher. Wow, this was great! We were able to see first-hand what really neat things were happening in the classrooms. Then we would be able to note the effective practices at our next staff meeting. We would talk about being in a teacher's classroom and that this worked really well, and on occasion address some things that didn't work. We would then encourage and ask if anyone else want[ed] to give it a try? Many said, "Yes, we'll try it."

So the process I followed was to address one or two teachers at a time, but teachers learn very quickly that it was an open door policy. My office door was always open, their classroom doors were always open, and administration was going to be in and out. We purposely didn't go in with a checklist. We didn't want to make teachers feel like they were being spied on, that we were in this together and it was okay to fail, as long as you tried something different. We had teachers who just took off and flew and who were amazing, and other teachers who really struggled because their classroom management wasn't really very strong, and so they needed some support that way.

In our staffroom we built our own learning wall from where we started with our PD at the very beginning of the year. And it was our learning highway, where along the pathway to the end of the year we put all of the different PD, all of the different activities we were working with teachers and seeing teachers use in the classrooms. The learning wall was a visual reminder of what we were doing. Teachers would say, "Oh yeah, I remember we did this. This worked really great in my class." Teachers would always see that, and so by the end of the year it was filled with all sorts of opportunities for them.

Interviewer: Whose idea was that?

Joan: It was mine.

Interviewer: Where did you get it?

Joan: Well, we talk about visual literacy and visual and kinesthetic learners and all of that kind of stuff . . . so it just kind of evolved from those conversations. We are talking to our teachers about engaging students from a standpoint of not just standing and delivering, but how do we engage them in something that's exciting and hands on? So it seemed to me a pretty logical step to say, well, our teachers need that too. That we can't just stand and deliver that PD, we need to demonstrate, and we need to show evidence that this is what we are building.

The beauty of a K to 9 school is that fluidity and intermingling between grades and divisions can happen. Great pedagogy typically happens in those early grades. What we needed to see was how do we continue to build those ideas and continue those great teaching methods into the junior high?

Interviewer: You make it a great place for teaching and learning.

Joan: Sure, yes. So in our elementary wing of the school much more collaboration was happening with the teachers than at the junior high wing. One of the things that I walked into were huge personality issues in the building, really poisonous to the staff, so the silos happened because of that. Not so much because they were subject specific, but they were people specific. So there was a lot of team building that needed to happen before we even looked at improving practice.

Interviewer: I want to move to this idea of learning community and of course one of the competencies is **leading a learning community**, so like a before and after snapshot, what would it look like? What would the PLCs have looked like in your school prior to you getting here? And what did they look like as you left the building?

Joan: Right. Well I think before I got to the school there were, and continue to be, strong teachers here, and they did their thing, and the weak teachers did their thing, and sometimes they shared, if it was beneficial to some of the people involved. Sometimes they didn't share, as there were a lot of different philosophies floating around in that building. So I would hear from some of them, "I'm a great believer in workbooks and worksheets, that's how I am going to teach." Or "I am a really strong believer and I am a tech person, and I really want a Smart Board, and that's how I'm going to teach." It seemed like these separate individuals and beliefs wouldn't get together as to why we teach the way we teach.

So when I came those conversations started to happen. Why do we teach the way we teach? Who are our kids? Who are the people we are teaching? I think those were the biggest questions that hadn't been asked in the school. We looked at ideas around whether it was curriculum that we're delivering or kids that we are teaching. Came to the point that we are teaching students and we happen to be teaching them curriculum, but that curriculum can take all sorts of different forms, shapes, and paths. But it is the kids that matter, I hope, was the change that we helped develop. That change in philosophy also led to a change in our PLCs. It was not just about people thinking, "I'm the math teacher, I'm the science teacher, I'm the language arts teacher, and we don't really need to talk to each other because we teach completely different curriculum." The change was, "Johnny is our student. He has these strengths and these weaknesses. How are you helping him in science? What are you doing in LA to engage Johnny? He's really great in math. Why don't we get him to do some math, but with some reading problems, math oriented. Would that meet your curriculum outcome? Sure, it would meet some English outcomes, but he's doing math so he thinks he is doing math, but he's actually doing language." It was more of a professional learning community team approach of: Who are our students? How are we engaging them? And then the curriculum piece, rather than this is my curriculum and I am just going to focus on that.

Interviewer: You mentioned earlier learner profiles. How does that fit in with what you just said?

Joan: We found that during the first week of school we waste a lot of time doing paperwork and doing items around the student account. What we decided to do was to engage students in learning profile activities, fun activities that were a challenge to the kids, but would paint a picture of how they best learned. Every homeroom teacher would do these activities with their students, and from there we built a group. Also there were, I don't know, three or four tests that we did, and for the younger kids there were games. So we had a whole kind of index full of learning activities that we could do to identify the strengths and weaknesses of the student. Then what we did was we combined that learning profile with any learning issues that student had—so whether they had an IPP,[27] an ISP,[28] whether they were coded but didn't have any support and we built that together. One of the issues we had was IPPs were just a document, a piece of paper, and for the most part that has always been a struggle. But what we tried to do was make that IPP or ISP for that student a living document, where a teacher could understand where that strength of that student was, how they could use some learning styles to help them achieve

---

27   IPP – Individual Program Plan.

28   ISP – Individual Student Plan.

curriculum outcomes. Our DL[29] teacher and CT[30] worked really hard in building those programs for teachers. Every teacher would have a copy of their students' learning profiles, and they were all colour coded, so they would know how many kinesthetic learners they had in any class, how many verbal learners, how many visual learners. We then offered lots of PD on different ways to engage that curriculum in different learning styles. And so that's where that learning profile came in.

The idea was that student profiles would be continued from year to year and passed on. This process led to a different way of building class lists for the next year. Instead of at the year-end, when a teacher might think he is competing with another teacher for the Grade 8 class, and where one might think I want to give the other person all the yahoos, and where he might get all the good ones—we quickly changed that thinking. It was more of a discussion as [to] whose learning style fit best with each other, to make sure we had similar learning styles in class so there wouldn't be just one kinesthetic learner in a class of verbal kids, and how would that kid fit in. We tried to balance the class that way. We also based class development along the lines of balancing with boys and girls, friends, all of the variables that kind of come into it. But it was more of a conversation about learning, rather than a hockey trade where, "I want to build the best class that I can because then it sucks to be you, but I've made for a great class." And that was the mentality we wanted to get rid of very much.

Interviewer: How many Grade 8 classes would you have?

Joan: Four.

Interviewer: And then, in the elementary say, how many Grade 2 classes would you have?

Joan: Our junior high was much bigger than our elementary, so our junior high was a feeder from other elementary schools. We would typically have stand-alone classes as well as combined classes in the elementary. We would have Grade 1, a Grade 1-2 combined, a Grade 2, a Grade 3, a Grade 3-4 combined in our elementary. So almost one-and-a-half classes per grade, but never a double.

---

29   DL teacher – Differentiated Learning Teacher.

30   CT teacher – Classroom Support Teacher.

Interviewer: So the next part I want to talk about, and lead you towards, is this idea of **developing and facilitating leadership**. What you do as principal in recognizing leadership skills, because in order to make this change—and it sounds like quite a dramatic change—how did you get other people involved, not just as doers, but as leaders as well?

Joan: I really believe philosophically that developing and facilitating leadership in others is one of the most important things a leader does. Leaders need to build capacity of leadership in others. When I first came to the school, I interviewed every single teacher, every single support staff member, and asked them a number of questions. What are you passionate about? What gets you up in the morning? Who is your family? What do you do that excites in you what you are currently teaching? What's your background? Would you like to try something else? Do you have any aspirations for leadership? Would you like to take on roles within the school? I built my own profile of each person, and while doing that I also found out who had issues within the building. And sometimes, not all the time, but there were a couple of teachers that I felt had the potential but either were never given the chance, and so they decided to see the cup half empty rather than half full.

I then focused on putting those teachers into positions of leadership where they could take ownership of learning profiles, or to take ownership of organizing some PD sessions, to deliver PD sessions, to represent me as a district person at a meeting. I would say to people, "You're going to go to this meeting. When you come back you're going to have to share what you learned with the rest of the staff. So make sure you go and make sure you pay attention." Those were the hard cases where I needed to get those people on board with the kind of the vision that we were kind of trying to instil in the building, so I tried to send them to PD that kind of replicated an evolving vision. I had one teacher in particular come to me in frustration and say to me, "You know what Joan, you just told us about differentiation three months ago. How are we supposed to know it by now?" I said to her, "I didn't invent differentiation, and if I did I wouldn't be here, I would be very wealthy. This is a pedagogical tool that you should have been well aware of. We have been differentiating in the district for years, so the fact that you don't know indicates that we have lots of work to do." And so we sent those kinds of teachers to see what is happening at other schools.

So I got on the phone to my mentor principal and asked if he had any really crackerjack teachers, and whether I could send so and so over. Instructional services can give me a sub, so I can send these teachers over to see what your teachers are doing. My mentor would always agree. This teacher-to-teacher development worked with my teachers.

I built leadership capacity in a small way, giving my inner circle, the teachers I deemed as having the same vision as me, that seemed to me to have the same kind of philosophical ideas, an opportunity to take on various leadership roles. "Are you with me?" "Yes." "Can you do this?" "Absolutely." "Can you do that?" "For sure." And through this process we built a new way of doing things in the school. Slowly that circle of influence grew, as I brought more people in. So that's how it worked. I am painting a pretty rosy picture, and it wasn't really that rosy. It was hard work. Some teachers never got there, other teachers who were on their way just exploded and are amazing teachers, and then there's the middle people who are still just content to kind of do their thing. But because everybody else has raised their level they've been forced to raise their level of teaching.

Interviewer: What did staff meetings look like when you showed up? And what did staff meetings look like when you left? Any change?

Joan: Well, I mean, I don't know exactly what they looked like when I got here, but I do know staff meetings were typically an hour-and-a-half long, with about 25 agenda items, and went on forever and ever. So I made the commitment to staff that our staff meetings would be no longer than 45 minutes, at the 45-minute mark we would be done, that there would be no more than eight agenda items, and anything that was informational would be communicated by email.

Interviewer: Good for you. Let's just change the topic a little bit and deal with the competency **larger societal context**. How did you demonstrate to the community your care for education and the important role it plays with the development of children?

Joan: Well, our community is a tough piece. It is [a] community that is very transient, yet we also have a population that are tried and true to that neighbourhood. And then we have around our school low-income housing, so a very transient population. We are really the first stop for many of our immigrant families. They came here before deciding whether to stay permanently in the community or move elsewhere. There was a lot of angst in the community against this transient group, and angst from the new arrivals and the group that has been here for a long time. But then again, for the most part, people got along. But there was certainly a pecking order of who's who in the community and who ranks. Within that there was that whole idea again about the have and the have nots, so there were certainly people in the community that had, and many of the people in the community that had not, and with that comes a different view of education than what maybe you and I have as middle class, born and raised in Canada, versus that whole idea of war-torn and all of that. So community sensitivity was an important piece for our teachers, as well as our messages sent out to the community.

So while we used all sorts of different ways to communicate, that idea of building relationships was the most important. So of course many of our community members didn't have access to email, didn't have computers, wouldn't use a computer anyways because that's not their culture, took great pride in their culture, but were really at a loss of how to manage and work their way through our system. We communicated how important education was by becoming what I would consider the epicentre of that particular community. So we had lots of community support. We had eye doctors come in, we had dentists come in, we had a nurse there, we had a social worker, we had all sorts of support. All we needed to do was help one family and then that family, from a certain ethnicity, would talk to all of their community people and then they knew. And so it was really about helping one family at a time to build the idea that [they could] come to the school for support. Come and we will help you.

Interviewer: Tell us about the relationship of **management** and leadership in your practice.

Joan: To have a great philosophy and great ideas about leadership, and all of that, but not have the management side can create all sorts of chaos in the things that require management. There are things that require management in a school and things that require leadership. You know the good thing about the management piece is you can often surround yourself with people who have those skills. So a great secretary who manages your budget is valuable, or you know a vice-principal who is crackerjack at scheduling, and those kinds of things. So if I had to choose I think I would choose leadership over management, but I think you have to have both. Everyone's personality makes us different, but it certainly helped me having a little bit of both.

Interviewer: So if someone were to ask you, Joan, after three-and-a-half years at this school, for three successes, what would you say to them?

Joan: Feeding kids. That is absolutely number one. Because it was more than feeding kids, and that was, I think I was more passionate about that than anything. To have students understand that people cared about them and people wanted them to be well academically, physically, emotionally. We did way more than feed kids. I mean we clothed families. There was lots going on and lots of people stepping up to do amazing things. The other piece would be that pedagogical piece of challenging teachers to build their own capacity, to not just rest on the fact that these are low SES kids and no one really cares. That it's important to be good at what you do, and take pride in what you do, and to be the best that we can be. The third piece is—I am going to count here—there are five teachers from the building that are in leadership positions in other schools. I take lots of pride in that, that I did my job. I have always believed that that's my job, to make sure people reach and build their own capacity to be leaders in our district, and they did, which is fantastic.

CHAPTER 9:

Interview:
Grades 6 to 9
School Principal

James has been a teacher for 32 years, has served six years as a vice-principal in various school settings, and four years as principal. His present school has 390 students in Grades 6 to 9. The school features sports academies with about 200 participating students. James is working on his Master's degree.

The interviewer (co-author) asks James about what role the competencies play in the district and then proceeds to ask him how he enacts each of the competencies.

Interviewer: In your district what, if any, use has been made of the principal leadership competencies in identifying potential leaders and in preparing them for a leadership position?

James: When I took the role of principal I didn't really think about that a lot. When the last principal moved to a new school the folks at the division office contacted me to see if I wanted to fill in. I took the job but never really thought about the competencies.

Interviewer: I was curious with the role that the principal competencies, the document, the PPCSLs, actually play in this district. What role does it have?

James: The role that the competencies play continues to grow. I know that when we had our previous superintendent we would go through a binder. We went through these professional competencies and we had to prove that we were doing those competencies. So it was kind of a laborious task to put that binder together, and proving that we are doing these things. I met with the new super the other day, and he said that I am up with my three-year term as a principal. As my three-year contract is due they will review my competency and go through the next formalized process. When I meet with the superintendent I will say where I'm at, he will say where he thinks I am at, and the professional dialogue will go through there. The new superintendent is not as worried about the portfolio as the old. He is more interested in the conversation that we will have.

Interviewer: I will now ask a question so as to get you to compare a process that you have already been through with a process that is yet to happen. I recognize that you may have to guess a little at a possible answer. However, please do compare the process of providing the binder of evidence versus being able to take a look at a rubric and trying to assess where you are at. Which of those two processes is more appealing to you?

James: The binder was good at that time for me to see what I actually did during the year. I think, sometimes, you don't really realize how much you do or where you are spending the majority of your time. So it really showed me where I was spending a lot of my time and where I needed to increase time or where I needed to decrease time. With the process I am going through now, I'm kind of curious to see how the dialogue will impact things, because we didn't do a lot of dialogue with the binder process. Once I presented my binder that was it. Like, you know, we didn't do a follow-up to it, and that was a little bit disappointing for me because I had spent all this time putting the binder together. I mean, it was close to a six-inch binder . . . but there was no follow-through, and so I was kind of disappointed with that. To me, it seemed like it was a make-work project, or was it something of value? I found it of value, because I again analyzed what I did, but I didn't get to share that dialogue with anybody. So with the new super we are looking at sharing what we each think. A dialogue.

Interviewer: Now we are going to go into the competencies themselves, and it is kind of like a repeat of your binder process—but with dialogue.

So the first part we are really curious about is **vision**. What is the vision of your school? Tell us how it was created, and when and why?

James: The vision of our school really relates to the role that the sports academy plays in our school. The school division had asked us to see about starting a sports academy. So we started at the ground level, which was exciting. Introduced three sports at the beginning and then increased to a fourth sport and we added soccer because we found the girls weren't coming into the program. Then after that, I think, the vision was developed. How can we best meet the needs of all our students? I have always maintained that a school needs balance in the program—a fine arts program, sports program, electives that kids want to go into. When you have that balance, then you will meet more needs than just trying to focus on one area. So we've tried to get away from just the one area, like being a sports-focused school, and to try to increase other areas. We started off as a sports technology school, but we found after about three, four years we couldn't keep up with the technology that the kids had in their own pockets, and so we kind of branched away from that. And that is why we have gone with the more hands-on approach to learning. Rockets, robotics, the bike building, the woodwork, the welding at the college, the foods lab now, and student publishers.

Giving kids a chance to try a number of different things, something that, hopefully, from which they will find that one thing that will spark them to continue on in high school and to a better path in the future. Another thing we did was ask the high school people not to talk to just Grade 9s. We wanted them to talk to our Grade 8s. We find that the Grade 9 year is the pivotal year, and that if students don't have the marks, or [are] not ready when they go to high school, they lose out on certain things. So now we bring the counsellors into our school about midway through Grade 8 to talk to kids. They let the students know what they will need to get into various programs when they go to high school. For example, they might mention what students will need if they want to get into a work experience program, if they want to go into an apprenticeship program. They will let them know what it is they need. We are not putting in kids that are failing; they have to have the marks to go into those programs.

Interviewer: The second competency we want to talk about is **relationship building**. Tell us about how you went about developing a positive working environment in your school?

James: I think by giving more control to different staff members, trying to cut down on certain things, building from the ground up. We have what we call our success team at our school, and every second Tuesday our success team meets to discuss issues that are going on in the school. We found our staff meetings were becoming way too long and we weren't able to handle what we really needed to work on. For example, next Tuesday our success team, which consists of a representative from Grades 6, 7, 8, and 9, will come in, and our vice-principal, myself, and our counsellor will discuss some of the issues that we are seeing at the school right now. One of the big concerns right now is second chances on quizzes. So we will discuss that with this group. The success team members then go back out to their groups and talk amongst their grade level, and then when we come to the staff meeting we are able to channel some of that stuff, and maybe do we need to cover this or don't we need to cover it? So we are giving the staff more voice. Sometimes it is a little tough because you have to bite your tongue. We are, however, finding it [to] be more successful than what we used to do.

Interviewer: How often would you meet with the success team?

James: Every two weeks.

Interviewer: For how long?

James: We meet for an hour during the morning.

Interviewer: During the school day or outside of the school?

James: Before school, outside of school time. We tried to look at some common prep time but I just couldn't do it. I give them a day in lieu to do this, so I give them one day off per year. I pay for a sub day for them. But it has been a valuable service for us. I mean it saved us a lot of time. Now when we get to our staff meetings we can discuss certain issues, but then we can spend more time on PLC work when we want to do stuff for the school, and we found that has increased our meeting time amongst teachers themselves.

Interviewer: We are going to come to PLC format. I am going to get you to give a longer description later on.

James: When we have a once-a-month assembly, we pick teacher groups to come out and then I can work with them. So for example we were just working on our achievement test results . . . our kids all went to assembly, so on Monday I worked with my Grade 6 and 9 teachers and we analyzed our achievement test results. We look at the PATs to see trends. See what can we do to improve them? What areas we need to work on. We try to build in that time as well.

Interviewer: Do you have an example, perhaps where you see your way of doing things is actually making a difference and an impact with the teachers you are working with?

James: Well, we had our vice-principal take over running our sports academies, so I gave up that role to my vice-principal four years ago. I said, "You are in charge now, so unless you need me to help out, this is your goal." Our Special Ed person, our learning facilitator, I gave them those roles. I said, "You know what? I can't do all of these things. I trust your judgement. We just need to meet once in a while and make sure that I'm informed of things." I have found that these new leaders have really taken charge. The process has decreased some of my role as administrator, and it has allowed me to do other things, such as acting as a learning coach. Tough to be a learning coach if I'm doing all these other jobs.

Interviewer: That answer is interesting because it leads right to where we are going next—**leading a learning community.**

Interviewer: Outline for us then the process you followed to increase the level of student learning in your school.

James: The first thing we did was we analyzed the number of minutes we gave to all our subject areas. We eliminated two of the option blocks right off the bat. We decided to get back down to the basics. And for our option periods we asked our option people to make sure that they were touching upon things that relate back to the curriculum the students are doing. So with rockets and robotics they look at altitude, so they also tried to relate some of what they were doing to the math and science program of studies. Next year we want to increase it and get more of those core subjects back into what we're doing.

Interviewer: How's that process being met by your teaching staff?

James: Very well. They enjoy it. I mean when we had our old options the kids hated them, so I spent most of my time during option time disciplining kids because they were causing a lot of problems in the class. Now if they don't do their homework, and if I say I'm going to pull you out of an option, they want to get that work in because they don't want to miss the robotics, and they want to be there when they're firing off rockets. So it's increased that way.

Interviewer: So who's come up with the ideas for these new options?

James: I approached the staff. I said, "Staff, we've got to get rid of the sit-down options where we don't do anything. We got to come up with something that is going to keep the interest of the kids, teach them something valuable but get them doing things, not just sitting." Now if you walk into our robotics group, or our rockets group, the teacher could leave the room and the kids wouldn't even know they are gone. They just work. They want to do this stuff.

Interviewer: So who developed this actual robotics class, you or the teacher?

James: We had a teacher develop it. We had the robotics kits way back, and now we are looking at trying to go to a second level. So I have asked my teachers to take a look at the robotics basics. Can we expand it a bit more and do something like robotics advanced? And do the same with the rockets? We are at this basic level, can we go up a little bit more? We are also doing something different with the yearbook now.

James: What also happened with options is my band students no longer wanted to take band, because for band you need to have a full-year program. When I approached the college about doing woodworking on their site in their apprenticeship program, all of a sudden my band numbers were next to nothing. So then I had to come up with a different way to offer band. We changed our year into a trimester system. I went to our band students and asked, "Why aren't you taking band?" "Sir, we want to do the woodworking at the college." So I asked, "Well, if I gave you the first semester for woodworking would you go in the band for semesters two and three?" They said they would. So that is where we have compromised with our band teacher. I have moved those kids into the option of their choice, and I do it for Grade 7 and 8 now, because the Grade 6 students didn't want band because they wanted rockets and robotics instead. The whole process caused me some different problems, but we just had to adjust our timetable to meet the needs of those kids.

Interviewer: So where do you actually find time to do the academies? What do the academies actually look like? Where are they in this deck of cards?

James: Our sports academies happen two days a week for each grade grouping. So my Grade 6s and 7s leave campus Monday and Wednesday afternoons. My other groups leave Tuesdays and Thursdays, the Grade 8s and 9s. There is no difference in academic time. The only difference that we have is our academy people do their big chunk of phys. ed. on those two days. So I run a daily phys. ed. program for our school that is five days a week, and then the one period we do for Health. So that is six periods. Our academies are two, three-period blocks. We schedule it that way as time lost was also a concern with our parents. They were concerned about students losing language arts and math time.

Interviewer: So your teachers themselves, do they meet as a professional learning community? If so, what does this look like in this school?

James: What we do is we ask our teachers to give us something that we need to work on. So when we met at our first staff meeting we will say, "What are some of the issues that we see from the previous year?"

Interviewer: PAT issues.

James: PAT issues, it could be as simple as the electronics policy, it could be something like new assessment policies, second chance policies. So that is one thing we have to work on in our next PLC, our group. So we asked our teachers to develop that. We do a staff meeting where we do a little bit of a professional activity at the beginning, about 10 or 15 minutes. I do my report. But now we have changed our whole format on that. We have cut down our actual meeting time with the teachers in a formal setting from three hours down to about 35 to 40 minutes, but then we have taken the bulk of that time now and put it into that activity that we need to do to actually help our school, and it has been great to see the professional dialogue that goes on with those staff members now. I will go out in the hallway, and I will just walk and kind of go in between groups, and these guys are meeting for a solid two hours and coming back with something that we really feel can be useful to our school.

Interviewer: What might be a curriculum-based project that one of these PLCs worked on that is now implemented within their area of this school?

James: Well, we went to a new assessment policy and we looked at rewriting math goals, rewriting different goals, how do we do assessments, common assessment planning, and exit cards? So when we did the manipulatives for math we spent that whole day just working on manipulatives. Everybody had to research a certain area, and they came in with how do we use manipulatives with this new math program? So it has been quite successful that way.

Interviewer: And as principal, as you wander around are you seeing some of the manipulatives in play?

James: All the time. Our Grade 6 teachers, they were the first . . . our Grade 9s are just getting on board now. But our Grade 6 teachers and a Grade 9 teacher were quite the lead on these. As well also Grade 7 and 8, because I've got the same math teacher, and the amount of time the manipulatives are used is quite high.

Interviewer: And was that a personal passion of yours, or would you say that truly arose from these PLC group meetings?

James: It arose from the PLC. It was something that we looked at, we discussed. But again they took charge of it, and they started developing it and just simple things that came out, just the ideas they came up with.

Interviewer: And it went from that one teacher, and would you say multiple teachers use them now?

James: Multiple teachers started using them. The other thing we did in our PLC is we said, "If you're developing something it has to be put into a teacher-shared folder."

Interviewer: On the Internet somewhere?

James: Yes. This shared folder is a great spot to keep all of the tools we are developing to help students learn. Also works great when we hire new teachers. We had two new teachers come on board. One was a Grade 8 guy that is teaching math and science. Our Grade 8 science and math teacher says to him, "Here's our resources, this is what we've done, here's our common test practices, this is what we do, here's the information you need, if you need anything else come see us." We also assign a mentor to our new teachers, someone who can make sure they know where all the resources are and how we do things at this school.

Interviewer: As soon as you say mentoring my ears perk up. So day by day, week by week, month by month, what does this mentoring look like?

James: The mentoring process was started by our school division. We are asked to pair up a new teacher with somebody that is an established teacher. The established teacher meets with that individual to discuss how things are going.

Interviewer: How often do they meet?

James: They will meet once a month formally in a scheduled meeting. But then they are also meeting informally on an ongoing basis.

Interviewer: They will meet on school time?

James: On school time, yes.

Interviewer: Do they meet all day, or do they meet half a day? Here at your school or in the Board office?

James: Here. They will meet here for half a day. Also at that time the new teachers are told, "This is what you need to do back at your school with your administration." So they come back to us and say, "Are you going to come see me?"—so that we keep in touch with them so that they are making that effort to go see other people. I always tell our new teachers that if you want to go see someone else do something, I will cover your class and you go watch this teacher teach.

Interviewer: How often would you be taken up on that?

James: Probably once every couple of weeks.

Interviewer: And they want to watch somebody else in your building or they want to watch somebody elsewhere?

James: Both.

Interviewer: And the content of the mentoring program?

James: Daily procedures they go through. When it comes to the first parent teacher interviews we will sit down with them and say, "These are some of the questions you are probably going to be asked at your first parent teacher interview. Do you have your marks ready? Have you made parent contact before? If you make a parent contact we need to know about it at our office because that way when a parent phones me and says, "Well no one's ever talked to me about the problems my kid's having," I will be able to reply, "Well no, I've got four contacts here that were made to you." I can let the teachers know that what I can say to the parents has more credence. We do a lot of monitoring of what kids are doing. We have a dreaded yellow sheet at our school. We force our teachers, if a kid has either a behavioural problem or there is [a] homework issue, to make contact with that parent through either an email or a phone call, and to write up the contact info on a yellow sheet. Then when the kid gets so many yellow sheets we contact the parent to say, "We are noticing a problem here." If they are a sport academy student, because we tell them at the beginning of the year, "You're student athletes, not athlete students. You miss an academy period"—and the parents know that right up front, so—"you are going to take that time when you could have been on the ice or you could be on the soccer field, you are going to finish up the work that you have missed." And then the regular students will lose an activity and they will come with me and work.

Interviewer: And that would be activities that matter.

James: Right, exactly. It has been a process and in many ways we are still developing it. You know, sometimes we take criticisms for that, but on the whole part we think it is working fairly well.

Interviewer: In your role of **instructional leader**, which, of course, is the ultimate role of the principal, tell us about how you see that role and what you do about it inside of your school.

James: I think it is getting tougher all the time, with all the other stuff that is going on, with the paperwork, the day-to-day work. Last year with my vice-principal I asked him to focus on instructional leadership with language arts and social, because he had more of a language arts and social background. I will do the math and science. So then we would go in and take a look at what is going on with the different groups.

Interviewer: And how do you ensure that your teachers are actually following current pedagogy?

James: Right now I am pretty fortunate, as our staff is quite up to date on all the different techniques and all the work. They are keen; they are keen on it.

Interviewer: How often would you be inside classrooms observing what is happening, particularly in the math and science classrooms?

James: Every couple of weeks I will be going in.

Interviewer: For how long?

James: Twenty-five to 30 minutes. Sometimes less. Certain people will get more of my attention if I know they are new instructors. With the new teachers I will spend more time because I just want to make sure that they are following some different techniques. We have our teachers put targets on the board that students need to reach for the day. I see right away when this class' targets are not written up on the wall, and so I say, "We need that target up on the wall." I said, "It reminds you what the lesson is about." But also at the end of the day I can say to the kids, "What was that lesson about?" Or whether they know what the target was at the beginning. One of our teachers came up with an idea about using a bull's eye board. This bull's eye was on a magnetic sticker that was put up on each bulletin board. In this way the targets are right there, so when the kids come in they know the target of that period. We have asked our teachers to make sure that they keep on that target. We ask them to write the targets in student-friendly words. The only issue I have had has been with our math people who aren't really crazy about student-friendly terms. They believe that we need to use the correct language from the math program. Using the correct math terms made perfect sense—so that is what we use in math.

Interviewer: With the 25 minutes that you are inside of a classroom, if I were a fly on the wall watching you, what would I see you doing?

James: Well, first of all I want to take a look at whether or not the targets are up, take a look at the lesson plan that should be on the desk, look at what the introduction for [the] lesson is like, and look at student engagement. I like to pay attention to how the teacher is questioning, the different instructional techniques being employed, checking to see if they are going to different students. Do I see them hanging around one side of the room compared to another side of the room? Are they active in the lesson?

Interviewer: How would you give the teacher feedback on what you are seeing?

James: We discuss it afterwards.

Interviewer: Would you have like a formal sit-down, or would it be a quick chat out of the door?

James: Just a quick chat afterwards. With the new ones I say, "Let's sit down tomorrow sometime and we will chat about it." When we meet I will usually ask, "What was your perspective of the lesson?" I like to give them the first opportunity to say something. Because a lot of times if the lesson doesn't go really well they know it, and then I will be able to give them some feedback afterwards. I often tell them, "This is what so and so does next door. I want you to go watch that lesson. Just watch him, how he presents."

Interviewer: And how do your teachers react to an encouragement to go watch somebody else?

James: They enjoy it. Even some of our veterans like to go and see other teachers. Sometimes you just pick up one idea and that one idea is powerful.

Interviewer: Teachers observing other teachers. Was that a practice in your school before you came here?

James: Not as heavily used as it is now. To me, I have always found that the best PD I have had is talking with other teachers. So I encourage it now.

Interviewer: In one of your answers, James, you mentioned that if a student isn't performing he gets taken out of this option block, which it seems is where kids want to be, and he has spent the time with you.

James: Right.

Interviewer: What does that look like?

James: We just go through some stuff. So the teacher will tell me these are the areas he's missing or weak on, and then we will meet. I also do all the new detentions, and I use that as math help, too. So I am in there monitoring what homework they are doing as well. So I have taken a lot more of a supervision role in terms of dealing with kids at lunch hour. I am hoping to free the teachers up to do other things.

Interviewer: All right.

James: And then we [have] a behaviour support room that we call the Pace Room. Students with severe behaviour issues can go to this room. The teacher who works in that room really gets these kids and can help them through some difficult times.

Interviewer: So they can be settled. I'm getting the impression, an insight, of your school that kids are not excused from actually getting the academics done.

James: No, no.

Interviewer: How have you built that into the culture of your school?

James: I think with our academy program, [when] we sat down with our academy teachers in the beginning to develop our academy handbook [we] started the process. We took a look at what do we want this program to look like? What was our vision going to be? Right away we went to a couple of other places to take a look at how their programs were run. From our own conversation, and from our visits, we said, "We can't sacrifice our academics for the athletics. If we do that, the kids aren't going to perform in the athletics either." The process built in-group support and a clear focus on what was important in our school—something that we all shared.

Interviewer: I want to ask you a very particular personal question right now. So you have Grade 6s and you have Grade 9s . . .

James: Right.

Interviewer: And the Grade 9s would have come in under your principalship?

James: Yes.

Interviewer: Grade 9, Grade 6 PAT results from prior to you being principal to, say, this past June—have they gone up, gone down, stayed the same?

James: Grade 6s, we have been extremely high.

Interviewer: All the way along?

James: It has increased. The use of manipulatives has made a big difference, just [to] give you an example. With our results with Grade 6 science we had 56% of the kids reach the standard of excellence.

Interviewer: This past year?

James: This past year.

Interviewer: And five years ago?

James: I am going to say probably about 20–25%.

Interviewer: Well, that's substantial.

James: Yes, but it's really increasing.

Interviewer: And what made that difference?

James: Our Grade 6 teachers are a strong PLC bunch, really strong. Like they get together, they discuss, they share, they are on top of it. Those four basic core teachers, they are on top of everything. They are not ones that let things go; they are always on the kids, really teach to master outcomes. They really take a look at manipulatives, how can we teach this better? When you go to our science lessons there are always activities going on. Our Grade 9s, we just got the Grade 9s three years ago. With the 9s we haven't reached that level yet. Like our PAT results are okay. This year we are a little bit low. Our group this year though was low all the way along, but we still got to get that culture of working together a bit more.

Interviewer: The 9s entered a different culture when they went from being high school teachers to middle school, and as they are in a new culture they have to be introduced to it to understand it.

James: And that was the thing that I found at the beginning. That was the struggle with these guys. They wanted to come in saying, "I only teach science." I had to tell them, "Guys, I don't have enough science courses for you just to teach science."

Interviewer: Oh, so they were in the high school with the Grade 9 . . .

James: Right.

James: So they went from teaching one core course to now two core courses. And then our one guy who's in an academy program, when I did my timetabling I said to him, "If you teach our golf academy you can't just teach Grade 9s, because I can't fit it into the timetable. You have to come down to one Grade 8 subject too." But it's getting them to buy into that dynamic.

Interviewer: So the next area is **developing and facilitating leadership**. The question I have for you is, how do you as a school leader identify and promote *different types of leadership* in your school?

James: I guess just recognize the model that I felt we wanted to go with, and one where we give everybody the opportunity to be a leader. So whether it be our academy personnel, whether it be our English department, whether it be our math department—giving those people that role. I approached one of our Grade 9 teachers to try to get him on board, and I asked him . . . they always look for a PLC facilitator from different core areas in our division. I said to him, "I need you to take on the role as a school division Grade 9 PLC facilitator." Hopefully by accepting the challenge he gets ideas from other schools and brings them back to our school. So I try to get them to take on leadership roles that are found in our school division.

Interviewer: If you are trying to promote leadership, what skills or attributes are you looking for in that person before you start pushing in a leadership direction?

James: What I take a look at is their ability to work with other people. That, I think, is the first thing. Try to determine if the person is somebody that the people respect. Will they listen to that person? Because if they don't respect that person they are not going to buy in. I try to find out if they have that ability. Do you have an ability to relate to other people? Are you a leader in the school right now? If I go to your classroom are you doing those things that we think we need to be successful? If we see people doing these things, that will be a person we will approach. We have had a number of our teachers in math, language arts, [and] science be PLC facilitators for the division, and they have come up with some good stuff.

Interviewer: Perfect. **Managing the operations of your school**, and the one area that I'm particularly interested in is the budget. How do you align the budget to the goals in your school?

James: That's been a struggle lately, I'm not going to kid you. I know my second year I spent over budget. We were close to balancing it, but we felt we needed to get some of that money into key areas until we got that established. Now we are fine financially, we are okay. I mean this year we probably had about a $7,000 surplus at the beginning. I want to keep the academy program costs down, so I eliminate certain things from that budget—like charging secretarial supports to a different budget.

Interviewer: What did you base that decision on? What was driving you to make that budget decision?

James: Well, I think with that one it was just the economy at that time. When the economy went down people were struggling to put their kids in the academy. We charge our students $950 a year to come into our academy programs, but that includes all the ice rentals for hockey, power skating coach, bussing, and all the works. So how could we make it cost effective for people? I knew if I were to follow a similar path as some of the models I saw in Edmonton and charge $2,000, all of a sudden I would have lost everybody.

Interviewer: What do you do in that context with kids who come from disadvantaged families?

James: We allow for monthly payments. So if they want to pay a $90 a month fee, we do that. We have never turned anybody away. We have a little bit of a reserve. I hold back 5% of the fees from the academies. So for example our academy brings in close to $200,000 of fees. I take 5% of that and keep it in a special fund. So if I know a family is struggling, if they contact me I can help them out a bit. Same with our sports programs. We have never turned away a student from being involved in anything. We will help them out.

Interviewer: I understand teachers are all assigned centrally. Have you ever had to hire part of a teacher's time from your school-based budget?

James: Not from the school-based, but from our academy. I guess that is part of our school-based budget, because I lose five academy teachers every day. Our academy program pays for 0.4 of a teacher to cover that fifth person going off campus. So we have to have that or else I wouldn't be able to run our core subjects correctly. Within that academy budget, though, they control how much money they spend for their teacher assistants. So for example our hockey people will hire some of the local Western Hockey League players that aren't going to school to come in and do some ice time with our kids. Get these players to be assistants. We go to the college and get some of their soccer players to come over and be assistants. So we look at the community for some other resources as well. For the golf program we have a golf pro that we have hired, and he comes in five months of the year. Assistant time, I bought a little bit of assistant time. I am running a cosmetics lab. We just developed that a couple of years ago, and we have a teacher in there, but she doesn't have the skills to do the hairstyling and all that. But we've had some people in our community that do have that skill, so I hire them to do the hairstyling part of the program.

Interviewer: How would you get to that point and the decision to actually put that program in place, or to hire that community person?

James: To put the program in place we surveyed the kids. So when we did our survey on our options we asked the kids what would they like to see? The two big areas were girls wanted cosmetology, because they heard they were going to get it in Grade 9 at another school, and when that was taken away when they came to our school they were upset with that. And we found a way to solve them being upset. For woodworking, I approached another school to use their shop. I was at the college one day, and a friend of mine who is in charge of some of the trades programs [was] there and I was looking through some notes. We just started talking about issues and I said, "Well, I have a big issue in that my kids want woodworking and we don't have any space to offer it." He just said, "Why don't you use the [community] college facilities?" Our use of the college, then, was purely accidental. Then once we got the program going, the college charged me $6,000 a year to use their facility.

Interviewer: Their staff too, or just the facility?

James: We have our CTS person go over but they give us a lab tech. They give us all their facility and all the materials for $6,000 a year.

James: That is very cheap and it includes our kids when we do the welding section. There are 14 welding stations. There are not too many high schools that have 14 welding stations. So we were able to do some neat stuff, and we have had some neat publicity with this, because the news came over when they heard about the program and they did a few shows on the program. After that we had people phoning us wanting to donate lumber to our school. With our bike repair option, one of the parents had asked, "Did you ever think of offering a bike repair option?" We hadn't thought about setting one up. It wasn't long before we met with one of the local bike businesses. I said, "I'll buy all my materials from you—bike stands, the whole works—but I need you to come help teach it just for the first year till our CTS [Career and Technology Studies] people get comfortable with it." Then we had Canadian Tire get on board and where they bought the bikes and our students assembled bikes for them. We assembled something like 250 bikes for them last year, and then they hired five of our boys to come work over there. So it was kind of a neat . . . it's been a neat situation that way.

Interviewer: You actually just went right into the next area, which is **responding to the larger societal context.** How do you advocate for the needs and interests of all children and youth?

James: I think that was the approach we took when we analyzed our CTS and our technology education, and when we looked at all our different programs and ask[ed], "Are we really meeting the needs of our students?" When I looked at our Accountability Pillar surveys we were very low. I was not sure if it was just because we were a junior high or if something was really up. Our ability to prepare students for later in life was low, probably about 40% satisfaction. We wondered about how to increase that result. We thought, well if we prepare students with jobs or little jobs or things like that, and if we got that information out there, it would certainly help prepare kids for life and also drive up our Pillar results.

Interviewer: Yes, because that's one of the questions on the accountability part.

James: It is. And the kids were right, and the parents were right—we were not really doing those things then.

Interviewer: In your time as principal have you seen a change in the Accountability Pillar results? Did you have any red areas that are now blue?

James: There was one.

Interviewer: Which one?

James: Satisfaction with certain courses was an issue. Sometimes, you know, we still have some of those results that come in a little bit poor, and I'm not sure why. When I met with our vice-principal and some of our success team we came to [the] conclusion that we will need to advertise more. Get our name out in the paper a bit more so the community will know we do the bike repair option. Get news people [to] come over to look at the rockets and robotics and the CO_2 car building, bridge building, the office technology program, the programs at the college. In that way people in the community know just how much we are actually doing.

We keep looking at new things. One other project we are looking at with the college right now is working with their international students, because they have a high number of international students that would like to do more conversation, conversational English. I took four kids over last year at the end of the year to meet with their Japanese students and Chinese students. We had them sit in certain classrooms with the international students where these students did activities where our kids were forced to converse with the international students. And since our students didn't know Japanese or Chinese they had to speak English, and the other students had to speak English back. This project will expand a little this coming year. The college will bus their international students over to us and our students over to them.

Interviewer: Is there any aspect of your leadership, or the leadership preparation, you would like to talk about that perhaps we didn't cover in our questions?

James: I still think the mentoring program sometimes for administration is weak. You know, a lot of time we are putting people into positions and it is a big change for them.

Interviewer: What great piece of advice could you give the superintendent in regards to a mentorship program?

James: I would say at one time we had a leadership pool where people would come together and learn some of the basics about leadership. I think that has to come back a little bit stronger. We have kind of gotten away from that, but I think we have to target our people that we know who have leadership potential and get them into leadership programs. We need to get them in and start training them in what they can expect when they take over that job. I know I did the leadership pool earlier in my career and realized it still wasn't enough. I never knew just how big the job of being a principal was; budgeting, all those other factors that all of a sudden I was in charge of, and it was like holy smokes I didn't realize this was going to be due. So many things were required the first year. That was an eye-opener for me when I took over as principal.

CHAPTER 10:

Interview:
Grades 6 to 8
School Principal

Katherine is a middle school principal with 29 years' teaching experience. She has 21 years of experience, either as vice-principal or principal in an array of settings (elementary, K-9, K-12, 6-12), and has been in her current school for six years. Her current school has 304 students and 18 teachers in Grades 6, 7, and 8. She completed a Master's in leadership in 2004.

The interviewer (co-author) asks her about mentorship and then proceeds to ask how she enacts each of the professional competencies.

Interviewer: When one becomes a school leader—mentorship sometimes plays a role, sometimes doesn't play a role—as you became a leader, did you have a **mentor** you could turn to?

Katherine: Yes, I would say I did. Now, you're talking right from the very beginning?

Interviewer: Or even more recently.

Katherine: Well, I have tons of mentors. That's the team, the admin team that I work with. I am very fortunate. I have a superintendent who spends time and works with me. If you want that, I would say I always have mentors.

Interviewer: What preparation did you receive prior to your first formal leadership position?

Katherine: None.

Interviewer: You were a teacher one day and you were the principal the next?

Katherine: Superintendent said, "The principal's out sick. And the vice-principal has to go on a medical leave. You just got moved to principal."

Interviewer: Yes, many of us know what that feels like. So then when you were appointed as principal of this school, because you were appointed, you didn't apply for the position.

Katherine: No, I applied.

Interviewer: You applied. It was an open competition.

Katherine: Yes.

Interviewer: You were selected to be principal. What kind of mentorship did you receive then, coming into this school, to prepare you for the task of leadership here?

Katherine: I worked closely with the superintendent.

Interviewer: So you went out and you sought your mentors and they were willing and able to be there for you.

Katherine: Yes.

Interviewer: Why did you choose to go into leadership?

Katherine: Well, first of all, I didn't.

Interviewer: But you have since made this conscious decision on a number of occasions.

Katherine: Well, you know, once you get a taste of it, what can you say? When I got that experience of being at the helm, and all of a sudden I knew that people could see that I could do it, I—and then you just started working and getting messy and people started seeing you that way. It just happened. Like, I don't know how else to describe it. It's—I don't always like leading in the front. I like being right in the messy, the middle of it. And it took a lot of people just saying, "Hey, you can do this. You are doing a great job." So, did I always say I thought I was going to be at the front or the back? I've always had ambition and drive. And I always wanted to be passionate about making a difference for kids. So I would say that is where that comes from, that drive to be a leader—I'm not going to let it happen to chance anymore. I'm going to make a difference. I'm going to step up. I'm going to walk the talk.

Interviewer: Awesome. We are going to go to your school division for a second. In your district, what, if any, use has been made of the **principal leadership**

competencies in identifying potential leaders and preparing them for leadership? It's part of policy. Maybe talk that way.

Katherine: Well, we went through the process once through CSA.[31] The competencies were introduced to me in a conversation with officials from CSA. So I immediately started sharing the competencies information with the superintendent and conversation started taking place in our school division. This is really something to work on. Now I also had something to put into place. When I did my Master's, I did it on the topic of leadership. And so I developed a mentoring program for administrators for our district. That was my goal. So we actually did start implementing it. I'm sad to say that, for some reason, the mentor program didn't continue, even though the individuals who participated in it said, "What happened? Why can't we have that again?" As principals we like hearing it from a principal's standpoint. So I need to put that piece in there because I'm disappointed about that piece. I'd like to know more, but I have never been given a reason why it didn't continue. But when we came to the competencies, what I do appreciate is when we started sharing it with the superintendent, and I said, "This is a great conversation for our administrators to have. Since then we model our meetings not based on business. We model our meetings on conversation and PD." And so that's how this came in. So we always start in the morning. Now, not all administrators like that. But I'm just telling you, I thrive on it. As a group [we] sat down and worked out what this process could look like. We did [it] through conversations—we wanted to know how it could be and how it couldn't be implemented. How does it apply for new individuals coming in? Right now I have a young lady that I mentor in a small rural school. We set this up ourselves and we get together and talk about school leadership.

Interviewer: But as a principal within the district, you have to submit to your superintendent evidence of you meeting each of the competencies as part of your supervision and evaluation process.

Katherine: Well, we do it maybe through our professional growth plans, if that is what you are talking about. Do I have to submit something, you know—like for

---

31   CSA – Council on School Administration. CSA is now called the Council for School Leadership and is a Specialist Council of the Alberta Teachers' Association.

example, my three-year plans? It might show in there. But anything formalized to the superintendent, no. I would say no.

Interviewer: Yes, okay, that is good to know. Now let's get to the competencies themselves. We are not going to begin with competency number one, but rather with the vision competency. I want to ask you: what is the **vision** of your school?

Katherine: The vision of my school? Okay, I really struggled with this one. I'm going to tell you guys why I struggle. The vision of this school is kids, the focus on kids and the practice. But if you ask my staff what the vision of the school is, they would say it is five simple words: believe, trust, honesty, respect, and responsibility.

Interviewer: And that would be the same five words that are printed right here on your wall.

Katherine: You will see them in classrooms. You are going to see them everywhere. And how that happened is when I first came I was talking to parents and to the staff about how excited I was coming to this school. And I had just talked about my heart and what I believed in. I talked about: "We are here for kids. That is our focus, the kids." And I know that is what we are all about. I believe in that, and I trust that I have made them a part of all that we do. Those words have just been absorbed into the school, and people live by it. And now we have added the word *be*. So if you talk about vision, the vision is kids-focus[ed], with kids being able to use—and community and people [being able] to use—these words in their everyday life. That makes us good citizens in the world.

Interviewer: Can you tell me then about a couple of actions you took to blend this vision, these five words, and encapsulated in the word *be*, into the practice of the school? What would it look like in the life of these kids?

Katherine: Well, okay. Teachers took to the words right away. It was amazing. I didn't tell them to. I didn't tell them at all. We just—I talked about them, and we talked about them. So the first thing I saw was in the classrooms. All of a sudden I saw the words everywhere in the classrooms. The words were being used with kids in the classrooms. And even teachers with parents were using the words. Whenever we talk with parents or with kids in this office, we use those same words in conversations, in that we believe in them, and that we trust that they will be able to make changes. So you see, it morphed right into the conversations that we live on a daily life. We even see parents coming in and saying back the words to us.

Interviewer: So how did you get them into the parent community?

Katherine: Using the words wherever we go, whether through newsletters, through parent meetings, through school council, through just—the kids were repeating the words. Who [is] more important to share the words about it than the kids sharing with parents?

Interviewer: Just a little bit of clarification from my part: this vision and the articulation of it, where did it come from? Did it come from here or was it—is it a district-wide thing?

Katherine: No, it is here.

Interviewer: Did it start with you, or did it predate you?

Katherine: When I walked into the building people were having difficulty in knowing where they fit into this world. There were people that were put on pretty high pedestals, and there were people that were injured. And these people were sort of— thought they were the master teachers and they weren't. So when I started looking at the big picture and what was happening in the big picture, I needed to do some healing in this building. And that is where the words came from, because I knew I had to help this culture get healthy and to remind them why we were here. And that is how that happened. Did that answer that one?

Interviewer: Yes, excellent, thank you. Say those five words again so we don't miss them.

Katherine: Believe, trust, honesty, respect, and responsibility.

Interviewer: And then you added a sixth.

Katherine: Be.

Interviewer: And how does *be* fit into the process?

Katherine: It's not that you just say it. You be it. You walk it. You talk it.

Interviewer: You be responsible . . .

Katherine: Yes. And that word just came in this year. And you are going to see it painted on walls. You are going to see it everywhere. It is just everyone's tired of what it was. They're saying, "Enough is enough. We're going to be this now, and we're going to do it."

Interviewer: And when you articulate that, and when it is spoken in the classroom or to parents or whatever, is there an expectation that it is not simply for professionals to have? That it is for the kids? It is for everybody—parent community. It is about the type of relationship that you want to have with every person in the building, in the school community.

Katherine: And how we treat everybody globally and everything. It is everybody.

Interviewer: Next question, slight tack on that. What role does that play in the accomplishment of this vision for your school? How do you know you are making headway?

Katherine: Well there is some of the data. It is more about actually hearing, the seeing, and the talking. But also it is what is brought into the building and the conversation around programs that are being offered, additional support, the health and wellness initiative. The data that shows from that—that decisions came from believe, trust, honesty, and responsibility.

Interviewer: Can you build that a little bit more? When you say the health and wellness initiative, what do you mean by that?

Katherine: That program came about through [the] kids' voice. Kids came to us and said, "How come in the cafeteria they don't serve healthy food? It is all deep fried, or it is this, this, and this. How come in our hot lunch that we offer, we don't have salads? Salads would be nice." Through our belief in kids and listening to kids and taking their voices seriously, we said, "So what do we do?" And that is how this all came about—to us, that is true, strong data. And the data they showed us, we can even go down into the hard data for the success of this program by looking at "Tell Them From Me" survey. We took the "Tell From Me Survey" on as a pilot. We used some of that data for our communication with kids—it led to kids surveying other kids about what they wanted—because we are making a new step [and] because we are having a hard time keeping up with this management-wise, sustainability, how we are going to address it? It led to kids have come up with a plan. We're trying.

So when you talk about vision, there is a real strong example of belief. Same with teachers. Okay, for example, teachers came to me and said, "We need time to talk about curriculum." But not just because they have team time to meet about kids and about curriculum in their dyads. But they said, "We need time across six, seven, eight. We need time with five and eight." So, believing and trusting people. And I said, "So what do we do about it? How do you go about it?"

Well, it's taken us three years. We got to it this year. And they are so excited because they actually made it happen. And the data is we had Grade 5s[32] sit with us for the first time this year to talk about curriculum.

Interviewer: Grade 5 teachers from the local elementary schools?

Katherine: Yes.

Interviewer: Your feeder schools?

Katherine: Yes. We have been searching for ways to meet with the Grade 9 teachers in the local high school. That has been a long, long journey. Long journey. But there, once again, it took a long time to gather the data required to meet with these teachers. Our teachers raised the desire to meet with the Grade 9s. I said, "Let's brainstorm how to make that happen. Let's find it, work through it. We can do this if we honestly believe this is best for kids. We will get there."

Interviewer: Go back to the *Tell Them From Me* survey for a second. You use that as a piece of evidence of data that supported the vision?

Katherine: That's one piece, yes.

Interviewer: Did you see any positive change in an element of what kids were saying in the *Tell Them From Me* data over a course of a couple of years?

Katherine: We only had it for a few years, and then we had a bit of a mess-up in part of it because their site went down partway through one of our largest groups. But in the results, yes, we did see some conversation areas. But the problem with that data device is the terminology used. So we went into it because we were allowed to make some changes and add questions. We changed it to the language our kids would understand.

Interviewer: And what did you see as a result of that?

Katherine: The kids that are really liking what we are doing, and they are seeing some positive change.

Interviewer: Positive change.

Interviewer: Awesome. That is a piece of data that I was prolonging the conversation for, to get to. How do you communicate and celebrate school accomplishments

---

32   Grade 5s – This school has four feeder schools. The meeting mentioned here refers to meeting with the Grade 5 teachers from the feeders.

and aspire to, or inspire, continued growth? How do you communicate what you are doing?

Katherine: Well okay, I've got a lot of just little tools. The big thing is, is that you have to have your team celebrating constantly and celebrating with kids. And so we do that. But . . . we've always done things same old, same old. Like I've been really working hard to try to change some old things and old thinking, because—since the development of this school, it was a very structured format. And it was always done this way. And you know what the words we were using [were]—"Oh, this is the way it's always been done." Well, what we have been doing the last two years is, "So why did we do it? Why have we been doing it?" So part of that process, one of the things was celebration, was our awards. In the old way of doing things we gave awards for the purpose of giving awards. Now we have a committee that developed a new award system. So we are trying to get engagement back in by inviting parents—they were disengaged from the school—in for these new celebrations four times a year about student achievement for citizenship and globalization. We have the whole list, the gamut, yes.

We celebrate every day. Every day when we have those kids we celebrate, especially the tough kids. I had a meeting this morning and this young man came to us pretty tough and he had a great year, just an awesome year. We could high-five mom, "Way to go." It was great. Just as important to celebrate with the parents. We celebrate every day, working with colleagues and having the time with colleagues.

Parents are welcome to come in and share celebrations about what is happening. We share the great things that are happening through school council. The media literacy class made a video for education week last year, where they interviewed people in the community and made this video. We celebrated it by showing it down at the town hall. We went to other schools and showed the celebrations and all sorts of stuff. Right now we see a lot of the kids' designs in different programs and publications.

Interviewer: **Relationships**. Tell us about how you went about developing a positive working environment in the school.

Katherine: The conversation right off the bat was about the importance of relationships. They get so tired of it, but I always say relationships, relationships, relationships. And I said, "In the success of any school, it's all about relationships. Relationships with kids, relationships with parents, relationships with colleagues, relationships with board office. It is relationships. We need to take time to build those relationships." So it is an ongoing conversation. We just had a really good PD on Monday where we had a guest speaker just come in and talk about strength focus. This is the time of year when we all get tired. We need to recognize everyone's strengths.

And so I had to really say, "I'm going to make mistakes as much as anybody else, and you will too, but it's okay because that's how we learn." And the same has to be true for kids. I had to let them have a voice. That is why it has taken a long time, because when we get complacent, too—some teachers are being complacent. I even had a teacher shake her finger at me and say, "Just tell me what to do." And I'm going, "No I won't, because I am not just going to tell a kid what to do. I want you to think. I want you to expand and grow."

Interviewer: How did you make that change?

Katherine: Time, patience, and walking the talk. When you say it, when I say it in the building, they know darn well we are going to do it. If I don't do it, they are going to be, you know, making sure they are at my door. I have had my butt kicked a few times. And I've had to stand up and say, "You're absolutely right." There are times that when we sit down and we make a decision as a team, it may not be what I wanted or envisioned, but it is what we needed to try. And some of them worked.

Interviewer: While you are thinking about that, almost along the same line, has there been any serious conflict that has happened in your school since you have become leader, and how did you go about resolving it?

Katherine: Well yes, there was conflict. You know, I think that is inevitable when you are dealing with personalities. Like I tell kids, I don't love everybody in this world, and I shouldn't have to be expected to, but I have to be respectful. At one time—and it still is a challenge—there was a situation in this building that two individuals were the kingpins of this building. I don't understand how they got to be in the kingpin role, other than I can best say it was a form of bullying. And that was really hard work. I actually went to investigate Todd Whitaker a little bit on dealing with difficult people and strategies, because this person would get in your face. In your face.

Interviewer: And into other teachers' faces.

Katherine: Oh, my teachers wouldn't even confront the individual.

Interviewer: How did you resolve that?

Katherine: Well, hard work, and it is still in progress. Conversations; [I] used a lot of Whitaker's strategies. But I also use strength-based [strategies] as much as I possibly can. This person is passionate, absolutely loves what she does. Loves it. But the problem is she doesn't see beyond. The second part is that I see she has struggles, not only in this building. So when I sit down and have this conversation, I can start with the strength. "I know you love kids and I know that you are passionate." Then I can start the next conversation. I say, "But I need you to know something." And then we would talk about it. So we have had a lot of those conversations. I have had a lot of temper tantrums in here, and it is not a word of a lie. But whatever I do with that individual, she has trusted me enough to know that I will be open and honest with her, tell her what I see, and if she needs support and is struggling with a parent or whatever, I will join them. Or if she is struggling with a teacher, I will join her and I will facilitate the conversations. How do I know there is progress? It is happening less and less. But I had to do one real critical piece. They used to team teach 60 kids in one classroom, and it was a nightmare. And I had to split them. And I just did it.

Interviewer: Sometimes you just have to be the boss?

Katherine: Sometimes you just got to do it.

Interviewer: And what is the staff sentiment towards this person today? Has it improved any?

Katherine: Yes. They are not scared to say, "No, I don't agree."

Interviewer: They can have discussions.

Katherine: Yes. And they also can—best way I'm going to say, sometimes she goes on a rant—let her go on a rant, because it doesn't mean that is how she feels. And then we can get back to where we want to be going.

Interviewer: How do you demonstrate responsibility for all students and act in their best interest?

Katherine: Talking about all students, being respectful of all students.

Interviewer: And that it is about all students, not just some students?

Katherine: Okay. I think it is also the bigger picture. We set up in our timetable true middle school team time, and we talk about kids. And during one of the team times, we have a counsellor there, IPP students or any others, [and] we will sit down and have a conversation about students, if there are concerns or—and it doesn't matter, IPP or not IPP, all students.

Interviewer: Is that something you brought in, by the way?

Katherine: No. That team time was there, but how it ran was different.

Interviewer: Could you speak to that a little bit?

Katherine: Originally when they did the team time, they had—once again, it's the trust factor, okay. So one of the things I wanted to implement right away was to let teachers know that I believed and valued who they were. So what I did was, we had one day that was meeting time where a team leader—I'll talk about that a little bit in leadership capacity—a team leader who ran their meetings and shared the business of what the week was going to look like. Then the Thursday was the time for them to talk about kids. So we started with that conversation and I said, "I don't need to sit in on those meetings unless you would like to invite me."

So at that particular time, teachers really started having honest communications about kids. And then if there were concerns, they said, "Could you come and join us? This is some of the stuff that is happening." And so I did—they happened frequently enough. Now it is interesting what is transpiring in a lot of the dyads. They don't wait for Thursday. They do it every day at some point in time, talking about kids. We are a very inclusive school, and that has been here historically and it continues. It is the one area that I have learned most about as a leader in the school: what inclusion can look like. So that conversation just needed to be allowed to grow even more.

Interviewer: Thank you. We are going to change gears a little bit into the competency of **leading a learning community**. Outline the process you followed or follow to increase the level of student learning in your school.

Katherine: Well, conversations, right? The conversation about student learning. We do have the important conversations around things like PATs, and looking at our Accountability Pillars, and the results and the reporting of that stuff. But it is also the open and honest conversation and sharing that and being—looking at those forms of data, *Tell Them From Me* survey information. Unless we are open and honest in the conversation, and deal with the elephant in the room, we are not going to make a difference. So in those conversations over the years that have happened, that is how we came to the point of unpacking curriculum, unpacking who we are, and revisiting about why we do what we have been doing. And that has a direct impact in the conversation with student learning.

And so I think—what people have to understand [is that] we are here as a team. We are not working in isolation. That we are not here to evaluate one another—we are here to support one another. When teachers have their dyad partners, they can honestly sit down with each other or their curriculum partners and say, "I am really struggling with this." They can cross over and visit one another and see each other's progress, and allowing that to take place or facilitating it through professional development. We are a staff, and we still promote that group identity idea. Our support staff play a real important role in our building in that they need to be part of that conversation too. And so we have them go to PD with our teachers as well, so that they understand what the teachers are conversing about.

Interviewer: Awesome, and we're going to pick up on that line that you just started us on. How involved are teachers in this school in setting the professional development goals, and determining sessions they would like to attend? And explain how this is done in a school.

Katherine: Well, it's conversation—the whole unpacking conversation that we have been using this year, which we are all very excited about.

Interviewer: What does that look like? Explain that to me.

Katherine: It is sort of based on Robyn Jackson's work on the rigour and relevance framework. That is sort of the process that we have developed. How that originally started was Bob and I had the opportunity to see Robyn Jackson. Well, we saw her two or three times and read her book and that sort of stuff. We have, in our admin team, book talks as well. And that was where some of the conversation started. So in our team time, as an admin lead team, we said, "Why don't we look at our PD days when we do our calendar? Get more of them so that we can do some stuff more on site? We have gone elsewhere, but why can't we do more of our own?" I think that could have been one of my kick-in-the-pants moments, too. And I went, "Oh. Okay."

Now Bob and I have organized it, but teachers also joined in. The admin lead team have joined into the process. So we put more calendar event times in. It is specified. They tell us what they want to unpack, or feel needs to be unpacked, what we need to do next, and what are the next steps—the hard part, where Bob and I come into a role, is we need to pull in the reins because they would want to unpack everything. They forget that we have to have a follow-through, too.

So it has always been since I have been here, that we have talked about professional development and what are [the] opportunities. Now historically, before, they didn't have that voice. I asked them to join me when I first started. But then pretty soon they went on their own. They didn't need me there and would phone me and harass me because I couldn't be with them. But then now they were starting to say, "Can we start here?"

Interviewer: So for a little while there was a teacher-run professional development committee unto itself? Am I interpreting that right?

Katherine: Yes. The division still has their ATA joint PD fund. But I utilized AISI as much as I possibly could because there are people that never left the building. And I didn't allow that to be an option either in the first couple of years. I said, "You get to come with me."

Interviewer: And how do you know who you are going to pick for this? How do you say that this teacher needs to get out and visit and see somebody else? How do you know that?

Katherine: Well, I can see it just in—well, monitoring and seeing what they are attending and what they are going to, conversations with them.

Interviewer: How often would you be inside of a teacher's classroom in school?

Katherine: Not enough.

Interviewer: But how often?

Katherine: I try to get in every day. But it is next to impossible.

Interviewer: Would you for sure have a reasonable idea of how every teacher teaches?

Katherine: Yes. Yes, I would. I can see what practices are put in place and what areas might be strengths. But we also have those conversations. I don't like telling them lots of times. I use the tool, say, "So what do you think?" And then they drive with it. Their mentors are really good for conversations that way. I don't always have to be the one. Like the admin lead team is very helpful in that because there are lots of times when I have to simply deal with kids more than anything else, and so they can help me out in that they are mentors, and they will come and talk to me and they will talk to the teachers they are responsible for.

Interviewer: Do your teachers meet as a professional learning community and if they do, what do they look like in the school?

Katherine: Well I would say the team time is definitely part of the professional learning community.

Interviewer: Explain that. What do you mean by team time in the school?

Katherine: Team time is a set time in our timetable where teachers are able to get together to have a conversation about needs of students and what practices work or don't work. In the admin lead team are people who would like to go into a leadership role at some point in time, even thinking maybe that they might like to possibly have my job and want to get a flavour. So we meet every Friday before school.

Interviewer: And how many members are there in the admin team?

Katherine: Well we started with only Grade 6, 7, 8, and Bob and I.

Interviewer: It has representative teachers from Grade 6, Grade 7, Grade 8, and you and your vice-principal?

Katherine: But it has expanded.

Interviewer: To?

Katherine: Nine. Now we have Grade 6, 7, 8, 9, the vice-principal, myself. In the past few years we added subjects reps, classroom support, and an office staff rep. Having the support staff rep has really helped.

Interviewer: And did they self-select or did you control it?

Katherine: No. The ones that I am more likely to tap on the shoulder are my teacher leaders, but most of the time they will express to me that they have an interest. They—historically the school had an admin lead team, but it was solely to tell people what to do, when to do it, and how to do it. My group helps me facilitate conversations at the other team meetings. Sometimes, as administrators, we get viewed that it is a top down decision. I don't want a top down. I want teachers to be able to have a voice and to express themselves and let their voices help shape and mould the school.

They would go and take a certain issue, like [the] calendar for example, to their team, the Grade 7 team or other team and ask, "What are some things that you would like to see?" They would have a conversation and bring the feedback back to the next admin team meeting.

Interviewer: And then they would bring feedback to the admin.

Katherine: Yes. And then we could decide if it needs to go further.

Interviewer: So these sessions where curriculum is unpacked would happen within a grade team meeting for the most part?

Katherine: We have been doing it on a bigger scale, but then we break it down into smaller groups. And then teachers can facilitate it in their own meetings. One of the things that I learned coming into this whole process too is that the support staff have always felt disconnected. Teachers and the professionals in the building felt there was a real need to have support staff to be part of that unpacking as well. That has been happening. We have used time—we call them discussion hours here—that teachers and support staff are part of. So there is time that we are all together. There are times we break off. And usually whoever is helping us facilitate it at that time will make those decisions. That is the leadership role—to know when it is best to do each.

My support staff that sits on that team right now just ran an unpacking of the inclusive classroom, what it looks like, with my classroom support teacher and myself.

Interviewer: How do you facilitate meaningful parent involvement in your school community and ensure they are informed about their child's learning and development?

Katherine: There is the standard process of just the conversation, with the report cards and interviews and that sort of stuff. I want to talk about a different process, though. One of the biggest struggles I believe right now that we face is apathy. That—and our parents are all so busy. Because in a school this size, I should have a really good school council. However, at a typical meeting I might get four or five.

I get from my trustees, "Everybody's really happy. They like what you are doing." But I said, "But I don't have their voice at my table." Now I have some real strong people in our school community. I do. But they are just—you know, they are not the whole voice. So things that we have done to try to get people more informed, to be welcomed in, we do—we have our phone, we have our email list to all parents.

Interviewer: Do all parents have email?

Katherine: [There are] those who don't, which is only about 5%.

Interviewer: You have identified them.

Katherine: We have identified them. So anything that goes out that way, we send out by paper. We also—we were really conscientious in working on our website. More and more people are web-based, and so our website has become very, very important. The other part is when curriculum comes into it. Teachers are getting more into Moodle and actually putting their stuff online. We are seeing more parents engaging in that particular way.

Now, what I had to break . . . [was] that these people with email . . . conversed [this way] with parents. And I just told them no. No, you need face-to-face. If there is a factual handout or whatever, you can do that via email. But I found that teachers were hiding behind the email. They were hiding. It was too easy and it led to too much misinterpretation. So we really told them, "You need to do phone calls at the beginning of the year." We do good phone calls. Celebrations. I got to make my phone call for my media literacy student, had a great visit with Mom, because there are times I don't get to have that call. Most of mine aren't that lucky.

But we do those kinds of phone calls. We are inviting—we are trying to get the community to come back in. They are supportive to the nth degree. They are here when we ask, but they are not here for meetings. They are just busy. I don't know how else to describe it.

Interviewer: Tell us about how you see your role as the **instructional leader** of this school. What does that mean to you?

Katherine: Well, I don't know it all, or profess to know all. And my philosophy on instructional leadership may not be true to everybody else. But my philosophy on instructional leadership is providing what they need to grow and to provide best practices. And that could be me visiting the room and saying, you know, "Hey, have you thought of this?" Or you know . . . But it's not just me. There are colleagues in our buildings, and within our jurisdictions, and in other schools that we can go visit, and they can glean ideas.

So when we talk about instructional leadership, I think it is talking about having the hard conversations. Sitting down and having a dialogue as professionals, and asking the questions. And so it may not mean that I always get to be in the classroom to have that conversation as an instructional leader. It is providing the opportunities for them to say to me, "Let's get it in the calendar and let's have those conversations." Like that unpacking that I talked about. I am excited about the unpacking because it has brought huge things to the table. And what the conversation of the same old, same old is, "Oh, I didn't remember that we did it for that reason. That's not good, right?" And so, when it comes to instructional leadership, it is not me. It is not just me. It is all of us working together and being able to collectively say, "So and so is really, really good." And facilitating that, allowing people to take leadership roles.

Katherine: And now what is happening is my teachers are taking that leadership role and working with other teachers, as well. And so what I am doing is building capacity within themselves. I can't do it all. I can't profess it all.

Interviewer: As leader, of course you are also mandated to ensure that your teachers are following current curriculum. How do you ensure that is being done?

Katherine: We have our standard policy procedures that we do through our course outlines and those conversations. And then going in and just checking in. There have been times where I have gone in and—for example, a science teacher had something that was going on. I said, "Tell me where this fits in the curriculum. Is this something that really needs to happen?" That is the intense conversation that takes place. But hey, I have had a teacher do it to a teacher too and say, "What the heck? Show me that in your curriculum," and had that conversation, a good conversation. They work it through. So opportunity is really important to ensure that that is how I make sure it is happening. That is how I make sure it is happening. It is always being out, visible, being seen.

Interviewer: And as an ancillary to that, how do you ensure that student assessment and evaluation practices throughout the school are fair, appropriate, and balanced?

Katherine: Same process once again—I rely on people like a teacher leader to take on that leadership role by providing continuing workshops, talking about it in teams, looking at course outlines, and to ask, what does this look like? We have reviewed past practices. We have gone back into why are we assigning marks for certain things when a checklist could be working just fine. We have actually had sit down sessions and teams and committees working on that sort of stuff.

Katherine: I would say I have to watch certain individuals who might not follow our approved procedures for student assessment. But on the whole, I would say the majority of the old practices are gone. We are not going to see lates as a deduction of marks. We don't see people trying to assign zeros anymore for work not handed in.

Interviewer: How do you get your teachers to focus on data and using that data to improve their instruction and student learning?

Katherine: That is why the conversations are always coming up. I don't think we do a good enough job in that department. But that is my personal perspective. We always hear the conversations about the PATs and that sort of stuff, but we need to go deeper.

Interviewer: Are PATs important in this building?

Katherine: It is not a driving force, no. Because look who I have. I have Grade 6. Grade 6s aren't the only ones responsible for the tests. Grade 4 or 5 teachers and programs are equally important. And the same—I tell my Grade 8 teachers and my Grade 7 teachers [that] we are responsible for how those Grade 9s do. So we have had those particular conversations, but they are not the end-all, be-all. I would say, in our building, when we talk about data, the data is about students, and very more focused on individual students and student progress.

We listed all the things about why we do what we do when we work with our assistants, when we are unpacking the curriculum. One of the things they said was that it really came down to the fact that we are not utilizing our assistants properly, not really as well as we should be. We are not communicating, we don't have the time to communicate with them as to what the expectations are. That the assistants are just coming in and hovering over kids instead of providing some really meaningful work to drive student learning forward. We called it fading. One of the things our teachers said was, "We need to ensure there is time near the beginning of the year for communication to happen between teacher and education assistant, for better utilization of the first two prep days at the beginning of the school year. We need to provide time at the start of the year to get on the same page in regards to classroom expectations."

So that conversation leads into our asking, "What about data and that sort of stuff?" We were just sort of getting it through these conversations, but now we need to look at universal assessment as everyday practice, and also the Individualized Program Plan information and that sort of thing. So we are not really good at using data, but we are quickly heading in that direction.

Interviewer: We are going to go to **developing and facilitating leadership**. How do you as a school leader identify and promote different types of leadership in the school?

Katherine: It is all about the levels of leadership we have in this school. We do have an admin instructor core—my admin lead team. We meet every Friday. They are people who like to step up in the leadership role. Others can then also go into that role. That way, they go into their team meetings and they actually know what it is like to run a meeting. There is a lot of growth that happens when teachers sit on the team. I had one teacher in particular—she's a superstar teacher—and she says, "I have a whole new understanding of what you do. I don't want to do this." So they get a mini taste of what it is like to be in a leadership position, and some people realize it is not for them.

When I'm out of the building, one of team becomes acting admin for the day. I provide a sub and the acting admin comes in and does my job, or the job of my AP, and gets to know what it is like to work in here, in the office, and see what we deal with. Each member of the team cycles through and gets to do the role at [some] point in the year.

Interviewer: Do they—these individuals that are on this admin team—do you invite them? Do they volunteer? Is it a combination of both, or how does that work?

Katherine: Near the end of this year, as we are looking at re-configuring what we have—because everyone knows about the admin lead team—teachers will ask, "You know, I think I am really, really interested in that." And then Bob and I will of course have conversations about it. But in the end we usually let them make that decision. A prime example was when our Grade 7 leader asked to take on this role. She took the role on this year and has already told me, "Not next year." And not just because she didn't like it, but she says it's hard work. "I don't know if I can put that hard work in." Most of the time, they decide it.

For the support staff I did select because it was a new position, plus I knew that this lady had a pretty good understanding of what we do. Usually the teams will give me their advice on whom to select.

I have a person that would dearly love to take on a leadership role but has been hesitant to accept one. I have had the conversation, "Why haven't you thought of it?" I told her that she gets the big picture and that I believed she could do my job. But the timing just isn't right for her. Now when it comes to the third in command, or after Bob and I, usually the team will make a recommendation to me. But everyone pretty well knows that I will go with it.

Interviewer: If I can paraphrase, here is what I am hearing: This team provides you with an opportunity to mentor potential leaders within the school community for the various aspects and roles of leadership.

Katherine: Yes.

Interviewer: They then get the opportunity to go back into their own team areas within the school, whether it's Grade 6 or Grade 7, and practice.

Katherine: And practice.

Interviewer: They practice the skill of running a meeting, practice the skill of facilitation, practice the skill of also being able to listen pretty actively, because I get the sense that they have to take what they are hearing back to this admin lead team.

Katherine: And use their voice.

Interviewer: To advocate for what their folks are saying.

Katherine: Yes, and understanding that our worlds are not cut and dried, and allowing them to see this, because often people think it is. Some people take that role on and some don't. But it is mentoring—I have lost teachers because of the process when they have learned the ropes here and then went into other roles in the division, which I celebrate too.

Interviewer: I am going to go to **management of school operations and resources**. How do you ensure that the budget reflects the goals for your school?

Katherine: No decision is made in our building unless we know how it impacts kids. We talk about that at great length. Now when we talk about budget, I sit down with my secretary and Bob, and even the admin lead team. We talk a little bit. But we look at our budget and there are certain standard things we have to manage. I go through these items with them and say, "Well this is how we spent this, this, this, this, and this historically." We then make a decision about which to keep and which to drop. But, when it comes to, like, managing staffing, which is the biggest part of our budget as much as anything, that is when we really start talking about programs. That is where the staff comes in and we say, "Okay it's a money factor," and we need to ask, "How much are you willing to spend? How much are you willing to sacrifice for that program?" There is a part of the budget that requires me to just sit with Bob and my secretary [and] do it—because it is management. However, even with these items I will share what it looks like with the staff. However, many other parts, the important parts where we spend money on things, texts and resources, I really rely on teacher feedback on what is valuable, because I am not going to put money somewhere if they don't see the value in it.

Interviewer: **Larger societal context**. How do you advocate for the needs and interests of all children and youth in the bigger community?

Katherine: I'm going to talk division now, because to be very honest, a lot of what I do I couldn't do if I wasn't under an umbrella that I am, and that I have a very trusting jurisdiction that supports the belief that sites can make decisions, which I thrive on. One of the challenges in our school division is related to the needs of First Nations children. So when we have conversations at that level, with the division, and we talk about First Nation students, we could enter into a problem-solving mode. Through the conversations, identification of key issues and solutions, and because of the faith the division puts in our ability to make good decisions for kids, we were able to get a First Nations liaison.

Another example relates to the education of a group of children in this community identified as Low German Mennonite, who are also known as Mexican Mennonites. As a school division we were really struggling with what to do with this group as they had limited English skills, historically would travel back and forth to homes in Mexico, had limited formal education in either Mexico or Canada, yet were starting to come into our schools in greater numbers and staying for longer periods of time. We knew we had to be better advocates for these children and to devise a system of education that would meet their needs. So now we have different programs that support these young men and women. As a division we have even established an alternate school to cater to some of the needs of the older children from this population. An important part of the process, as far as this school is concerned, has been our efforts to engage the parents and to help them to come to know our school and the people who work here so they will trust us with the education of their children. We are starting to see greater numbers of Low German Mennonite children in our school and also seeing improved school results.

CHAPTER 11:

Interview:
Grades 7 to 12
School Principal

Thomas is principal of a junior/senior high school. For seven years he has been a principal for a school that has 276 students and 16.5 full-time equivalent staff, Grades 7 to 12. He has a Master's degree.

The interviewer (a co-author) asks Thomas about his mentorship, and then proceeds to ask about the professional competencies.

Interviewer: We are curious, in addition to the competencies, about your experience of **mentorship** as you moved into your first formal leadership role. The first mentor who was assigned to you—was there a formal process put in place to go along with it?

Thomas: Yes, but nothing too formal.

Interviewer: Then what about with the superintendent? How often would he actually come by to see you, interact with you?

Thomas: We were a smaller school jurisdiction at the time. I saw him probably—I'm going to say probably at least biweekly, it seemed. He would stop in the school and say hi and have a coffee and talk about how things were going and ask a few questions. Then I would bounce ideas off him and sometimes used him as a sounding board. I felt like I could ask him anything. He was that type of person.

So yes, maybe it wasn't quite that much. It sure felt that way. Whether he was there in the building, or a phone call away, or whatever, it felt like I had that connection.

Interviewer: What about here, as you moved into a new province, new jurisdiction. Would you have had a person assigned to you, or a person you would look towards as your mentor?

Thomas: In short, no. There was no mentorship program set up at that time. Not for me. And I don't know if that's because I had some whiskers or not. I have no idea. And I mean, obviously from the standpoint of having had seven years of experience. I can tell you honestly that the person who I turned to at that time was my vice-principal. I would bounce ideas off her. She became a great go-to person. It was funny, because she was somebody that applied for that position and didn't get it. She was already the vice-principal, and I'm sure had some feelings, had the feeling that, not unlike myself, that there should have been some form of promotion and yet didn't get it. Yet over a very short period of time, we became the closest of colleagues, I can say very good friends today.

She was somebody who always showed support, didn't always agree and yet we were a team anywhere beyond these office walls. There was no question. She was my biggest mentor, helped me through a lot of the tough times—or not tough times, but the questions, because I will say moving to Alberta, it was a huge learning curve. Just understanding some of the terminology that was used, whatever the case is, how diploma exams are operated, and they are very different from the world we came from. PATs, the whole nine yards.

So there was a lot of support that I got from here. I also have to say I had a teacher who retired, I think a couple years after I came. But the first year it was somebody who had all those years of experience in this province, really did a nice job of questioning, "Are you sure you want to do this, or what do you think about this?" And that person became a, I can say a mentor, you know. I would turn to that person at times, too, for various questions about things, and it was always very supportive. It was always very involved in terms of my growth as an in-school administrator.

Interviewer: Let me ask the question a little bit differently as well. Now that you are a leader within the school division, your evaluation—what does it look like? What is it based on?

Thomas: That is a good question. Of course you know as well as I [do] that evaluation today should be very much based on those standards or indicators for principals. I have had two evaluations and neither one of them even remotely looked like that. I was kind of baffled a little bit in my last one, which happened about two or three years ago I guess. I was kind of baffled because it was kind of like—I never received an evaluation, I never provided any evidence of how I met these particular indicators and so on. There was none of that.

I think—and I'll be honest with you—since the superintendent now goes through an evaluation every year, he is providing his own evidence of how he is meeting particular qualifications or standards or indicators. Since that process has happened that way for him, he is now starting to apply that process to the rest of his in-school administration team.

Recently the vice-principal went through the evaluation process. I was with her in her evaluation and basically it was left to her to show evidence. It was "take me through how you are meeting these indicators." And she had various evidence that supported that growth and supported that documentation. So like I say, my own evaluations—and I'm sure the next one will be totally different—but my own evaluation was very dissimilar to what should be happening as far as I'm concerned. I think the model that they are using now is exactly the way it needs to be. It needs to be that process where I show evidence of how I am meeting those particular competencies.

Interviewer: The competency we want to talk about first of all is one based on **vision**. So what is the vision of your school and tell us how it was created. When, why, that sort of thing.

Thomas: My vision of this school? I want a school that accepts everybody and has something for everybody. I have had arguments with people about this before, because they are saying you can't be everything to everybody. If you do, you will spread yourself too thin, blah, blah, blah. And I think, you know, maybe that is true.

So I was able to quickly get support for the vision of "something for everybody" and that was, I will tell you, very fortunate, I have had support throughout my career in terms of decisions that I wanted to make and implement. I got support for bringing in a band program and a band instructor. Last year we brought in somebody who was kind of multidisciplinary in terms of being able to provide visual arts to kids. Probably I think one of the premier art teachers in the province, but that is my own biased opinion.

We now have visual arts, we've got drama, a drama program that I think is outstanding. We have 50, almost 60 kids involved in our drama program this year. In a school of 270, that is pretty unheard of. We also brought in a hockey program. It was a dialogue that kind of happened over time, and it was about providing an opportunity for kids to hone some skills and that kind of thing, but give those hockey players a bit of an athletic opportunity and develop as players. We have two sections of it running right now in our school. We have close to 40 kids taking part in hockey programs out of 270 kids in the 7-12 school.

Interviewer:　At the high school level as well, or—

Thomas:　The hockey program is at the high school level only. So when you think about it, it is 40 kids out of 175.

I believe that we needed to be a safe and caring community first and foremost. I believe that kids will learn in many places, but that they will learn best in an environment that they know is conducive to learning, that is safe, that they feel cared about and loved.

I remember walking into this place and you could cut the tension with a knife. We needed to first and foremost look after that safe and caring piece. So we have done a lot of things.

I developed three teams in the school to help lead some of the change. I developed an atmosphere team, an athletic team, and an academic team. Every staff member in this building is part of one of those three teams. So the atmosphere team, they are responsible for looking after the atmosphere of the building, making sure that we are doing things to promote healthy young people in a positive environment and that kind of thing.

The athletic team works to also provide some of that aspect of things. We brought in a banquet for our sports, for our teams and our players and our coaches and everybody, and it is quite a celebration that we have. And some awards and stuff, and it is not just about being the best, it is about having the greatest attitude and things like that.

We brought in things like our Christmas dinner, which we have every year, and this will be the seventh year now that we will host it, where everybody sits down together as a community and a family, and we break bread together, so-to-speak, in a non-religious environment, but certainly have the opportunity to sit down and have a festive meal with each other.

Every two weeks we have an O Canada assembly. I am sure that there are schools that, you know, they get all kinds of pressure about having O Canada assemblies as a result of various groups that are opposed to that level of patriotism. And we have some people, who for religious reasons are opposed to the singing of O Canada in our building. But there is a work-around for everything. We celebrate each other at that time, and we celebrate the academic achievements, and we have draws and things like that that the academic team brought in on a term-by-term basis.

So we have looked after that safe and caring piece. That had to be first and foremost. Finally, I really believe in moving technology forward. I believe in the whole aspect of moving our school into the new age to really grasp this new learner that we are blessed with. Finding creative ways of doing so. We are a school who believes in "bring it if you've got it" kind of an approach. But we also now are ready to take the next steps into moving our school forward with technology so that kids are able to embrace what we have.

I think I can safely say that we are moving in the direction of making assessment an important aspect of what we do here and using various assessment for learning approaches in classrooms so that kids are responsible for their learning.

We talked about assessment for learning. It has been one of our goals for the last four years and will continue to be one of the goals for the next four.

Literacy approaches that we have built right now with guided reading, and you name it—those approaches are really a part of that whole umbrella in terms of an assessment for learning. We believe in second chances. We believe in giving kids the opportunity to make mistakes and learn from those mistakes and then try and try again. That is something that has been a work in progress, but I can tell you that that is built into the fabric of this building.

We don't believe in zeros. We don't work with zeros. That is just not even in the dialogue that we have amongst professionals in this building. We believe in holding kids accountable for what they want to do, what they need to do. And then through that approach, making sure that if they don't get something done, they haven't handed it in, then by gosh, they get it done. And we find ways to do so.

Interviewer: I am going go from vision, but right into its twin, which is **fostering productive relationships**. I would like you to put it into the context of what you alluded to, a culture and climate of this building when you took over as principal, and then something happened. Now, I put a few of my own interpretations on that as a lead-in, but correct me very quickly if I am wrong.

I would suspect when I hear that language about the culture and climate, teachers may have been acting as bullies towards each other, certainly acting as bullies towards kids. That if your gut reaction when you walked into a building says there is something going on here where kids don't necessarily feel safe and secure, therefore, it is going to impact learning in a negative way, we know that.

Thomas: I can tell you, I think there was a lack of trust between people in this building. There was a lack of trust that existed between teachers. There was a lack of trust that existed between teachers and administration. Not that kids—you know, in classrooms kids weren't being picked out or picked on or anything like that. I have to say that I didn't get that sense.

I got the sense that there was just a lack of trust between each other. That was something that came out very clearly as I moved further into the position, that we needed to somehow rebuild that sense of trust, that people needed to feel like they were valued for who they were and what they were doing. The stories that came out afterwards and stuff like that, some of them were pretty vicious. Like, it seemed to me that there was a sense within the administrative practices that were going on— you know, that bullying mentality that you referred to—I think there was a sense of that. And teachers felt that. Not all, necessarily, but many did. I think that created a real wall between people.

You dialogue. You communicate with people and you show them that things are not going to be that way in how you deal with them. Did I have situations? Yes.

Interviewer: So what did you do?

Thomas: I will tell you it wasn't easy, but we got to a place, and it was a good place, where—there was a confrontation that needed to occur. And it was all simple, crappy things, stupid things. But it was continuing to kind of propagate itself, and so I pulled the two people together and we had this dialogue. It seemed like the relationship between two people in particular was a root cause of some of the lack of trust in the building. I had to bring the two of them together.

It was important to bring the two of them together in [a] non-threatening environment, one of reconciliation to let them say what they needed to say, and have that dialogue, and open up and really deal with the root issues. The difference it made in the relationship between those two people over a period of time was huge.

It wasn't just that one piece. It was forcing them then to begin the process of communicating with each other. Took a while, but in the end it made a big difference to the health of this building.

Those kinds of conversations were invaluable in terms of the process. I can't really pinpoint one thing in any situation that made a difference. But just even little things like when I would have a conversation with a staff member about something, I would begin the conversation with, "What we talk about here is going to stay in this room and nobody else knows about it." Building that sense of trust with them, where they would say, "Oh, you mean, you're not bringing the vice-principal in to sit here, and you're not going to berate me right in front of my colleagues?" Comments like that told me a lot about the past culture, but also the increasing value placed on trust.

So many times I think we sit in a chair on a different side of a table, and all of a sudden think we are better than somebody else. I think if you ask people around here, I would hope that they would say that Thomas never feels like he is better than somebody else. We are colleagues here working together. Yes, I wear a bit of a different hat at times, and I have to exercise that hat once in a while, but in the end, there is nobody here that feels threatened or intimidated—well, I am pretty sure there is nobody here that feels threatened, intimidated, or in any other way, shape, or form with things.

Interviewer: Usually the threatening comes in as soon as we enter into the role of evaluator. So how do you deal with the **relationship** piece, with your legal mandate to **evaluate your teachers**, but yet at the same time provide for some semblance of trust and professional growth? How do you blend that together?

Thomas: That is another aspect of things, too, and I am a big believer in walk-throughs. I am a big believer in just walking into a classroom and ensuring that the person who is in that classroom [is] not feeling threatened in any way, shape, or form. That is something that, I mean, even this morning I probably was in eight or 10 classes, just doing a walk-through. It varies at different times of the day, but I am always checking in with teachers.

I walk into a room—honestly, teachers don't stop what they are doing. "Oh, the principal's here." They just keep doing what they are doing. I will stop in and sit down beside a kid and chat with a kid for a second if I get an opportunity. It is completely unthreatening. So I think teachers feel like when or if it comes time for evaluation, it is just me sitting there giving some notes and making observations and that kind of thing, and ensuring, you know, looking at ways that I can provide evidence that they are meeting the TQS.[33]

So I will talk about it as well, ahead of time, especially in an evaluation process. I will talk to them about it ahead of time and say, "Here is what I am looking for. Here is the TQS, and here are the kinds of things I am looking for, and here is what you need to show me evidence of. Planning? Okay. Well, show me evidence of planning." Then through the evaluation process, I go through and I am usually in a classroom. If I am evaluating somebody, I am in there about six times to get a good read.

Interviewer: For whole class periods?

Thomas: Yes. For pretty much whole class periods. Sometimes I get pulled out late in a class or something. But for the most part, yes, the entire class period. I am a visual kind of person. I like to have evidence that is visual; I want to see it. So I ask a teacher when we are having a post-lesson dialogue, I will ask, "Show me your evidence of planning. I want to see your evidence of planning." And so they will flip open their day plan books or get on their website or whatever it might be, whatever that planning looks like. I will snap some photos with my camera and then use that, use some of those images in their final evaluation so that they get that it is not just a bunch of gobbledygook, but I have pictures that demonstrate the evidence as well, as I go through the process. It works really well for us at this school.

It is always most difficult for a beginning teacher because they don't know me or how long I have been in the classroom or developed the sense of trust that is so important to make the process work as it should. One of my newest additions to my staff I have visited seven or eight times this year so far. Sometimes just for a 10-minute pop-in, and sometimes more formal observation where I spend pretty much the whole 90-minute period in their class and just kind of got a good sense of what the person was doing. In the end, when we are doing the post-discussion, we can go over what I saw—and I love the iPad for that. I take my iPad in, I use the

---

33   TQS – *Teaching Quality Standard Applicable to the Provision of Basic Education in Alberta.* See http://www.education.alberta.ca/department/policy/standards/teachqual.aspx.

notepad piece and I can send my observations to them right away and any suggestions and things that I've put in.

I try to make sure that my teachers get a sense from me that what they are doing is good stuff. I pinpoint those positives so that when we can look at what the suggestions might be, they can take that as, "Oh yes, okay, I could improve on that by doing this," you know, and that kind of thing. We have to build that trust and it has to be quick.

I walked into a new teacher's classroom this morning, a CALM class, and it was just good teaching going on this morning. The teacher kept going about his business and had no sense of me being in there doing anything connected to evaluation or worrying about me going to tear a strip off him or something like that when the class is over. It is just a normal part of the process that we follow in this school.

Interviewer: Have you had any teachers that have been on the marginal side, where you have had to render the opinion that they have to leave?

Thomas: Yes, I have.

Interviewer: How did you handle that?

Thomas: That was not an easy one. The first year I was here, I had a teacher who was a new teacher to the building—not a new teacher to the profession, but a new teacher to the building. And so [according to provincial policy] I have one year to make my assessment. I will be honest with you, through various dialogues and so on, I found that things were just not going as well as I had expected. I mean, I had a veteran teacher here—I didn't hire the person, not that I'm blaming somebody else or whatever the case is, it just was the reality. And the reality was not great. I knew I had to have a tough conversation with this person. As time wore on I found that things were not improving. Plans for improvement and things that we were talking about were just not being executed. The teacher in question took on [a] "You told me to do it that way so that's what I'm doing" kind of an approach. I just said, "You know, I am looking at next year and I am not certain that maybe you shouldn't being looking elsewhere. I can't make that decision, but maybe you should start thinking about that."

By the time the final decision was made, and of course I don't make that final decision, but when the final decision was made, the teacher understood. I am not sure the teacher was happy with it. I am sure the teacher wouldn't walk across the street to say hi to me. On the other hand, I can't look back. I can't. In the end, I have in my mind's eye major league baseball [as a metaphor]. That is what I am looking for. Major leaguers give great service to students.

Interviewer: That's a perfect segue into the next competency, **leading a learning community**. The question I want to jump to: Do your teachers meet as a professional learning community, and what do PLCs look like in this school?

Thomas: In a Grade 7 to 12 school where one teacher is the math department because she is the only math teacher in the high school—or, I have three different teachers teaching math at [the] junior high level, that kind of thing is occurring—it is sometimes difficult to build PLCs that are subject-based so we can do some vertical kind of collaboration and sharing. Not that we don't, but I think the biggest thing that we do together is we learn together as a complete community. That is what I say—our staff meetings, they are one big PLC.

Then within that, we also have a high school PLC and then a junior high PLC. Administrators are part of all of those teams, and it has now come to the place where it is teachers teaching teachers, and that is what is happening in our environment now.

Interviewer: Give me an example.

Thomas: So many people are actually involved in the process—veteran teachers, the vice-principal, me, all teachers are involved. Everybody gets to take a piece and do some instruction to staff. It is a PLC where teachers say, "I'm going to show you my best practices," kind of a thing. So I have a teacher, first-year teacher, bought right into the whole SMART technology and so on, with the little clickers. He wanted to demonstrate to the rest of the staff how he was using the technology in his setting and put on a PD session at a staff meeting. After finishing a first year of teaching he could put on that kind of a demonstration—it was just a powerful thing. I always say I am the leader of leaders as far as I am concerned. Everybody has leadership ability. It is powerful when you see people feeling like they can—they are not threatened in any way, shape, or form to try.

Interviewer: And how do you know these professional learning sessions or professional learning communities are actually making a difference?

Thomas: That is a good question, because some things are tangible and some things you can't really put your finger on necessarily. But I think in the end, it allows teachers to see that these are professionals who are very capable in what they are doing. These are people who have not necessarily ever seen each other teach but this first year teacher opens up possibilities. Conversations around, "You should see this, we can do it this way" are happening. Is that making a difference? I think it makes a difference to each one of us in a way, that we feel like we are part of a learning community together. That is how I think personally—I know it is a bit of a fluffy answer to a more difficult question but, I don't know, I think we have a successful school. We have built on our successes. I know I don't put a lot of emphasis on it, but the data are the data.

Interviewer: Where I want to go is **providing instructional leadership**. You made the statement that you are a leader of leaders. But ultimately there is a place in a school where the buck stops and that is very often at the principal's desk. One of your prime mandates is to be *the* instructional leader. So how do you live that? How do you provide that evidence of giving instructional leadership to this building?

Thomas: I hold kids accountable for what they are doing. In the end I think that is what matters. I remember at one time thinking it is all about zeros and approaches to zeros and things. I think over time I realized that it is about accountability, not just about the mark or lack of one. I realized what accountability means, and not only am I accountable to you but you are accountable to me, too. So I believe to be an instructional leader I have to be an instructor. I believe that. I think I have to be in the trenches, and when I am in the trenches with my colleagues every day, doing what they do every day, it validates me.

It puts me in a place where I feel like I am able to walk that talk. So many people get into administration, and now they're away from classrooms for a period of time—and I'm not saying it has to be this model, I don't mean it that way—but I think sometimes there's a disconnect that occurs.

But like I say, I honestly think that the biggest thing is being in the trenches, battling through, learning and trying new things myself and failing, then trying again—all of those kinds of things. I think that—if I am living that on a daily basis, how can't my teachers feel like they can?

Interviewer: I want to push that question in a slightly different direction but actually go a little bit deeper. Assessment—and I think you have said the word assessment about 15 or 20 times in the 45 minutes we have been together. Let's say as you are going through that process of assessment change, your teachers are studying an Ann Davies book or someone from your district office comes in and provides direction. Where are you throughout all of this? What are you physically doing as this learning is taking place?

Thomas: To be honest with you, I am going [to] just say it the way it is. In the beginning, I led it. In the beginning, I felt as an instructional leader I needed to provide instruction as well for my staff, and give them new ways of thinking about things and new ideas. I mean that is life-long learning as well. So I first did the learning myself. As a result, I felt I have got something that I can share with these people. And I have always believed that.

I think that the professionals within this building have as much to offer to each other as many people around the world. So we can make use of that. So I began the process of two years of extensive PLC time that was focused on assessment for learning, and the beliefs and the learnings and all of that kind of stuff, and they were learning and we were learning together in that process.

Interviewer: That is another segue to the next question area, and that is **developing and facilitating leadership**.

Thomas: I believe in us all taking part in some role, giving people leadership roles, giving them those opportunities—whether it is through our teams or through budgetary processes or whatever. Giving people the ability to lead is so important. Even our TAs do a lot of leadership around here and I think that is a good thing. They have a lot to contribute.

I always said, if you are asked who is the most important person in your building, probably number one—the people that you meet at the front as you walk in, and number two—the people who are spending the time cleaning the floors at the end of the day. If you look down on any one person from on high, then by God, I think it will make for a hell of a rough ride.

CHAPTER 12:

Interview:
Grades 9 to 12
School Principal

John has spent 37 years as an educator, with 31 years as a school leader in various types of schools, often rural. His present school is in an urban setting, has 1,800 students in Grades 9 to 12, and 104 full-time teachers. He has a Master's degree.

The interviewer (co-author) asks John how he tackles the competencies.

Interviewer: Tell us about the context of the school when you came into the building as principal.

John: The staff was in flux for an extremely long period of time over renovations. It was a difficult renovation, and the principal that they had was more of a caretaker kind of principal, a manager kind of principal. The person just focused on keeping everything calm, everything going, moving forward. Wanted to just keep it on stable and moving at a set pace. It was a very successful school when I came in here. However, it became very clear to me that we had to do some significant changes, because what made the school a success in the early 1990s and late 1980s was not going to make it a success this year. Education had changed, so it was about changing the school and making the school something different than what it was before. And making it much more successful.

Interviewer: As you moved into the school, in addition to the conversations with district leadership, what did those initial days, months, year look like with your interactions with staff members? What did you actually do to get an in-depth understanding of how the place was operating?

John: Well, we spent a long time talking. I had four vice-principals at that time. I still have four vice-principals. One had been an administrator here, a vice-principal here, for eight or nine years at that time. The other one had been an administrator for the district for about five years. The third one, who had just transferred in the September before, had been a long-time administrator in the district, but always a vice-principal. And then I had a fourth vice-principal who had just gone into administration. So we spent a lot of time as a team talking about what we saw happening in the school. As we had these early discussions we started bringing in curriculum leaders and started to talk with them about, "What do you see? What do you see us having to do? What do you think about this idea?" As we answered these questions over the years, we have done a number of different things. For example, one of the big changes occurred when we changed our assessment practices. We also made our budgeting process completely transparent. The flexibility project also needed attending to so I took curriculum leaders to various schools around the province so we could see what others were doing. So it is about trying to be transparent and trying to be as open as I possibly can be.

One of the very first things I did was I had a staff meeting—and it was a short staff meeting—and I went through and identified the things that were holding us back. There were poor relations with district office. There was kind of a cult of personality surrounding the former principal, where everything was compared to what he had done. There were financial issues, and there were issues with upward education. So what I had to do, or one of the first things I did, was to say to the staff, "We need to move on. Walk away from these things and put them in the past and start deciding what we are going to do."

We were going to become an entirely different school. And that was when we started talking about different things throughout the year that we were going to do to the school. Identifying the staff I thought were holding us back, setting a plan in place. So we had about a six- or seven-point plan that I had shared with the superintendent about what we were going to do. And then as we moved into that plan, we learned an awful lot about what we did wrong, and what we did right, and how to do things better than what we have. So we were continually looking at our practice.

Interviewer: Within that six- or seven-point plan would there be an item that you would have identified as **vision** for the school?

John: Well, there are a couple things I would identify. The one thing I did identify was the financial situation. As I talked to the staff, I said, "What we have to do is we have to raise our CEUs[34] so that we can begin to play." The other vision for the school that I had and gave to the staff, and I think it is one that we have been very successful with, is we are not just going to let kids walk out of the door. So when I came here—the year before I came here—we lost about 16% of our kids between September and June of that school year. Last year we lost about 2%, so we were working at keeping the kids in school, providing support for them, making sure that we do everything that we possibly can in order to make them successful here at school.

Every year we do something different to add to our peer intervention. The first year we got staff calling parents. We brought them into the process. We started talking about interventions that teachers could do in their classrooms. This year we are talking about creating a room where kids can go during the day to get caught up on assignments. There will be two teachers working in there—very much the same as Adlai Stevenson High School did under Rick DuFour.

Interviewer: Stay on that same tack, John, if you don't mind, please, and build for us a little bit more of the story of that pyramid of interventions at your high school level. And to have a 16% attrition rate drop to a 2% attrition rate is a story that needs to be told. Flesh that out more for us, please.

John: We started off by talking with the staff about what we needed to become, what we needed to do. We were going to be about keeping kids in school. So the first thing that we did is we changed our attendance policy. The attendance policy that they had previous to that was one where you had eight absences and you were gone. And I said, "No, we are not going to do that." There is no defined number of absences a kid is going to have. We are going to work with kids and to say,

---

34   CEU – Credit Earned Unit. At the time of the interview school boards received high school student funding based on the number of CEUs the students earned.

"You need to be in class." Part of that was working with the staff to get them to work with students and to hold students accountable, and at the same time bring parents into the picture. So one of the first things we did is we gave staff access to our discipline program that is built into our attendance program. We require staff to contact parents and make sure that whenever there is an issue going on, that they are talking to parents. The conversations with parents need to be documented before it goes in to an administrator.

An administrator or vice-principal will look and see what a teacher has done already before they start to deal with the student. So a typical situation would be if the student will be sent down to a vice-principal. The vice-principal will check what has been done as far as discipline is concerned, and then go back to the teacher and say, "Okay, you haven't done anything with this kid. Let's talk about what you can do and what I will do if this doesn't work."

The other thing we started doing—we brought in our reluctant zero policy in the second year. We fleshed it out, what it was going to look like for each department, as each had a different process for different needs. What we have done now, since that time, is we now take our retreats early in February, and do all that planning then. So we have the whole second semester to get staff on [board]. So we brought in our reluctant zero, where kids earn a zero, but they have to work at it. We extended our special education program. So we brought in a school avoidance program that was part of the district. It was a district program. We brought that into the school, and we worked with those kids to make sure that they started attending. The other thing is I increased the counselling staff. When I came here, we had four counsellors. I added a career counsellor for students so that they had some sort of vision of what they want to do after they get out of high school. We added another counsellor that was strictly for Special Ed programs. This counsellor was for our K and E, our Foundations program, and our Pathways program. Pathways students had some type of diagnosed severe disability or cognitive delay. Foundations would be kids with IQs slightly below what K and E would be. K and E is known as Knowledge and Employability, and is a program for students who are destined to go to work after high school. We started bringing in support for these children—counselling supports for them—so that there was that support there, bringing in the parents.

We required each department to have a pyramid of interventions about what they are going to do when kids don't complete assignments. It was key for us that these plans were passed down and made known to the kids.

For next year we are going to combine study hall and the opportunity room, put it in our learning centre. The learning centre was another intervention we put in place. In this centre students could go online to do their courses. Through the introduction of the centre we were able to put the kids in one area, and have it manned—instead of by EAs, by one humanities teacher, and one science teacher. Students will have access to computers, which they didn't have in the other programs. They will also have access to teachers that they didn't have, and specialized teachers that they didn't have in the other programs. Then when kids come back from being absent for a period of time, teachers can send them into that area, get them caught up, get them ready, and bring them back. So the kids aren't being overwhelmed by missing stuff, but they also have a very short, concentrated time to get caught up as opposed to, "Well let's try and figure out how to get you caught up over the next two weeks to a month." That never happens.

We also improved our relationship with the various alternate programs in our district so that we now have a clear transition between us and the alternate programs, if that is required. We also have a clear transition back from the alternate programs, where we require that the principal of alternate programs recommends the kid to come back, and that provides an opportunity for him [the student] to be more successful.

So those are some of the things we have done.

Interviewer: Can we go back to the item that you called reluctant zero? That is new to me. John, can you flesh that out a little bit more?

John: Okay, reluctant zero is the student has to work at getting a zero. We just don't automatically give zeros. That was a tough one for the staff to swallow. It was very difficult for some of the more traditional teachers on the staff. We do have a lot of teachers that were more traditional and have a lot of experience. What happens in a reluctant zero is that each department must have a specific timeline that they will take in marks without deduction, take in assignments or things along those lines without deducting marks.

So depending on the department, we have any time between the start of the unit and the end of the unit to hand in an assignment, based on the fact that zero is not a true assessment of what the students know. So we have some departments that do it on a unit-by-unit basis. In that way a student will have any time up until the end of the unit. We have some departments that will take any work up until the end of the year, or the end of the semester. So it is up to them, based on what their needs are within their departments. So an NR … if the student doesn't hand in an assignment, an NR is recorded in their grade book—their online grade book—which tells the student they can still hand it in. But students will also see what the impact of the mark [is], because the system reads an NR as a zero. Okay, and then if things get out of hand, teachers are responsible and accountable to contact parents to let them know that these kids have not been doing their assignments along those lines so that we can track it.

Some departments had some difficulties. Like the math department has daily assignments, so what we have asked them to do is not to count those zeros if a kid doesn't do the homework. We want them, instead, to find some way to assess it, so they can make that determination as to whether or not the students have accomplished what they need to accomplish in the curriculum. So all along we have said that a zero . . . giving a zero, that is a behaviour issue for kids not handing in assignments. That is a behaviour issue, and we want to deal with it as a behaviour issue, not as an academic issue.

Interviewer: So when does the reluctant zero become a formal zero and calculated in a mark? Work me through to the end of the semester, and what does that look like for you?

John: Okay, I'll give you social studies because they are the ones that do it for the full semester. So the teacher will give out an assignment, get a specified time for the students to hand it in. If the students don't hand it in, they will mark it as an NR. As the semester progresses, we will be working with them to get that NR replaced. Lots of the social studies teachers, for example, will take one day and say, "Catch up on your assignment today." All the teachers keep a list of what outstanding assignments the students have. They will from time to time contact their parents. In the social studies department, that actually becomes a zero. It is a zero in that it is an NR, but it translates into a zero at the end of the semester. This year they tried, and they didn't like it.

At the request of district office they wanted to take a couple of days during exam break to have students finish overdue assignments, and bring them in when we are on exam break. They were much happier being more proactive about it. The same thing works in English. Only, because of the amount of marking that goes on in English, they don't want a whole bunch of stuff coming in at the end of the day—or the end of the semester—so they set theirs up at the end of the unit. You could hand in anything up until the end of the unit. What science did was that they held tutorial classes at lunchtime, and the expectation was that the student will be in that tutorial class the next day working on that assignment.

The teachers that do that tutorial class know when the assignment is due, so they are working with the student to make sure the assignment is completed. And so that is how the science department is.

But the two things that we learned was that we couldn't make a reluctant zero fit all kids, in all situations, in all courses. The other thing that we learned, was I needed to bring staff into this stuff, into these discussions, much earlier than what I was doing. The other thing I learned was I didn't tell the students what we were doing and why. We didn't explain it to the kids. I had made that conscious decision not to explain it to the kids and found, instead, that we were apologizing to the kids the next year at the beginning of the year ceremony by saying, "Look, I [am] sorry for not telling you what a reluctant zero was. Because I didn't tell you, you made your own definitions." And the definition that the kids came up with was that we don't have to hand in any of the assignments. So at the first assembly after one year of doing it, I told the kids, "Yeah, you can earn a zero. The deal here is that you have to work at it. We are not just going to give it to you. We are not going to give up on you. We are going to make sure that you do the assignments, because if I have made this assignment, or [I am] giving you this assignment, it is important for you to do it. I need to hold you to it. I need to hold you accountable. If you are not going to do it, I am not going to punish you academically, because it is a behaviour issue. It is not an academic issue." And that was the process and the philosophy in which reluctant zero is available.

Interviewer: So after doing this for a few years, do you have any either anecdotal or hard evidence to say it is making a difference?

John: I think it is making a difference for kids in terms of getting their assignments done. I know that there are still some issues around it and that we are continually fine-tuning it. But I think it has had an impact. The trouble with what we have done is we have done a number of different things over the last couple of years, so it is hard to say whether this has had a significant impact, or whether this is more of an impact. So it is difficult for me to quantify it. I know kids are doing the assignments. I know kids are getting things done. Whether it has a long-term impact on their achievement, I can only guess. I would think if a student was doing the assignments, and the assignments are important, then it is going to have a long-term impact. The side bonus of setting the system up the way we did was that it forced teachers to look at how they were doing their assessments. Were there assessments that we were doing that weren't really all that valid?

Interviewer: The change with attrition [story that John told about reducing the dropout rate] is very dramatic. Did you see comparable change in things like your graduation rate, or with items like the number of CEUs getting completed?

John: Our CEUs right now with a high school population of around 1,600, 1,500, is the same as what the school was completing when they had a student population of about 2,000 kids—about the same amount. In terms of our graduation, we made our graduation policy very clear, that students had to actually be in a position to graduate to walk across the stage. So our Grade 12 vice-principal spends all of the second semester working with kids and to make sure they have got the right courses, the right programs. To go through graduation, students must not only be enrolled in courses, students must also be passing. They have to be passing on that date. Our date is May 30 for our graduation, or the last Friday in May. So what that has done is kids—when they walk across the stage—they know they are in a position to actually graduate. And so they just have another couple of weeks, and so they want to maintain those grades and graduate. So it provides an example; last year out of all of the kids that walked across the stage—and I think it was about 400 kids, somewhere between 390 and 400 kids—out of all of those kids that walked across the stage, only seven of them ultimately didn't graduate.

Interviewer: Good numbers.

John: Yes, very good numbers.

Interviewer: I don't know if it was a mandate of change, but it sounds like you are actually changing the culture—from bureaucratic to much more kid-friendly—is that what the language is? Is that what I am hearing you say? What did you do to go about **building relationships** with your teachers in order to accomplish some of this?

John: Well, the first thing that I did—and it is an absolute must as far as I am concerned—I ran an open door policy. I literally run an open door policy, so staff come down and they are welcome to walk into my office any time. I made it a habit—to be walking around the school a lot of times.

Prior to me coming to this school the vice-principals each had a teaching assignment. Each one of them taught two blocks, so they were basically three-quarter time. My first full year here, that September, I took away their teaching responsibilities. So they became full-time administrators. What that did—and I explained this to staff—this makes it more, the system [more] proactive. Instead of teachers sending kids down to us, we were able to go to teachers' classrooms.

We worked hard at being in classrooms, around classrooms, being highly visible. We took on the difficult situations. The administration took on the supervision of the cafeteria. We were in the cafeteria every day. Teachers see us on supervision every day. We took on the supervision and dealing with the smoking area. Those changes did two things. They showed the teachers that we were walking the talk of what we needed to do. But it also gave us contact with kids that we wouldn't normally have contact with. Lots of in-classroom visits—I took on the staff members that were at best marginal. And I made sure the teachers saw me doing that. So we did clear out the number of teachers that were marginal the first couple of years. And that made a lot of the other staff members at least sit up and take notice. We tried to make sure that we dealt with staff in a fair manner, and we tried to make sure that they were valued.

One of the things with the school is that it's so big that we don't have one staff room. We have 12 staff rooms around the school, so we instituted something called fraternizing Fridays. We purchased soup and buns for the staff, and we all met in the staff room just to socialize. The admin was there. So we tried to do a lot of different things with the staff. We tried to make sure that the teachers understood the reasons for us doing what we were doing. We tried to be very transparent with this staff in terms of what we were doing, why we were doing it, and what the background was.

We established a faculty council. We knew it was going to be difficult to bring 100 teachers together and explain something to them. So [we] used the faculty council as a sounding board and as a mechanism to get ideas out to the staff. Through this structure the staff could respond back to the various curriculum leaders, or they could respond back to their vice-principal, or they could respond back to me. Each one of our administrators had a responsibility for a particular department. I took on responsibility for our counselling, Special Ed, and our careers areas because they [are] critical to the school and the success of our students.

Interviewer: Talk us through the move with the vice-principals and yourself to become active inside of teachers' classrooms. That speaks directly to the whole aspect of **instructional leadership**. So when you go into a classroom, what does it look like? What are your vice-principals looking for? What are you looking for? What are you doing when you are there?

John: The first thing we had to do was make sure teachers were comfortable with us in the classrooms. This is a very, very busy high school. I just got a new vice-principal who can't believe how busy this school is in comparison to his former, smaller high school and how much work actually goes on, and the amount of contact we have with the kids. So we had to get teachers comfortable with us being in those class-rooms, and walking through those classrooms, and walking in the door. We got people comfortable first, and then we started moving towards what is it that we [are] looking for?

And we played around for a little while with check marks. We went and we studied the walk-through and all the criteria that goes along with that. And we did that for a while. And then we've abandoned it. Now what we have done is we have basically said there are a couple things we have to do. We have to make sure that the feedback that we are giving to staff is useful. We cannot just interrupt their classes for no reason at all. We've identified what it is that we're looking for. What is our goal? And the goal is really truly to see how kids are being engaged in the classroom. So we have no checklist, but we always send back an email where we talk about the level of student engagement. We also ask the teachers how they were able to get to that level of student engagement. We tried to bring in some aspect of their learning, so we can comment on what teachers focused in on as we see it in their classrooms.

So we try and stimulate more of those discussions that are going on between admin and the teachers. It is a tough, tough thing to do to keep on that, because depending on who you are, you can let distractions take the priority. So it is a constant battle of reminding us all that this is what we are going to do today. So every email for every response that is sent out to a teacher I get a copy of it, and I track which teachers are being visited. I also track which administrators are visiting which teachers. We have had to deal with things like three of us going into one classroom on the same day. We focus, for the most part, on our liaison areas or our grade levels. So I have got one vice-principal for each one of the grade levels, and then I am just across the board. I took a department that I am going to spend the week with, and I am going to get into each one of their classes.

Interviewer: So in a typical week, how many teachers would you have an opportunity to visit?

John: We tried to set a goal of 20 a week. Each one of us would do 20 a week or four a day. We are not anywhere near that goal, but we are trying to get into classrooms often. So typically, each one of us would probably get in, in a week's time, 10 or 12. We are going through a bit of flux right now because the district is taking on a project. We are now having to redesign what we are doing with our walk-throughs, and we had a bit of a lull in that.

Interviewer: I am getting the sense that prior to your principalship the vice-principals or the principal would not have been in the classrooms other than first-, second-year teacher evaluation. Then once you pass that, never the twain shall meet. Am I interpreting this correctly?

John: I think it wasn't the same priority as it is now. I know the vice-principals didn't get in because it was very difficult for them. And that was what happened in the first four months that I was here—first five months—was that it was even difficult for us to meet as a team because of the differences. So that was one of the reasons why we decided to take away the vice-principal teaching assignment.

Interviewer: And your superintendent was fine with that?

John: Well, I think he was a little bit leery of some of the things that I was going to do, because we were going to do a lot of different things, and he didn't know how he was going to fund it. We were talking about a significant increase in CEUs. We were talking about things like no preps for Grade 10 or Grade 11 students. He thought I would have a wholesale rebellion on that. I put it in, and it had no impact whatsoever. The kids just accepted it.

Every student can take HCS 3000, or that time it was CTR 1010. We have a huge number of kids going through work experience. So we had each kid do a CTR 1010, or HCS 3000. We still do that, and that is a prerequisite for work experience. So it would increase the number of CEUs that we earned. But it also meant that when the kid in Grade 12 got to the second semester of Grade 12 and was short a credit, we could put him into work experience without him having to take one course before he could go in. So it was a proactive move, knowing that we were going to grow our work experience. So work experience has taken on a huge career aspect. I do have a full-time career counsellor. It has become a real focus of the school. We have created a department which focuses on this ... they are called career counsellors. That is all they are, and that is all they look after. And so in that department we have got the career counsellor, and she has her career centre. We had this year three full-time people working on work experience. Between our K and E work experience and our regular work experience, we're going to cut that back to two next year, because of the funding.

And then we have people who look after the learning centre, which is also part of the careers. So that is our distance learning centre. We also have the individuals who look after our partnerships. We have a partnership with the daycare society in town ... and we have daycare on-site, where we have kids that take the modules for daycare and then do practicums with them. And they get their first year's credit, credit towards part of their training in post-secondary daycare.

Interviewer: The next area I want to explore a little bit, John, is this idea of **developing and facilitating leadership**. Can you speak to that competency, but from two directions if you don't mind? What you do as principal with your vice-principals, and mentoring them in leadership. But then also the other side—what you are doing with recognizing teacher leaders, and how you are promoting that level of leadership.

John: What I tried to do with the vice-principals ... I try to model—we spend a lot of time talking about what we should be doing and how we should be bringing it out. It is not the same as what I used to do because what I used to do in all my other schools is I would go to the leadership academies with all my vice-principals, or any teachers that were interested in leadership. We would spend the time—I would do the leadership academy with those people, driving with them back and forth and talking about leadership.

The big discussions were what went on in the car. With the vice-principals here, because this division doesn't have a leadership academy, what we end up doing is spending a lot of time talking about how we are going to do things, and what is the best way to get them done, and what do we have to do? At different times, different vice-principals have had different responsibilities they needed to attend to. I had one vice-principal who is now working as the district's principal. I worked with him for about four years, trying to get him to recognize that an aggressive style wasn't the way to work with teachers. So whenever he got into a situation where he was going to deal with the teacher that wasn't going to go particularly well, he and I would sit down and talk about it first. And we would talk about how he should respond. Then he would respond and send me whatever email he was going to do or whatever he was going to say.

And then I was going to respond and say, "Okay, this is not exactly how you should do it." So we talked . . . it was more on an individual basis. I don't have a specific mentoring process with them. I do know though that two of the vice-principals have gone on now to be administrators. One has gone to become the district principal for a year. The other one has become a principal in the middle school. I do know that when I came here, these two people were not considered administration material at that time. In many ways it is just working with them one-on-one. Right now, with both the staff and the other building leaders, I try and get them involved in the decision-making process and to give them many opportunities to take part.

Our school is about to become involved with the provincial flexibility project. To help us get ready we are going to go visit other schools and blend the visits with the admin retreat that we do every year. In the retreat we usually spend three days together. This year we are going to take two days and go visit high schools in Edmonton and high schools in Calgary. In addition to the admin team we are also going to take curriculum leaders with us. So whenever we start to think about a sort of plan, or talk about some sort of change, we bring curriculum leaders into the mix and bring them into the discussions early on in the process. We also do the same with teachers who are not curriculum leaders. We need their perspective too.

A good example of this process was when we introduced the Rater program—that's another intervention type program. The Rater program is for Grade 9. We set aside 10 days during the beginning of the year. We use it as a transition program—10 days at the beginning of the year for a half an hour a day, another day later on in October, two or three days in January to talk about exams, and then right now we have five days for talking about transitioning to high school. The program was designed by a vice-principal and two or three staff members. We told them what we wanted, how we wanted it to look, and they took it and built it. And we gave them time in the timetable to do it. The process gave them some responsibility and ownership of the programs. I try and bring staff into the discussions in particular areas of real interest and importance. We do the same thing for the students.

Interviewer: Just a point of clarification, when you say curriculum leader, are you referring to department heads? Or other types also?

John: Department heads.

Interviewer : All right, thank you.

Interviewer: How are the department heads selected or appointed?

John: Department heads request or apply for the position, and then if there are more than one that is looking at a position, then we bring in members of their department to do a kind of an interview or selection process. That is the same thing we do with teachers. We model it after teachers. So when we hire teachers or EAs, I bring in members . . . the vice-principal liaison does it, is part of it. At least two or three teachers are a part of it, and I am part of it in staff selections.

One of the things the division was a little bit hesitant for me to do was to bring parents in on these decisions, but I still do include parents in Special Ed hirings. I include students in a different way. We have students taking prospective new teachers on a tour of the school. Then I talk with the student tour guides afterwards to see what their impression of that individual was. In that way they don't sit right in on the interview process. We used this process with the last vice-principal that we hired. He still laughs about it. He had 16 people in the room when he was interviewed for the job. He said it was the best interview he ever had, because he was talking with kids, he was talking with parents, he was talking with staff, he was talking with administration. And one of the things that we are the most proud of around the school right now is the staff we have hired in the last five years. Because of the process, they are really top quality people right now.

Interviewer: That is interesting. I want to move the conversation to your **budget**. I am sort of picking up the sense from you that your budget is along the lines of what I would call site-based. So your budget must be into the millions. How do you take your total budget allocation and make sure it aligns closely to the priorities of the school? Who do you involve in those conversations? What does it look, taste, feel like?

John: Well, when we talk about the budget there are a couple things you need to know. First of all, we have changed the way we budget here at the school in the last two years. One of the things that concerned me about budgeting was it was done in the office. And what would happen is that staff members would submit what they needed for a budget item to the business manager, and then the business manager and the principal would give them whatever they wanted—whatever they could give them. They wouldn't give them what they wanted. So it was a bit of a joke with the staff because it didn't matter what you put in. You were going to get whatever the administration gave you. So what we did two years ago is we developed a policy whereby, first of all, we have a capital budget now. We have the capital budget and an operational budget. Capital budget is done in a process where departments send in what they want for new capital purchases for the year. And there is a committee of three curriculum leaders and myself and the business manager, and we go through the capital budget.

I make recommendations to that committee about what I think is capital and what isn't capital. And then we take that back, and it is approved by the faculty council. So that is a new process. The other process that we put into place was that we wanted it to be as transparent as we possibly can. So when curriculum leaders make a proposal of what they need for their operational budget for the year, we sit down as a team and we go through that. And we, as a team, kind of decide what the operational budget will be, what is actually needed to allow the department to operate. Once the budget is set, the departments get monthly statements showing what has been spent and what is left to spend. So they have real-time ideas of what's being spent on the budget. The budget itself is very, very transparent.

In terms of the priorities of school, the best example I can give you is this change that we are doing to the opportunity room. We showed the staff the data about the opportunity room and study hall. It showed that these spots could be more effective than they were. Then we took to the faculty council our suggestion of putting two teachers in there instead of having two EAs, and how much that would cost . . . what it was going to cost us, and how it would impact the operations budget. The staff got a real sense of what the proposal was, what the goals of the new program were, and how specifically we were going to fund it. In this particular case, they were concerned that we were exchanging two EAs for two teachers. We then had to go through the whole process of how the complete staffing of the school worked. We explained we already had a .5 teacher up in TLC, that we were already paying for two full-time EAs—one to run TLC and one to run the opportunity room. To make the new process work we had to remove those two positions, and by so doing put the money back to create another teacher position. In this way the project would only cost us an extra $50,000. Less when you talk about the EA who does study hall. So we were very clear and very transparent about the financial operations of what we were doing in the school and how we were going to meet the goal. And last week, I went through with them just exactly what was going to happen in terms of our cuts, and how we were going to try and deal with the cuts because we were facing about a $350,000 cut next year with all our programming.

Interviewer: And where is that cut coming from?

John: That cut is coming from the Alberta government. We are losing about $80,000 from ADLC. We are losing $230,000—somewhere in there—from work experience, because work experience has gone from about $184 a credit to $112 a credit. And we do have a lot of work experience here. Then the other cut is we get about $100,000 for our AISI project; $50,000 of that goes into our literacy projects. We have one woman who works half-time in our strategies program doing literacy with Grade 9s. And we are likely going to lose that. And then the other $50,000 pays for 50% of the career counsellor's position. So I am going to have to find that money somewhere within the budget.

Interviewer: That cut to work experience was a budget line from Alberta government?

John: Yes, they added a tier. There were three tiers to CEUs before. Tier one was $184; tier two was a little bit more money; and tier three was a little bit more money than that per CEU, because it was based on the fact that CTS shops need smaller classes and are more expensive to run. They created a tier four that is just strictly work experience. So where work experience was $184 a credit to the district, it is now $112 to the district—so a $70 cut, a $70 cut per credit.

Interviewer: Fascinating. Again, as I said, that is something new to me I hadn't picked up on in this budget document.

John: Yes, that was cut. ADLC was cut. Funding for ADLC was 80/20 previously, so we would basically get our full funding for ADLC before, at a full $184 a credit. It is now going down. It is going to be 44/56, so it is going from a $184 credit to $56—or $86 a credit for us. So that is another big cut. And of course AISI was cut right across the province.

Interviewer: The next question I have for you is related to your role as an education leader and as a **spokesperson for education.** When you communicate to your parent public, when you communicate with the Chamber of Commerce, when you are out in the public speaking as principal, typically what are your messages? What are you trying to reinforce? What are you trying to almost educate the public about?

John: Well, there are a number of messages I send to the public. And you have to remember that we have a very strong public relations, community relations individual. A lot of the messages that go out into the public go through him. But the things that I tend to promote here for the school, I promote our successes as a school. I promote the idea that we offer more programs than any other high school in the Province of Alberta. We offer more options to kids than anybody else. I tend to promote the career aspect of it and the support aspect about it—our SAC—because it is the largest counselling department in the province. So those are the messages I tried to get out to parents. In addition, I try to get the parents to understand just exactly what is it that we stand for? Much more of my work with the community is done through our school council. So we have a very strong school council. I typically have about 35 to 40 parents that come out each month. And what I tried to do is include them in the decision-making process, to make them feel a part of what is going on here at the school.

Interviewer: Expand a little bit more with school council. You are the only high school principal I have ever heard say that 35 or 40 people show up for a school council meeting.

John: Well, what I do at school council . . . I always bring into our school council meeting some aspect of our department, of our school. So I will have a presentation, a 15-minute presentation being done by somebody. So on Monday night we had a teacher who just came back from an Australian exchange. He spoke about the Australian exchange. I have had the career counsellor come in and talk about the career centre. I have had the work experience people come in and talk about the work experience program. In February I took them to a 20-minute performance of our musical—a practice. The kids were doing a practice, a rehearsal. So we went there and we watched them for 20 minutes. I always bring in something that is some aspect of the school so they can see what we are doing. I also bring them into discussions and on issues that we are having.

So right now we are in a discussion about our cafeteria. Our cafeteria loses about $70,000 a year. It comes right out of the instructional budget. With the cutbacks and everything that came up, I made the decision that we have to make a choice. We either have to change what we are doing in the cafeteria, or we are going to have to close it and do something different. I brought school council into the discussion. So they are part of what is going on. So with the cafeteria, what I have created is a management committee, which is going to make recommendations to me after we look at all the findings of what we have discovered about what the cafeteria is doing, and after we talk to different people.

A number of parents that are on that management committee are from the school council. We are fortunate that some of the parents from the school council have a background in restaurants. They are now helping us change the way we operate the cafeteria and are making recommendations.

I tried to bring school council members into anything that is going on in the school. Any policy that happens at the school—they have a say in policy as well. So if we are doing grad policy or something along those lines . . . the latest one would have been our valedictorian policy, how we select the valedictorian. They have a say in it, and they support it or don't support it and make recommendations that may change . . . they understand that [at] the end of the day it is my decision, but they have a say in it. And I make sure that they know exactly what is going on. So I send them out a letter before our meeting, and I outline the things we are going to talk about. So this last meeting on Monday night, I told them I was going to talk about the cafeteria. I was going to talk about the cuts to our budget and what that meant. But they have a say, and the meetings that they come to on the Monday nights, they have told me that they feel like they have learned something. They have learned something about the school. They have learned something about the way we operate. They have learned something about what I'm thinking in terms of the school.

They very much appreciate it. The president of the Home and School Association sits on my school council. So it has been very good, and to be truthfully honest, it becomes very easy for me to say to a parent who is complaining about something in the school, "Well, school council approves," and that ends the discussion. "Were you there?" No. So I took it to parents and they have approved it. It is a very, very good tool to use when you get yourself into an issue and parents are complaining or concerned about something. It just takes it away right now.

Interviewer: Is there something about your leadership in relationship to the competencies that we didn't hear? Is there something that you think we should know that might be of relevance to other people?

John: I think probably the most important thing about my whole experience—and I often think about this because I'm getting at the other end of my career—is that all the help that I've had along the way, and the individuals that are there helping me along. And I go back to my first principal, who was the first I worked under as an administrator. That mentoring process is absolutely key. And what you learn as you go through is absolutely pivotal. Does that make sense? I completed a Master's. I have also done the equivalent of another degree through the National Staff Development Council. I have been to, I don't know how many, leadership academies because I used to go with staff. And in spite of all that, I still think the most practical learning I had was working with people who were just before me, showing me how to do things and showing me what I can do and the pitfalls to watch out for.

And the other thing I think is being very true to who you are. I know for the first year that I was here—the vice-principals and I would get into arguments all the time because there would be a tough decision, and they would say, "Just let central office make that decision. Pass it on to them." And I kept saying to them, because it's very core to my beliefs, "I don't want central office making decisions for this school. We make decisions for this school." And that is what I mean by being very clear on who you are, and what you are, and what you stand for.

CHAPTER 13:

Interview:
Grades 10 to 12
School Principal

Mary is a high school principal in an urban setting that is not economically advantaged. Teaching for 29 years, she has been a formal school leader for four years: three as principal of a large urban junior high, and one in her current high school. This school has about 1,200 students and 70 teachers in Grades 10 to12. She completed her Master's in 1998.

The interviewer (a co-author) asks about her mentorship, and then asks how she enacts each professional competency.

Interviewer: The **mentorship.** Probably more so as you moved into your junior high school principalship. Was there a mentor assigned? Did you find a mentor? What was that whole process like?

Mary: So it was sort of both. I was assigned a mentor and he was also a principal of a junior high. Had been a vice-principal and so had been through that process. I also tended to choose people along the way, colleagues, that I would be not afraid to call and ask the stupid question or "what would you do if" and so on. So it was both.

The nice thing about being assigned a mentor is right from the get-go I had someone that I knew I could rely on when it came to doing some of the paperwork, to staffing, to that sort of thing. It was really important, I think. In fact, I now assign a mentor to every new person in my building. So whether you've been around the block for a 100 years or you're brand new to the job, you get a mentor inside the building as well. Same reason.

Interviewer: To go back to the mentor, particularly the assigned mentor you had when you first became principal—maybe talk us through a little bit of the expectation the district might have had for that mentor-mentee relationship. What sorts of things did they expect to have happen?

Mary: They wanted us to meet on a fairly regular basis, so they actually—there were set meetings throughout the entire year.

Interviewer: Do you remember how many?

Mary: I think there were five, if I remember. When we met, and there would be a set agenda and it was always timely when there were certain things coming up, which was really important. So whether it be staffing, and so here's your staffing process, here's how to interview, even though you may have done all of that—[it is] really helpful to sit there with your mentor and be able to discuss that. Often then there was work that we could do together.

But they also wanted us to meet informally at each other's schools. So I had my mentor at my building twice, and I went to his once, where I could just observe what was happening in the building and sort of see what the culture and climate were like in his building. He would come and see the same in mine. So it was really helpful, like really, really helpful to do that.

Interviewer: When you said you also took a look around for informal mentorship, who did you turn to there?

Mary: It was just colleagues. There was one gal who was in the same boat as I was, but she had already been a principal for two years. We had a relationship already. I think what was different about this person was that I got to choose that relationship. So there are things that maybe socially I would be connected with outside, whereas sometimes with the mentor that was assigned, it wouldn't be that. So it was nice to have both sides. She was, again, fairly new, but had lots of experience and was someone I could trust and work with.

Interviewer: If the school district had not assigned a mentor to you, do you think you could have found what that person provided to you in other people? Or did it just happen because it was the natural arrangement?

Mary: No, I think I would have found it in other people. But the difference with it being set up by the school district was it was instant. My job previously, I had worked at the district level for 10 years, so I knew a number of the principals, but not as that kind of colleague. It was a little bit different. So I would have still sought out people because I knew them, but the difference with that is that for example, I went in right after Easter into my last school, and we were looking at staffing and our numbers going forward.

I had never had to do that before, so right away my mentor called and said, "Okay, tomorrow you're going to get this form, and this is what it's for, and this is what you need to do. This is how I do it. Other people may do it this way. Play with it and see what you think." And then I could call him back and say, "Okay, this is what I've done. Can I send it to you?"

So I didn't have time to sort of go, well, I think I'll find that person who can help me. It was done for me. And I think that's the difference.

Interviewer: This district has used the principal competencies as part of the process you follow. When the district is looking for a new leader, how active are the competencies used in the search process? Or what role do they play as they are trying to designate folks as school leaders?

Mary: I think it is pretty key now. I think anybody who is beginning the process needs to know those competencies. Our district has taken the competencies and really expanded them into modules we use to work with potential and new leaders. The process we have is ideal, but it's long, long, long. We are working to try and make it actually a little bit slimmer. But really, when I look at what in my opinion is a strong leader, I really like looking at their skills through the lens of the competencies, because I can see yes, this person has this particular strength, this level, will be working at this level. But that's fine, that's a goal, it's an opportunity.

So I know that in the vice-principal pool, for example, they needed to know them and be able to speak to them. I know in the principal pool we all have to know exactly what the competencies are and what they mean. I also know at the upper level you need to know them as well.

Interviewer: When you are evaluated, is the competency document used as part of the evaluation process and in what way?

Mary: Yes, it is. We have to demonstrate. I find the best way to improve any practice is that reflection piece. There is not a day that I don't go home and think, "I didn't do that very well, how am I going to change that for tomorrow?" Or I go home and go, "That was really awesome." That is something that I need to make sure I start embedding in what we are doing in our building. So I think it is ideal. I really, really like it.

Interviewer: I'm going to make an assumption first and correct it if I am wrong—I am assuming it is your area superintendent who would be doing the quote-unquote evaluation of you.

Mary: Correct.

Interviewer: How does your area superintendent know you are actually—I am not going to say truthful, but that you are very accurate in the evidence that you are presenting to him or to her as part of your evaluation? How do they know that? What else do they do?

Mary: That is a good question. My superintendent is here a lot. She is in other schools more. We invite her as much as possible. I share with her as much as possible the good things that are happening here, and she knows all the bad things because we are all dealing with them together.

How does she know? That is a good question. I think in how we demonstrate it, how we have to show the evidence. In mine for example, I have got photos. I think as well there is word of mouth. I think by being in the building, talking with staff—I mean, there are lots of ways of knowing. I can't speak to certain things. It is a good question, really.

Interviewer: So when the superintendent or the area superintendent is here, when you say, "be able to speak to staff," how often would she actually be inside of a classroom to check on instruction? Or would she?

Mary: No, she wouldn't be.

Interviewer: So what would her visit to this building look like?

Mary: It can be for a meeting here with a number of staff. It can be just at our gala on Friday nights, so she was here for that with our drama production. It could be just being in the halls and wandering through. So we might be walking. I take her on tours, try to show her anything new that is happening, and so she might be stopped in the hallway or chatting with other people. And it wouldn't surprise me either what she hears in the community because she is out there a lot. She is very busy. She is seldom in her office.

So even going to the junior high, it is how the parents there are feeling about their child going to the high school. You know, we hear things are really wonderful there. Or we are not very comfortable having our son or daughter go there. But is she in the classroom observing? No. I might take her into a classroom and show her, but it wouldn't be for something very specific.

Interviewer: Good. Thank you. Let's go on to **vision.** And I am curious about either school here—because you are still, relatively speaking, a new principal—or at your most current school.

Interviewer: When you were at your last school, did you actually have to lead the process of creating a vision? Or did you inherit one and you tried to live by it?

Mary: Neither. And the reason I am going to say that is yes—I mean, the one side as the principal, I do have a vision. And the vision I had for that school came from a lot of data collection. So I was fortunate.

The best thing that happens in this district, when it can happen I think, is when a new principal can go in right after Easter, say, or the first of May, because the school is going to keep running. No change has to happen between May and June or April, May, and June, because everything is running along. The school plan for the next year has already been done. But you get to really get a sense of what is happening in the school.

So I was fortunate. I got to go to my last school right after Easter, so that was in March, and I got to come here in March of last year. I think it is fabulous. It is hard on the school you are leaving, and it can be hard coming into the school, because if they really liked the principal that was here, then they are sorry to see that person go. That is all, you know, we are human. We understand that. But you do get a sense of what is going on in the building.

So at my last school for the example, their PAT results were not good. They were about 33% ESL kids. Engagement was pretty good, but just observations in the classrooms—the doors were often closed, very much like a silo in certain areas. And the layout of the building I didn't like. So I started to create a different environment and asking the questions, "So why are all the Special Ed kids down one hallway? Why is it that they are on the far side of the school?" To me, that sends a loud message.

So they said, "Well, it's just the way it's always been." There was no, well, because of this or this, that is just where they always were. So we completely changed that.

We looked at the PAT results and really tried to drill down to what the issues were. When I looked at them and I looked at common threads in the results, I could see it was literacy. When I stood in the classrooms and observed, it was clearly literacy.

So that became the vision. But it was how you get it to the staff and get it to be their vision [that] was the biggest part that I could see. So when I say it was neither me leading it, nor walking into the vision, but by planting the seed over that March to June, and then September to June the next year, it became their vision, and the champions in the school took it on.

It wasn't the principal or the vice-principal. Every staff member started, and it started with some people who said, "I'd like to try this, is that okay?" And it was around literacy. "Sure. Let's do it." What is the worst that can happen? No one is going to get hurt and there is going to be good learning, either that it didn't work or that it did. So slowly those champions evolved and it became their vision. Then it became the school's vision.

Interviewer: Could you articulate that vision in a sentence or two?

Mary: The vision of—

Interviewer: Of your last school? So what you were able to create inside of that building with these champions. What would it be?

Mary: It was a collaborative environment where all staff were seeking with the same core vision in mind for the success of the students. And it was around literacy, it was around co-teaching, it was around sharing of plans. The doors were all open—there was never a closed door in that building—so somebody might pop across.

In staff meetings we started doing—all of our staff meetings were—at least half of it was PD time, so it was embedded PD. Staff felt that they knew the purpose and they saw the success of the students, and then they wanted to try more and try different ideas. And I think they weren't afraid to ask or to just attempt it themselves. Does that make sense?

Interviewer: It does. And I want to push this further, because there is a huge story in here. And I am going to go right to the end of the story. So you referred to roughly 33% as ELL, and provincial achievement test results. For a school in this district to not have good provincial achievement test results, that is an issue. So when you left, you still had 33% ELL students, but you must have had a change in what was the output in something like PATs. What was the change?

Mary: Yes, slowly. Slowly, the change—and I guess I should go back to one other point, too, is that we told the staff that—and then this was something that there was a bit of a panic [over] and I didn't realize, because the staff, when I first started presenting this to them at the end of June and then that first full year, the staff thought, "Oh, here is another flavour of the month," or "Here is another new principal with a new idea."

I didn't realize—unfortunately. There was one staff member that was brave enough to come and talk to me, and he said, "You know, Mary, this is like one more thing being done to us." I went, "Whoa, whoa, whoa. I guess I didn't say this is like three to five years that we are working on this. This is all we are going to do. I give you my word." The sense of relief I saw in his face was almost funny. I thought, "Oh my God, I missed the key point here." I said, "This is something going forward over three to five years."

So what was the output? We saw an increase in our PATs, they were slightly better, because it was not going to happen overnight. Probably the biggest thing we saw change [in] was collaborative instruction, where people wanted to work together. The other thing is—because my mind is more of a high school person—I created their departments. So an English department, a math department, and so on. But then I said okay, that was the first year. Then I said, "Now we are going to do across departments."

Math and science were working together, and they weren't afraid to try and do the joint planning. So then it became people used to going to their colleagues and saying, "I'm doing this unit and it is not working. Have you done this before or something different?" And I will think, "Oh yeah, but look, let's try this. Let's do it together." And so they would actually plan together and have the class together.

That to me is what a school should be, is people working together for [the] success of students. So we saw a complete change in the environment in that building and watching it grow where they were very collegial, really working well together.

Interviewer: It just begs the question of how were you able to accomplish that? Getting teachers to work together who historically work in silos is one of the toughest—if not *the* toughest—thing for a principal to do. So how did you accomplish that?

Mary: I set the standard, I guess. I said this is what we are doing. But again, I think it goes back to, to be honest with you—I don't think a principal has to be the one standing right in front saying top down, this is what we are doing. I think you need to be able to first of all see what is going on in the school. Find out what the culture is within that staff. Find your champions, and get them to feel the leadership opportunities for themselves as well. And see success starting to build.

It is like a kid. They feel like, you know, I can't believe I just did that. And look what I got? I got a great mark. Staff want that, too. So it is that supporting of the staff. I told them I would never say no, and I don't say no. I will ask what are the pros and cons or why not. Why are you asking if you can do it? Why wouldn't you do it? So I think just that empowerment, to help them feel like this is a good thing.

Not everybody was on board right away, either. So part of that, then, is setting standards, and I guess in so many ways maybe the message got out there, although not said—either you swim along or you float away. I hope that wasn't a message that they felt that they had to do. But they all came along.

Interviewer: Let us go to relationships, because competency number one actually is **fostering effective relationships.** Tell us about your relationship style, your interaction style with your teachers, and maybe a good example of "here is what it looked like when I was at my last school."

Mary: It was definitely transparent. I told the staff when they met me, what they see is what they get. I feel it is very important to develop that relationship, but it is definitely, you know, it's friendly, it's warm, it's engaging. Family comes first. I tell them that, "You know what? If there are issues at home, that is going to come to school. So you need to make sure that home is as best as it can be, and if you need help, what does that look like?"

I do set the expectation and the standard that they are to be their best. And if they can't be their best, then what help do they need to get there? I try to engage them as much as possible. I'm not going to get everybody, but I also am in the classrooms a lot. And I said, "I am not necessarily watching you teach. I want to watch the curriculum. I want to see what you are doing, I want to see how the kids are doing." So they see me often. They see me in the halls.

I think the other piece that was really key is I don't feel I'm up here and they are below me. They have the hard job. My job is pretty easy. So I want to be alongside with them and I really work hard. So an example is when I see garbage, I pick it up. Why should a caretaker, why should that be only their job? So I encourage other staff to pick it up as well. So it is that community piece. We are all in this together, and the core is the success of our students. If our students aren't successful, then we all have done something wrong. So we have got to work harder to try and figure out what is it we need to do to make it better.

So relationship, yes. They know if they come to me, I will do what I can to try and support them. Sometimes I had to make the tough call and say no, or I had to make the tough call and evaluate. But because I am transparent, there were no deals, there was no, you know, if you do this for me, then I will do that. Or can I have this if I do that? That was not how we operate. It has got to be for the good of all.

Interviewer: I am going to flip to **leading a learning community**, because there is a natural tie here. I want to go back to your last school, but then I want you to come back to the present school experience with the fine arts again, if you don't mind.

We could almost say within the junior high school that you put a high school stamp of bureaucracy into a middle school climate. What did those departments look like? Did they take on more of the flavour of what recent writers would call PLCs? Or did they become a department chair who would meet with you on occasion? Talk to us [about] what these departments called PLCs actually look like, and maybe also how they function.

Mary: It was more like the PLCs—what we did was we found a champion in each department. Someone who was really passionate about English or passionate about math. That person became someone who we would use to start running our PLCs. They weren't CTs, they weren't department heads, but they were passionate. So they got the advantage of doing a little bit more PD, whether it be external, outside of the city, or here—whatever it might look like.

We would have an assembly for all the students in the gym. The assemblies would be 45 minutes. That way all the staff could meet. So we began by developing our vision through what would be a strategy. When the PLCs met there were very specific things each was working on.

So the first year, it was really looking at literacy within their department. What does it look like? Well, English, they said that is pretty easy. What I am looking at, it is easy to do. But not really, because they had to drill deeper and deeper and deeper. And with that was differentiation and assessment, all of those things. So they started developing it and looking at it.

Then the next year we said, "Okay, how do we make it cross-curricular? Where are the connections that we can have so that we can be working all together on that?" And we started developing that. So each of the meetings became very plan-full. As an administrator, I made sure I was in every single one.

So my vice-principal would be in the gym. I would go around to every single PLC. Get a sense of what was going on, what they wanted to do, what they felt they could try, what kind of PD they needed, and we made sure they got it. Then I made sure the vice-principal got in, so it wasn't just only me either. The vice-principal needed to get in and be part of what was happening as well. So that's how we developed it.

Interviewer: Did they have to submit any reports to you periodically, or did you have enough sense by your visits?

Mary: Yes, I had enough sense by my visits. And then the meetings that we had. So our staff meetings, because they were focused on that as well, we would get a number of different types of information. So for example, the math department would say, "We want to show a strategy that we tried as a department in math in Grade 8, and we want to show it to the whole staff because we think they can benefit from that." So PD in the last year I was there, very little of it was external. It all came from inside.

Interviewer: And was that the third step in your process?

Mary: Yes. Because I knew I had experts in my building. But they had never been allowed to show their stuff in the past. One guy I asked for three years straight and who would never demonstrate to other teachers in our staff meeting PD. Just didn't want to do it. He was nervous. He said they can come in and they can watch. I said I really need you to do it. And he finally did. And it was amazing.

Interviewer: As in he presented it himself?

Mary: He presented his ideas, how he ran his classroom as teams. He would mix them up all the time. There would be opportunities for students to plan their own learning. They could choose using how they wanted to present a particular topic. The kids got to plan all that themselves, and then there was a lot of peer marking, and then of course the assessment by the teacher. It was just a different way of doing it, almost like the reverse classroom, if you will, that we are just starting to explore here.

So he had that going and he wouldn't present on it. And then I asked him again. So he finally—he said, "Yes, I think I really want to do this." And he actually asked for two staff meetings after the first one.

Interviewer: So he could show.

Mary: He could show.

Interviewer: Did any of the teachers try it?

Mary: Absolutely. Yes.

Interviewer: Would teachers go into his room to watch him?

Mary: Yes.

Interviewer: How did you get that to happen the first time? Or did they come to you to ask if they could do it for the first time?

Mary: No, no. Again, that was something—so if I find out somebody was doing something neat in the classroom, we would bring it up in a shout-out or something. Every staff meeting started with that. So I would say, thank somebody for drama, or I would thank them for the coaching, or whatever happened.

Interviewer: And by the time you hit the third year? Or did you have a different structure in place?

Mary: No, but what was starting to happen was it was just that there was so much collaboration happening that they were in each other's classrooms all the time.

Interviewer: How would they get freed up to be in each other's classroom?

Mary: They would either look at their own spares or their own prep time. They would go in. I would cover, my vice-principal would cover, a counsellor. Whatever needed to happen, they would do it.

Interviewer: Would teachers in this district at the middle school level still get the infamous, roughly speaking, 40 minutes prep a day?

Mary: Ours did. For sure. Some schools not so much. It just depends. It really will depend on their staffing and their numbers. But we were able to make sure, and actually I think—so everybody got six out of six.

Interviewer: Six out of six.

Mary: Yes.

Interviewer: And then over and above that, would there be times during the day that the various departments or PLCs would meet? Or was it somehow factored into their prep time?

Interviewer: Would they also meet outside of regular school time?

Mary: That was what started to happen. People were—I mean, some of those staff were there—I would leave at 6:00 p.m., I still had staff there. I would get there at

7:00 in the morning, I had staff there. So we have people that were willing to take their own time and do some of that planning as well.

Interviewer: Was that happening before you showed up in the building?

Mary: Not as collaboratively. I can't speak to whether or not I noticed it. But there wasn't collaboration, for sure, that I observed.

Interviewer: They were just doing their own thing.

Mary: Yes.

Interviewer: So with **instructional leadership**, so you make the move from your last school and you come into this school and you've identified a requirement to develop—let's just call it a first-rate fine arts program. So how did you use the power that comes with being principal to make that happen?

Mary: I supported the people who wanted to develop the first-rate fine arts program. They came to me. They said they wanted to do it—I didn't know that they had never done a musical in this building in 20 years when I said I wanted to see a musical. So I didn't know that. But I said I wanted something where we got band kids involved, we got choir kids involved, we got dance kids involved, where we got the art department doing all the art. I said, "You guys do whatever you want, but that is the expectation." They came back and they said that that is what they were going to do. And I mean, it was unbelievable.

The comment that was made back to me was, "Every time we asked to do something in the past, the answer was no. So you have allowed us to do this." Was I nervous? Absolutely. It was going to be a big show, and it was either going to be good or it was going to be really bad. It was really, really good. Thank goodness they weren't afraid to try.

Interviewer: How do you find the money to do all the initiatives you tried to start in the school?

Mary: That was a challenge. We were able to get community sponsorships for things like robotics. We set up budgets that the various groups in the school could access. We had a phenomenal business manager. He has really done a really good job. He recognized the importance of spreading out the money, and the right to make decisions, out to everybody. So no one group gets more than the other. And we work within their needs.

Interviewer: How do you make those decisions—everybody gets to share in it equally? What formal process do you have in place for **budgeting** in the school?

Mary: It again involves all our department heads. So it starts with the business manager and myself, with the admin team, and we look at—because there was quite a debt when I walked in. So the first priority is we got to get ourselves out of debt.

Interviewer: Do you mind sharing that amount?

Mary: To the tune of about $37,000. So we had to be very creative and work really hard. And again, part of it was working with our parents. We explained why we have school fees and why and how we spend them. There were issues in this community with money, obviously. But it is not everybody. Again, what I found was that, working with parents, to be able to say to them, "What can you afford? Whatever you can afford would be great."

Interviewer: The budgets in this district are everything that you require to run the school, except for staffing and except for operation and maintenance.

Mary: Yes.

Interviewer: So a lot of the instructional needs of the school come from your school-based budget. Is that correct?

Mary: That is right.

Interviewer: They have a pool that they can draw upon to take care of specialized needs?

Mary: Teachers at this school told me for instance, "So even though there were budgets, let's say athletics needed new uniforms. So athletics needed new uniforms, but another department had a surplus because they were saving that money to buy four Smart Boards for their department for the next year. When they arrived back in September, it was gone. Where did it go?"

So one of the things that we insisted on this year is everything is transparent. So that is why I need to know what their wish list was from the very beginning, and once the budget is set they are in charge of it. They understand where their money goes. If you say you need new microscopes, then we have to have them. So what is the budget for that, what is that going to be? But I'm not going to rob from another department to buy them. It will come out of the department budget or school specialized capital budget, which is just that global piece that we have. But it won't come from another department's budget.

The musical had to break even. I think we are going to be up a little bit because of just the amount of sales. We had a full show, so it was good. But again, if you want to do that, our way of doing that was, "I am going to charge $3 per student to the junior highs that come." Well, they were thrilled to do that. So that again added money.

Interviewer: The way you lived your life as an instructional leader—did that change from the way you did business at your last school to the way you now do business at this school? Or what is your instructional leadership style?

Mary: No, it's the same. Everything has to be data-driven. So I need to know if our results are poor, because, by the way, our diploma results here are poor as well. We spend a lot of time analyzing. So now we have had three sets of diplomas written. So I was able to see January of last year, I saw June of last year, and now January again. By the way, literacy is a big issue here. Kids don't understand what they are reading.

Mary: I said, "No, the poor results are not good enough." In the past, at this school, students could walk the stage even if they were not going to qualify for their high school diploma. You only had to have a 45% average to walk the stage. Why? To give them the experience of something that isn't real. They didn't work for it, to get that 50% that everybody else had to have. My belief was if I just keep raising the bar, the kids will rise to it. They will achieve.

So in terms of that vision, our job in my opinion, yes, is to teach curriculum. But our job as a staff at this school is to prepare these kids for post-secondary. I work with the assumption that every kid that wants to go to post-secondary will be able to go to post-secondary. If kids have to retake a course or do an upgrade, that is okay. But we have to prepare them as best we can to get there. And that is what I tell them. What I started to do the moment I walked in here, that was my expectation.

Interviewer: So when you say post-secondary, you're thinking university? Or what are you thinking?

Mary: No, no. It is any kind. So I am very much into the trades. I am a strong supporter. For university, post-secondary, we have a culinary arts program here where students can actually get their first-year apprentice, or they can go Red Seal chef, or they can go into another program. Whatever a student wants to do. I don't care if it is a 10-month diploma. But if they have a vision of what they want to do, and they know how to get there, and that is our job, and our job at the end of Grade 12 is to make sure they are prepared to be there as best as we can, then that is what we have to do.

Interviewer: You talk about three opportunities now to review diploma examinations, and you say we took a look at them. Who is the "we" in this case? What does that process look like?

Mary: The entire staff. So what it looks like from the admin standpoint is we all look at them first. I look at the entire package and then I have three vice-principals, so each will take their own department. They go through the same package line by line, looking at what the common threads are, come up with the data that we have. From there, we take it to our departments.

So each vice-principal has one or two departments with them. They take them and say, "Now, here is what we see. Now you as a department need to explore them and have a look at them as well." Then the last part of it is, "What's the plan?" We have a number of our staff meetings, and the development days, where part of those days has to be to sit and look at the results and map out a plan.

So in chemistry, the kids did really, really well in five of these areas, but in two areas they didn't, and that affected the overall. What are we going to do to improve? And what do we do well? So it is not always about what we have to do to make it better, but we have to celebrate what we have done well as well. And they do. They focus on what the right stuff was. And is that transferable somewhere else? So it is a whole school, whole staff.

Interviewer: I am going to have you think back to your last school again, because you had a longer experience there. What process did you follow **to identify leadership in others**, and then to promote the leadership?

Mary: I call them the champions. They are the ones that want to test the waters early by coming and asking if they can do something. I will use the reluctant teacher as the example. He was a champion. But he didn't want to be the guy out there. He didn't want to be the leader. So I saw that, because I was in every classroom.

So at my last school, I got into every classroom a minimum of twice a day. That was my job. My job was to be in the halls, to be in the classrooms, to be present to the staff and the kids. I do it as best I can here. I can't get into every classroom every day at this school. It is too big. I am in the halls every bell. Like for example, the bell just went. I would normally be out there.

Interviewer: I saw you move.

Mary: Yes. Because presence is so key, and I think when I am present, I see those leaders. I see them, and I merge their excitement to teach—how they interact with kids—with how they interact with their colleagues. So I kind of start seeing them and then start looking at—and again, it's not my decision. It is working with my team, the admin team.

So at my last school, I had a vice-principal. So we would sit and look and I would say, "You know, what about asking so-and-so if they want to kind of try doing some of these things?" Then we would get groups of staff together. So we actually worked with Pearson, a very large project with literacy, and again it was a group of teachers who wouldn't have interacted normally. But through this work all of a sudden they start pulling together, even though at the start they all had different ideas with literacy. One was our LD teacher. Another was an English teacher. Another was a science teacher. They naturally start evolving.

I think the other piece is when people have ideas to try and make things better. If you always say no, then everybody will stay the same. So our view was—and I said this right from the very beginning—if you've got ideas, I am not going to say no. But if you can come to me and talk about what you would really like to do and can present the value of what you want to try, let's try it. And that is what we did. The process just naturally grew and allowed me to identify leadership skills in others, and to promote their leadership.

Interviewer: You said you worked with Pearson on a project. Can you describe that project? Was it meant for ELL children or was it meant for children, period?

Mary: Lots around ELL. But my view was good instruction hits every kid. And so a lot of the ideas in this could have been for the ELL. But we found, you know, the example that we used in a staff meeting was, "Who knows what a boy is?" Everybody kind of chuckles. "It's a male." "Okay, what about a buoy—B-U-O-Y?" Some people will call it a boy, some people will call it a buoy. So we know that language, and especially in English, is very difficult. And context means all the difference in the world.

So we started looking at that kind of thing. And the staff, you could see them saying, "Yes, this all makes sense." And that is all this did, was it just helped us with that.

Interviewer: So if we go into science—and you said literacy became a huge focus in every subject area—what would literacy in science look like after you were there for three years?

Mary: Again, it would be the strategies that they were using. So one example was we had a fellow who started using different strategies to teach the concepts. Visual, hands-on, contextual. He would use his Smart Board and, for example, talking about a pulley system, and showing the pulley and going up the ramp, and it was around friction and whatever, the math of it and so on. So he was demonstrating it. He would demonstrate it so kids could see it.

He always made sure that he had a physical demonstration so they could see it and then try it. Get their own understanding. Then they would have to reteach that piece. But there are also kids who needed it on a piece of paper, and so he always had that available. I would say more of it was just strategies . . . Instead of evidence of showing it being done one way, he would show it a multitude of ways to get to all kids actively engaged. Made a huge difference.

Interviewer: One of the competencies deals with **responding to the larger societal contexts**—the message you give out as principal to the community and the degree to which you are an advocate for education. What does that look like now? What kind of advocacy for education do you take part in within the bigger community?

Mary: I think part of it is that I do have high standards. So just like I said, when a staff member would say, "Well, Mary, it's the nature of this school." And I would say, "You know what? That is not good enough. These kids are as good as any other student in any other part of the city. Just because they may not have the money, or they may be first-generation Canadian, or they may come from a home where the parent works three jobs in order to put food on the table, the standards that we set for these kids and the amount of work that we put in might be more than what would happen in better off schools. So we have to work harder, because our children may not have the same things as kids in other parts of the city. That doesn't mean our standards, our expectations, have to be any less."

I tell that when I talk to parents as well, and to the students obviously. But I tell them they are the best all the time. But I also thank the parents for letting their kids come to our school. So at the gala after the play—and this is a message I always do—it's about community and it's about family. And I thank parents for letting their children come to our building and be part of what we try to do at the school, because that means that they are spending more time with us than they are with you in your home.

I think the parents like that. The parents like the standards. The parents like the way we work with them. You don't see that. But it is that respect piece. That mutual respect is what is required in a community. So we work on that.

CHAPTER 14:

Findings:
Making Sense of What
the Leaders Told Us

In this chapter we identify a series of big ideas about leadership derived from the stories told to us by the highly effective principals we interviewed. Valuable to note at this juncture is a serious overlap between the competencies and the lived experiences of the school leaders. Whether school leaders had a few years' experience, or decades of time in formal leadership, they all articulated stories around the important role the competencies played in the way they lived their leadership mandates.

Mentorship

We begin by addressing the role of mentorship in the development of leadership capacity. We wanted to see if the principals had been provided with a mentor when they became school leaders, or whether they had sought their own mentors on an informal rather than formal basis. Finally, we tried to assess the degree to which the mentoring process impacted the way they fulfilled their roles as school leaders.

Most of the principals did not have a formal mentor assigned to them when they entered their current positions. All who were asked identified a person who served as an informal mentor. Various principals shared comments like: Valuable, very helpful, showed me the ropes, helped me answer the dumb questions, and allowed me to deal with tricky managerial tasks right away. In a couple of cases, mentor and mentee shared teacher expertise between their respective schools. In another, the mentee used the mentor as a sounding board of sorts to generate ideas on how to tackle some issues impacting the school. Most positive were the soft skills identified by the principals in our study, knowing they always had someone they could call upon to be of assistance and to "be there" for them.

Of the four principals who indicated they had a formal mentor provided, two were from the same school district. Both commented glowingly about the power of relationships developed through the mentoring process. The mentorship program established by this urban school district rose to the level of attending to both the theory of school leadership and the day-to-day practicalities that often arise in running a school. The two principals identified the value of working with their mentors. They also valued the leadership preparation program they were engaged in with their school district, especially when it came to understanding the mission. In addition, they also related the power of having someone on their side when trying to master the managerial aspects of their jobs in compliance with school district policies and procedures. The immediacy of the help they received proved to be the most important aspect of the mentorships. These principals indicated they didn't have to search for answers to some of the procedural issues they dealt with; the answers were just a phone call to their mentors away.

Most of the school leaders interviewed indicated they would have liked to have been part of a more solid mentoring process organized by their respective school districts. They recognized the value of the mentorship process from the informal arrangements they had set up, and often wondered how much more powerful the connections could have been if organized in a formal, purposeful, and timely way through the school district.

Lived Competencies

Fostering Effective Relationships

All 10 principals were asked how they went about fostering effective relationships in their schools. Based on their responses we developed a *Wordle*. Often-mentioned words included trust, process, team, learning, together, know, talk, support, and think. Trust and team appeared in the responses of all 10 interviewees. Key to the practices of the principals was a general sense of needing to act with fairness, dignity, and integrity. The following quotes highlight ways in which individual principals attended to practices of fairness, dignity, and integrity:

> "We tried to make sure that we dealt with staff in a fair manner, and we tried to make sure that they were valued." (John)

> "Power can go to a lot of heads, and I suppose this could be construed as a position of power. It is certainly a position of authority when it needs to be. But the position is not carried out in any way, shape, or form that isn't with everybody's dignity maintained throughout. I think that is a big, important aspect of being principal." (Thomas)

> "And it's about trust, all about those relationships, and that takes time— time, and consistency, and integrity, and knowing exactly why we made certain decisions. I think early on I made a real conscious, concerted effort to tell the 'whys.'" (Donald)

Climate and culture were identified as important elements in developing a relationship with students, staff, and parents. These principals attempted to develop a climate and culture based on sensitivity and genuine care and concern. The word "respect" was heard from many. Mary articulates the way in which respect plays a key role in relationship development and a healthy school culture and climate:

> "I think the parents like that. The parents like the [moral and ethical] standards. The parents like the way we work with them. You don't see that. But it is that respect piece. That mutual respect is what is required in a community. So we work on that." (Mary)

An extension to the idea of building healthy climate and culture through the use of respect was the articulation of the necessity of building inclusive communities in which diversity is honoured. The example presented by Katherine was the integration of Low German Mennonite (LGM) students into the everyday life of the school. These students came from a cultural group that spoke German at home and were transient in nature, many travelling back and forth between Canada and Mexico. While in Alberta, the LGM men often worked as farm labourers and the women remained in the home to care for the house and children. Katherine related that her school worked hard to help the LGM children feel at home, and their parents welcome to visit and see first-hand what the children were learning.

Mary spoke to the need for making her school a service hub; a place where people, many of them recent immigrants, could come for help and support. Joan blended a deep respect for diversity with moving special education classrooms to the centre of the school to help create an atmosphere of acceptance.

Many principals indicated that a foundation of trust was the cornerstone upon which relationships were built. However, they also noted, in a variety of ways, trust was built with purpose, through hard work, and attention to detail. The purpose, these principals noted, was to support learning for all students in the school. Relationships, in other words, were used to build a climate and culture in which the best interests of all students could be invoked as a moral imperative and acted upon. A number of principals identified that building trust and establishing healthy relationships, while acting in the best interest of students, were often preceded by tough conversations. Donald said it in this way:

> "I'm a shoot from the hip, fairly direct type person, because that is the way I like people to treat me. And I think staff appreciate that. They know exactly where I stand on things, and so if conflict does arise, you know it surfaces at times, but we deal with it head on. But it always comes back to what is in the best interest of students at this school. And can we make it work for you? Absolutely. But I am not apologetic to say we need to make it work for those kids."

Principals also addressed the ways in which they worked to make relationships real and impactful on student learning. A number said they promoted open dialogue, and almost all did so through establishing a collaborative working environment. Dialogue, for Donald, started with listening to staff, students, and community members. He also felt it was important to begin the dialogue by ensuring teachers and students knew the "why" of school projects and goals. Steven stressed the importance of being visible in halls, classrooms, and the community, and that visibility led to increased two-way dialogue. Both Ellen and Katherine said it was important to be visible in the school, and through observations of what was really going on to have tough conversations with teachers whose actions were not consistent with what was perceived as good for student learning. Collaboration was recognized by many of the principals as a means to focus the process of dialogue on the primacy of student learning. For example, Steven said, "My role was just build all the structures and supports for that collaboration and conversation to happen."

Another relationship building strategy used by the principals was effective communication, facilitation, and problem-solving skills. Key to this area of the relationship competency was identifying what was expected of teachers, support staff, and students. The focus for teachers was the Teaching Quality Standard; for students it was routines and procedures; and for support staff it was their active integration into the decision-making processes of the school. In other words, with some of the principals communication began with the identification of key priorities and what would matter. Next, facilitation came into play with the process of making people aware of what the principals deemed to be priorities. For some, facilitation took the form of both formal and informal conversations about what was important; for others it was being visible, and for others it occurred through the establishment of leadership-type committees. Facilitation with students took the form of getting to know students by name and inviting them to provide feedback through conversations and surveys. Ellen emphasized the importance of speaking directly to students and asking their opinions on school matters. Donald stressed that even lower-grade elementary students needed thoughtful and age appropriate dialogue with adults about what they were learning and how the school could better serve their needs. A number of principals underscored the importance of transparency in the facilitation process with parents. However, it was also apparent in the answers of all the principals that relationships with teachers dominated much of their language, and we were left with the impression that they were purposeful in the ways they spent their time. Many of the principals related that, whether through formal PLCs, committees, or with school leadership teams, problem solving became the dominant mode of addressing the dynamics between communication and teacher involvement in school decisions.

Many of the principals also addressed the issue of conflicts and their impact on school-based relationships. Principals noted it was important to deal with conflict in an honest, open way. These principals did not hesitate to identify and communicate what was really important in the school community, and have conversations with people who were neither "buying into" the program nor adapting to the culture and climate being established.

Embodying Visionary Leadership

When we examined the language around embodying visionary leadership, words like "school, kids, teachers, staff, knowing, and data" dominated. As we asked principals about the vision of their respective schools we noted that all were able to articulate what they considered to be the school's driving force. They didn't necessarily quote a printed and formally approved vision of the school. Rather, they addressed the big idea of vision from the point of view of what was generally considered the feature that made their school unique, and around which they and their school community rallied. For Donald the vision was very child-centred:

> "Our vision is that children need to do their best, they need to feel good about themselves. We need to get along, and we need to build a sense of community. So everybody has a part in a child's education."

For Timothy the vision centred on the role of the community and the school's historic position as a community school:

> "The vision of our school is based on the community school concept. We were designated as a community school when that program was in place, and we felt that it did so much for what we were trying to accomplish, we kept community in our name without the funding.
>
> Basically what that has done for us, and our vision for our school, is that we want to make education as relevant as possible for students, and so we take the basic curriculum and we try and give it that practical aspect by involving the local community."

Katherine worked the concept of vision into a simple yet powerful set of words: *believe, trust, honesty, respect, and responsibility.* The word *be* was added when staff wanted the vision to be lived and put into daily practice by students.

In addition to articulating a vision, each principal shared stories that emphasized ways in which the vision was lived and expressed by themselves, the staff, and/or the students. They also aptly demonstrated that being the keepers of the vision was a significant role they played within the school community. Joan told of arriving in her school and witnessing first-hand the number of children who came to school hungry. She also noted various data she turned to in order to verify that what she was seeing related to hunger in her school. Her vision became centred on the necessity to feed and clothe children so they could learn. Joan also related that she had to hold true to the vision of "kids being able to eat anytime, anywhere" when staff wanted to judge whether kids were hungry or not, or when staff thought certain kids had enough money to buy their own food. Her vision went to the heart of children being able to learn only if they have enough to eat. She was forced on a regular basis to get staff members, especially teacher assistants who lived in the community from which the children came, to stop judging and start feeding, and then teaching.

Principals consistently told us they were driven by their own vision of education, yet also worked closely with their respective school communities to develop a shared sense of vision, mission, and goals. Donald spoke of the need to develop a common language around vision and mission. In turn, he provided examples of how the school's vision aligned with the educational goals established by his school community. In order to keep the *vision common* he revisits the big ideas every year and speaks to the language of the vision with students, staff, and community stakeholders. Ellen noted it was her clear, unwavering vision of making all decisions in the best interest of kids that led staff to jump on board and work toward achieving what has become a common vision. Thomas worked through the idea that vision, mission, and goals are for the long term. He emphasized in his school community the need to stick to things over extended periods and not jump to new fads just because they were the "new way" of the day or flavour of the month.

The principals noted the important role data played in the accomplishment of the vision, mission, and goals of their schools. Data sources mentioned were varied and appropriate to the plans outlined by these principals. In some cases the focus was on the effective use of Provincial Achievement Test data and the ways in which groups of teachers used this information to refine their practices; in others it was in pouring over results received from the Accountability Pillar data and the information gleaned from parent, teacher, and student surveys. Some used the wealth of information obtained by asking the appropriate questions in the *Tell Them From Me* surveys. In all cases the principals made a direct connection between the data that was important to them and the fulfillment of their vision. Many organized multi-grade committees to emphasize that learning outcomes were not just the responsibility of the PAT year teachers.

One of the most powerful stories of vision in use came from Timothy who explained how he moved his school community in the direction of a total focus on literacy and a response-to-intervention model that was created. The vision in this school grew out of the community school concept, and as such he actively integrated all elements of the community into developing a school-wide literacy program built on a pyramid of interventions approach. Teachers and teacher assistants worked in collaboration to plan and deliver an exceptionally rich, individual-student-focused program. Of all of the schools included in this study, Timothy's excelled in both the Fraser Report and the C.D. Howe rankings.

There is a common understanding in educational circles that "context matters." Context certainly showed through in the vision, mission, and goals developed by the highly successful principals in this case study. The approaches taken by the principals, though similar in philosophy, were widely different in practice. In many ways principals articulated that when they first went into their schools they had to come to know the place before making major changes. They spent the first year looking, talking, and coming to know the school and the people who made it unique. Once they had the lay of the land they went to work leading the appropriate processes to develop and bring to life their respective vision, mission, and goals. The significant impact of English Language Learners and the existence of poverty greatly influenced the development of vision for education in both Joan's and Mary's schools. However, the visions and the approaches taken to meet them were different, as Joan's school was elementary-junior high and Mary's a high school. Age of student certainly influenced the context, which in turn influenced the vision and the eventual strategies that were developed.

In most cases, the principals spoke to the importance of establishing a trusting relationship prior to tackling the development of vision, mission, and goals. Either on purpose or by accident each principal in his or her own way attended to the issues of trust prior to the process of change. With trust also came the second key component of backing up with appropriate data what was being proposed. In many cases the data, both soft and hard, led the vision conversations. In other words, these principals were strategic in their attempts to improve the overall quality of education in their schools by attending to the personal needs of people in the building while moving forward based on a solid understanding of the students they were tasked with educating. Building trust was also seen as critical in promoting risk-taking and innovation.

Leading a Learning Community

In our interviews we asked the principals to describe what *Professional Learning Communities* (PLC) looked like in their schools. We asked questions that allowed them to highlight ways in which they attended to the essential purpose of educational leadership, ensuring all students are offered optimal conditions for learning and development.

From an organizational perspective the principals approached teacher collaboration, as indicated by some form of PLC, in various ways. Grade level teams, whole staff PLCs, groups working on common goals, division PLCs, dyads, high school and junior high school PLCs, and department structures were some of the examples given. The level of direct involvement by principals in the PLCs varied, but it was clear they made sure they were informed, one way or another, about issues and decisions.

Interestingly, for several of our principals the level of their involvement in these structures evolved over time. At first, they tried to be at the centre of agenda making and activities. Then, they would often choose who was to lead these teams or committees. Many started with the idea that their active presence in all meetings of all types was required. However, over time, many warmed to the idea that allowing for more professional autonomy and teacher-directed actions was a desired reflection of facilitating leadership in others. As their confidence in their colleagues grew, they saw more wisdom in allowing teachers to make many of these choices on their own, as long as concerns and decisions were shared with the principal.

Through the PLCs the principals were able to enhance the idea that the work of student learning should be a shared responsibility of adults in the building. The following statement by Timothy highlights the increased sense of collaboration leading to an increased sense of shared responsibility:

"I'd say the biggest change is now people working together in teams, even sharing teaching. It's opened up teacher collaboration. We are much more team-oriented than we were previously."

We certainly got the impression from evidence presented by the principals that as collaboration grew in their schools, high expectations for teachers and students took hold, and indeed rapidly became part of the school culture. Examples of this culture of learning included teachers presenting what they were doing in classrooms at staff meetings (Mary); a clear and unwavering focus on providing good feedback to teachers and students (John); bringing teachers reluctant to try new ways of teaching out to conferences with her (Katherine); staff meetings based on professional learning and problem solving (James); enhanced use of collaborative conversations (Ellen); and grade level teams attending professional learning sessions together, and then sharing how they implemented what they learned with the rest of the staff (Steven). In all cases, we saw what one principal referred to as the importance of "pressure and support" (Steven). It is not enough for school leaders to set the context for continuous student learning growth; they also need to actively support the process and be seen valuing its importance, providing the resources for it to occur, and checking to see it is being done. The shift to a team focus, rather than an individual-based supervisory policy, induced a greater sense of collective responsibility for learning outcomes, and simultaneously opened the doors of both the principals' offices and classrooms throughout the schools. For many principals and their schools, the culture of learning extended beyond their own walls through visits from other staff members and their own visits to other schools, which both helped to develop networks of educators.

A change from what has been understood as professional development (as denoted by something that is "done to") to what we understand to be professional learning (as something "actively sought") was noted in these schools. The term embedded was used in many of the examples given to us by the principals. Focusing school-based professional learning around teacher- and student-identified needs was a common feature in the processes followed in these high-yield schools. Donald indicated that the PD Committee in his school was comprised of five teachers along with administrator support. Professional learning in the school was ongoing, organized around needs identified by teachers and confirmed by data, teacher-driven (teacher buy-in was high), and engaged in by the principal and vice-principal, who were actively learning alongside the teachers.

From a structural perspective we were struck by the varied and highly imaginative ways principals found time to allow teachers to meet in collaborative groups. In a number of cases, school-wide, or part school-wide, assemblies were held with one of the school leaders in attendance so teachers could meet in PLCs for extended periods of time. In other cases, the typical monthly staff meeting was changed to a PLC format, and instead of dealing with administrivia during this time, teachers were actively engaged in professional learning and collaboration. In a few cases, principals were granted school district permission to close the school early on a particular day so teachers could use that embedded time for PLC work. Other methods were also used, like groups attending conferences together, teachers using their own time right after school to meet, and judicious hiring of substitute teachers to allow for teacher meeting time. In the end, each principal identified one or more imaginative ways to carve out time so as to let collaboration happen.

The terms pressure and support used by Steven—although not always articulated in those words—were evidenced in the language of the other principals. These educators did not leave it to chance that the collaborative work of the PLCs and other teacher-driven initiatives were making a difference in the educational lives of students. Most mentioned they were actively engaged in classroom visits, teacher observations, student conversations, data checks, and other methods, all designed to ensure improved student learning was occurring. It is fascinating to note that a number of principals spoke of more frequent teacher-to-teacher observations as the amount and diversity of collaborations increased. Perhaps, in the end, the greatest growth in enhanced teacher practice came about when teachers observed each other teaching. In doing so, they affirmed what their colleagues were doing, while also applying some peer pressure to do better.

Providing Instructional Leadership

The 2012 version of the Alberta *Education Act* (Government of Alberta, 2012) stipulates that the principal must "evaluate the teachers employed in the school" (p. 120). The *Teaching Quality Standard Applicable to the Provision of Basic Education in Alberta* clearly establishes the knowledge, skills, and attributes for which teachers are accountable (Alberta Education, 1997). In the Alberta context, teachers are accountable to the principal. Finally, we know that the *Competencies* document used throughout this book highlights the requirement for principals to provide instructional leadership. This competency blends the provisions ordinarily found in school district *Teacher Supervision and Evaluation* policies, the need for the principals to exercise powers incumbent in the various acts, and the ways and means instructional leadership leads to increased student learning.

The principals gave powerful witness to the ways in which they carried out their mandates of instructional leadership. In most cases, the *Teaching Quality Standard* was used in their practices, as was the skilful integration of *Teacher Professional Growth Plans*. In addition, they mentioned they were frequent visitors to classrooms in order to see for themselves that great teaching was happening. Finally, we note that most principals had systems in place for other leaders in the building, both formal and informal, to share in the responsibilities associated with instructional leadership. In larger schools, vice-principals also visited classrooms, often engaging in subject-specific supervision.

It was evident that the principals took on the role of instructional leadership in meaningful and deliberate ways. A number said they "enjoyed" the role. Donald spoke to the need of "setting up a sharing process." Joan noted the importance of "breaking what they were looking for in the classrooms into manageable chunks." For Timothy, the structure entailed "creating time in the schedule for teachers to meet in PLC." Steven introduced the idea of not only building the structures but also providing the necessary supports. He said he made "effective use of team meetings to determine where teachers were at in their pedagogy." The high school principals in our study all addressed the idea of structure by indicating ways in which they actively involved vice-principals, department heads, and lead teachers in the process of teacher supervision and evaluation. Katherine had mentors working with new teachers. Thomas used his vice-principal as his own mentee and actively integrated her into the process of enhanced student learning through focused work with teachers in changing their practices.

Most principals articulated a belief in the power of teacher collaboration as a means through which teacher growth could occur and result in enhanced student learning. In a number of cases the process led to a change in the way PLCs were either introduced or altered. Timothy noted, "The teachers themselves run the meetings (PLCs). They identify the areas that they need help with and they run with that. They do the research. They support each other." Steven's practice was similar. "We make effective use of team meetings to determine where teachers were in their pedagogy." Katherine tied the process of teacher leadership to teacher growth in this way: "I rely on people like a teacher leader to take on the leadership role by providing continued workshops, talking about it in teams, looking at course outlines, and with asking 'what does this look like?'"

Some of the principals also changed the way staff meetings were held so as to focus on increased teacher collaboration and pedagogical growth. Donald said, "Staff meeting processes changed. Changed to focus on teaching." Joan spoke to the value of finding really effective teaching practices and then celebrating them during staff meetings, getting teachers themselves to share their successes and conduct mini lessons demonstrating for their colleagues what was working. While many of these teachers did not wish to play teacher leader or formal leader roles, their contribution was focused on pedagogical innovation, such as classroom organization and technological innovation. Teachers were encouraged to visit the classrooms of innovators.

Just as teachers were being encouraged to use differentiated instructional practices to ensure all students have the opportunity to learn based on their various learning styles, a number of principals noted the need for differentiated teacher supervision and evaluation. They recognized not all teachers needed the same degree of oversight, guidance, and/or supports. Donald said, "I am like the conductor of an orchestra. I need to recognize the strengths and areas of growth of each member of staff and come to a determination on how to use each in the most effective way." He went on to say, "Put people in spots where they can be most successful." Steven said, "Use differentiated teacher observations and go where the need is."

A number of principals articulated the ways in which they used data to help them meet their instructional leadership mandates. Mary said her instructional leadership work started with data. She went on to explain how data use allowed her to make substantial changes in student academic achievement. For Thomas, data use enhanced and added meaning to student and teacher accountability. A couple of principals spoke to the value of data obtained from reading every report card. One principal even made data use very public by recording the nature and impact of teacher professional development events on a data wall in the staffroom. Increasingly, skills in data use were extended to focus on individual students.

In the end, most principals recognized the need to be where teachers do their work. They spent considerable time in classrooms, talking to students, observing teachers, and being part of the daily life of the school. Whether running a school of 1800 students or 200, they each articulated the need to be where the action was. What changed from principal to principal was the format used, but what didn't change was the actual doing. They were all active participants in the learning processes established in their schools.

Developing and Facilitating Leadership

Most of our principals mentioned that in order to develop and facilitate leadership in others they needed to embrace the notion of distributed leadership and to devise structures that supported this concept. For example, principals noted teacher leadership in PLCs, grade level teams, subject area teams, and active involvement as mentors to other staff members. Principals also referred to the formal leadership distributed in their schools: vice-principals, associate principals, department heads, lead teachers, and instructional coaches. As we interviewed principals we listened for ways they identified leaders, and what they did to help develop latent leadership potential. There was wide acceptance of the notion that facilitating leadership meant building on the strengths of individual colleagues and not viewing perceived weaknesses as "deal breakers."

Many spoke to the value of getting to know the people they were working with as quickly as possible. Leadership positions to these principals grew out of knowing individual teachers' strengths and their desires to impact the school as a whole. Joan spoke to the value of interviewing all staff when she first came to the school. She built what she called "teacher profiles" based on a series of questions she asked. Through this process she identified potential leaders, but also noted people who had previously been held back from leadership positions, and she looked for ways to empower them by giving them increased responsibilities. Mary followed a similar route, but paid particular attention to identifying leadership traits in others and then encouraging their development.

Once the principals identified potential leaders they went about putting people into key positions. Katherine described a process of building capacity through a judicious use of teacher leadership of various committees established in the school. Timothy provided an excellent example of leadership when he offered to two teachers the opportunity to lead a student behaviour program. The pair of teacher leaders made fundamental changes to the program and brought other teachers along in the process of serving the needs of the students—especially students who were experiencing difficulty with student-to-student relationships.

Some of the principals used what they described as an invitational style of leadership appointment (James, Katherine, and Joan), while others encouraged teachers who were serving on various teams, committees, and PLCs to appoint their own leaders (Donald, Steven, and Mary).

We found that some principals recognized they had a role to play in actually teaching various aspects of what could be called leadership skills to the teachers they invited into leadership positions. They recognized that they couldn't simply assume a teacher who might be great at in-class instruction would also know how to lead groups of adults. John, for example, spent a considerable amount of time talking to his vice-principals and various teacher leaders about leadership. He even mapped out a course of action for some vice-principals if they were dealing with a particularly tricky issue. For Joan, leadership skill was enhanced when she brought key teachers into what she referred to as the "inner circle." The inner circle was not intended as an exclusive club for Joan—rather the contrary. The inner circle was meant to be an ever-widening group. However, Joan recognized the importance of working closely with teachers who were in leadership positions so she could help them enhance their skills. Katherine followed a similar process. She had numerous teacher leaders working within the school, but she had key teachers sitting on her admin lead team. For this group she modelled the leadership type skills she hoped they would employ when they led their own particular groups.

Managing School Operations and Resources

School operations and management can be massive and all-consuming in a typical school. In the past, management was the part of school leadership that dominated many principals' professional lives, it was nice to see that this practice was not as evident with these principals. We asked principals about their budgeting process: alignment with goals, involving others in decision-making, and following through with how money was spent and who could spend it.

The principals shared stories that highlighted their philosophical beliefs regarding management of the schools they led. It was obvious from their stories that the budgeting process was in reality another way to garner maximum input into key decisions impacting student learning. We didn't get the sense that these highly effective principals wanted to keep the money close to their own vests. School monetary resources were to be used to drive the overall instructional program of the school. With this type of attitude, principals articulated processes that supported their beliefs.

Timothy mentioned the importance of school goals connecting to school division goals. He also noted that his school had set the big goal of keeping class sizes small.

Keeping class size small resulted in the staff coming together and deciding to reduce the number of teaching assistants and dedicating more dollars from the school-based budget to teaching staff. Teachers knew that fewer hands in the building would result in more work for each of them, but they also knew that when it came to class instruction they could make more of an impact on their students. They would live without some things they might formerly have considered priorities by adding to the overall teaching numbers in the school. James also followed a process of matching budget decisions to goals and priorities. As his school was introducing sports academies, his teachers wanted to ensure there was a balance with the fine arts. They made budget decisions to positively impact both priority areas and sacrificed some teacher preparation time to pay for the programs.

From many of the principals we heard the word "transparency" on a regular basis. The processes they established in relation to setting and spending the budget had to be open and transparent to all in the school. For a number of principals this transparency carried over to the parent community. In all but one case teachers were actively involved in establishing school budgets. Teachers were also given a fair degree of decision-making authority over how to spend the monies allocated to their particular areas. They were kept informed as to the status of each budget as the school year progressed, so there were no surprises at the end. Surplus departmental or subject area budgets were not "raided" at the end of the school year to fulfill the wish lists of other groups of teachers.

Understanding and Responding to the Larger Societal Context

We know from research that school context plays a role in the overall operation of a school and the ways in which it attends to its mandate of educating children. The principals in our study clearly illuminated the social contexts of their schools and the ways in which they went about blending context into vision and mission, and in turn their school's educational program. They also responded to the need to keep various publics informed as to what school life entailed, and used various media methods to ascertain community expectations of their schools.

Both Mary and Joan were placed in environments dealing with a high number of English Language Learners as well as a very high proportion of new Canadians. These two principals used the social context of the schools to their advantage. They ensured students who were coming from homes where poverty was an issue had enough food to eat and proper clothing for the cold Canadian winter. They also put in place programs to help new Canadians understand the Alberta education system. However, both of these educators didn't stop there. The schools they ran became community hubs; go-to places for community services and supports that helped new Canadian families integrate into society. School newsletters were printed in multiple languages, translators were hired so parents who didn't speak English could play a significant role in the educational planning process, and liaisons were put in place for home visits. Both Mary and Joan became spokespeople for the needs of the children and for education in its holistic sense in the school, as well as in the community. They thanked the parents for allowing the schools to educate their children.

On the other end of the spectrum were two rural principals, Timothy and Steven. They led schools best described as stable. The children, for the most part, came from families who had lived in the area a long time. English was the language in homes and the community. However, both of these educators also played active roles as advocates for children and education. Newsletters, school webpages, Facebook, Twitter, blogs, and other electronic means were used to get the message about education out into the community. Timothy ensured each principal's message reinforced one of the priorities the school community had developed and was implementing. Steven noted a connection between collaborative planning developed in the school and how it was carried out into the local community. From there it reached the wider educational community, which resulted in many visits to the school from educators around Alberta.

Donald provided a terrific example of how the role of education advocate and school leader combined and impacted education in his school. He spoke of the value of giving parents voice. He believed that parents were true partners in the educational process. Through various programs he put in place, after paying attention to the needs of the community, he started to see as many as two dozen or more people attend school council meetings. These meetings became two-way sessions focused on sharing with parents what was happening at school, while parents shared with the school what was happening in the community. Each class in the school had representatives elected by class parents. Each rep was to bring the voice of the class to the school council meetings, and report back to class parents what council was saying. School council hosted information sessions with parents on how to support their children and the role the school can play in the process. In addition, Donald recognized that the school didn't exist in isolation from the school district. It was important to him to know the roles played by various people and what their perspectives were. As principal he needed to see how the school fit into the district plan and be able to articulate that to the school community.

The principals indicated that technology, in its many facets, provided wonderful means through which communication could take place with various publics. However, a number cautioned that face-to-face or voice-to-voice (phone calls) were also critical in ensuring teachers and parents were effectively communicating with each other. They noted that an over reliance on email had ended up in disputes arising between teachers and parents when misunderstandings occurred.

Each principal, when asked, articulated a particular way in which they could bring the school to the community and the community to the school. They addressed the ways in which they needed to advocate for education and the role it played in the lives of all children. Throughout the interviews it was evident that this group of principals knew their communities well, and viewed that knowledge as an essential piece of what it took to develop highly effective schools.

REFERENCES

Alberta Education. (1997). *Teaching quality standard applicable to the provision of basic education in Alberta.* (Ministerial Order (#016/97)). Edmonton, AB: Government of Alberta.

Government of Alberta. (2012). *Education Act.* Canada: Queen's Printer.

CHAPTER 15:
Analysis and Conclusions

In this final chapter we connect some of our key findings regarding principals enacting professional competencies within the theoretical framework we developed in Chapter 2. Before moving on to the competencies, however, we need to address the issue of mentorship, added to our study because of the significance it played in principal development.

Mentorship

The benefits of mentorship were mentioned by most of the principals. They mentioned supports gained, greater levels of empathy, counselling availability, shared ideas, problem-solving help, professional development enhancements, and a growing sense of self-efficacy (Hansford & Ehrich, 2005). While much of this mentoring would best be described as procedural and substantive in the way that Timperley (2011) conceived it, we also think that this mentoring played a large role in grounding the novice principals emotionally. Most in our sample did not have a formal mentor assigned to them when they began their school leadership roles. Informally, through their networks, they sought the advice and counsel of, in one case, the district superintendent, and in most others peers and more experienced principals.

Trust, mutually agreeable personalities, and knowledge of similar contexts played a key role in their choice of mentors (Camburn, Rowan, & Taylor, 2003). On the other hand, the principals from the large urban area had a much more formalized relationship with appointed mentors. The substance of their discussions and frequency of meetings were informed by district policy. The principals who received mentorship of any kind often said they were not afraid to ask what several referred to as "dumb questions" concerning procedures, paperwork, managerial, and leadership issues. This underscores a theme apparent in several of the case studies: that while many teachers think they know what a principal does, the specifics of the school-wide and community perspectives—and indeed, the relationship with central office—are not really known to them until they are actually serving in the principal's role. The weight of the new responsibilities came as a surprise to most of them.

Katherine invited teachers to be on the admin team so as to view what administration and leadership was all about. Once their eyes were opened to this new reality, some recognized they were not prepared for this level of commitment. What is required of the principal is a preparation and development related to, but also different from, the preparation and development of teachers. This fact, we think, was correctly highlighted in the Alberta Commission on Learning report discussion of recommendations for more appropriate principal preparation, and the role that an articulation of standards (later called competencies) could play (Alberta Education, 2003).

For some of our long-serving principals expectations about their changing roles meant adjusting to issues of accountability, school improvement, and distributed leadership. The perception of the principal as first and foremost a manager was withering on the vine, although we know that some principals not in this sample still prefer a manager's role. For principals who were inducted over the last decade, emphasis on accountability, procedures and paperwork, school improvement, and distributed leadership became the focal points of mentorship.

Bedard, Mombourquette, and Aitken (2013), in a study of district leadership practices, noted that the leadership preparation approach of the large urban district in which two of our principals worked and the approach in the more rural districts were quite different. The period of induction in the urban district is much longer and is structured by a step-wise progression through various pools (prospective principals and VPs). In the urban district the program of preparation is equal parts competency defined and performance based, and by the time one assumes a principal's position much learning about procedures, policies, professional knowledge, and a demonstrated capacity to perform leadership type functions has been addressed. If mentorship is as important as the literature and our principals tell us, then it might be useful, we think, to revisit more informal models and see if direction and cohesiveness, over a period of time, might better prepare principals for their manifold tasks. Rural districts with far-flung schools face hurdles that the large urban district does not, but at least one of the districts in our study has used various information technology media to close the gap.

The Seven Competencies of Alberta School Leadership

Fostering Effective Relationships

"Fostering effective relationships on the basis of appropriate values, ethical foundations, and within the school community" (Alberta Education, 2009, p. 4) are the foundational bedrock of our 10 principals in the varying contexts in which they were placed. The principals spent much time, school-wide, team-, and individually-focused, identifying and supporting relational networks, norms, and trust—structural and functional forms of social capital. This was not done on the basis of an end in itself, but rather as a means to create unity and cohesion around the central goal of serving students and their parents and making student need the focal point of professional adult conversations and activities. These mutually supportive roles are dependent upon principal leadership style (Aydin, Sarier, & Usyal, 2013) and supporting student achievement through principal-teacher interactions (Wahlstrom & Seashore-Louis, 2008).

In our present age, fostering effective relationships also means recognizing and making room for diversity of communities, socio-economic conditions, language, religion, sexual orientation, and student learning abilities. If the students were hungry they were fed, and when children were cold they were clothed. If the parents were reluctant to enter a relationship with the school, special invitational means were devised. Compelling rationales were created for school stakeholders, and data were used extensively to track instructional and developmental changes (Elfers & Stritikus, 2013; Higgins-Norman, Goldrick, & Harrison, 2009). The common purpose articulated was to prepare all students for post-secondary futures, academic mastery, training for the trades, or entry into the world of work. Conflict and lack of trust were endemic when several of our principals entered their schools, and they met these challenges head-on (Kutsyuruba, Walker, & Noonan, 2011) with effective communication, facilitation, problem-solving skills, and by being more accessible to teachers for advice (Friedkin & Slater, 1994). The doors were opened! When faced with those who made it clear their attitudes and teaching performance were not about to change, several principals did not shirk their obligation to remove recalcitrant individuals from the building.

Embodying Visionary Leadership

That school vision influences student learning gains is supported strongly in the literature.[35] Based on our assumptions that because districts had ready-made visions articulated for schools, and there is lively professional skepticism that the visioning process produces more hot air than purposeful direction, we were not sure our sample would be as engaged in visioning as we found them to be. Principals showed us their articulated visions in a number of visual expressions, but what was noteworthy for most was that the "official" language of the vision was frequently replaced by more down-to-earth language, such as "we are here to serve the kids and their parents," or some related theme close to that sentiment. Mintzberg (1979) pointed out that one tendency of "professional bureaucracies" like schools was that of "provider capture," where professionals with high job autonomy and a great deal of discretion to work directly with their clients (students) may bend the vision and goals of an organization to serve *their own* needs at the expense of the clients. The exhortation that "we are here for the kids and their parents" we think has its power in refocusing teaching professionals, at regular intervals, to consider whose interests they should be serving. Schools and educators are not immune to the seduction of provider capture.

Ylimaki (2006) notes that the most often used definition of vision is related to a principal's ability to see and articulate a compelling future for the school (Bennis & Nanus, 1985; Westley & Mintzberg, 1989). She signals a more collective approach to visioning, involving staff and the school community. Bedard et al. (2013) found that aligning school vision and goals with district vision and goals was an important consideration for schools. In our data for this book, we found that both of Ylimaki's definitions (individualist and collective) formed the ideational core of the organization, and that the ability to engage others in buying into a realistic but challenging vision begins with the commitment and passion of the formal leader's belief and his or her ability to communicate with and engage educational stakeholders about preferred destinations (Copland, 2003).

---

35   See Bottoms & Schmidt-Davis, 2010; Chappuis, Chappuis, & Stiggins, 2009; Gronn, 2002; Lambert, 2005; Marzano, Waters, & McNulty, 2005; Joseph Murphy, Elliott, Goldring, & Porter, 2007; Naseer, 2011; K. Seashore-Louis, Dretzke, & Wahlstrom, 2010; Ylimaki, 2006.

In some cases identification with the local community was seen as an important factor in refining the pedagogical and affective goals of the vision. School goals are more concrete expressions of vision statements, and in our sample principals made sure that the number of goals was small and their objectives significant. Gone are the days when school goals took on the characterization of a laundry list that keeps getting bigger each year, to the point where trying to do everything means accomplishing nothing. Data played an important role in making sure the vision was actualized and impacting student learning (Barnes, Camburn, Sanders, & Sebastion, 2010; Bowers, 2009; Copland, 2003; Datnow, Park, & Wohlstetter, 2007; Knapp, Copland, & Swinnerton, 2007; Luo, 2008). Data came in many forms: the PATs, of course; some standardized assessments; student exemplars demonstrating learning outcomes; and frequent visits to classrooms by principals and vice-principals who engaged students in conversations about what they were learning as much as they engaged teachers about lesson objectives and pedagogical and assessment aspects of the learning. Our principals were less impressed with the information provided by yearly assessments such as the PATs, although all included PAT discussions in their agendas with teachers. They were more comfortable being informed by varying types of data they observed in visits to classrooms, and by what grade teams told them about progress in learning or issues that impeded it. Making a vision operational, like so many aspects of K-12 education, influences, and is in turn influenced by, the prevailing school culture (Karen Seashore-Louis & Wahlstrom, 2011), a connection that most of our principals underscored.

From what the principals told us about the visioning process it was clear that they had a strong sense of beliefs that they communicated to teachers. For example, several were committed to ensuring that inclusionary practices were embraced in the school community and they would not allow complacency on this issue. The work of Branson (2010) about the leader's need to define and balance his/her own values and beliefs and those of the collective are important considerations to understand this tension. Donald, Katherine, Joan, and Mary eloquently spoke of this tension.

Leading a Learning Community

"The principal nurtures and sustains a school culture that values and supports learning" (Alberta Education, 2009, p. 5). Our principals had a strong sense of themselves as agents of cultural change, linking and influencing the values, beliefs, and practices of the professional staff with an increasingly informed and engaged community of parents. Various media tools were developed and scores of face-to-face encounters with parents were encouraged by principals to reach out in an invitational style to the larger community. Shaping a professional learning culture is an endeavour in building the social capital of the school, with relations among individuals built on trust, collaboration, and a sense of obligation (Richmond & Manokore, 2011). It is all about honouring high expectations for *all* the students, for the staff, and for the community (Brown, Anfara, & Roney, 2004; Hays, 2013; Reynolds, 1999).

Heading a learning community took on a number of formats led by principals and assisted by vice-principals. The notion of teacher professional development *done* to someone changed to the concept of professional learning (Timperley, 2011). The latter concept is driven by an "inside-out" approach, in which the learning needs of teachers are directly connected to the learning needs of students, collectively and individually. Much of this new learning was job-embedded. Grade level teams, clusters of grade level teams, and PLCs became the focal point of teacher activity for the identification of problems and development of solutions. Time was created for this endeavour before, during, and after school hours, with varying degrees of autonomy. The principals were not always present in these discussions but they all were apprised of issues, concerns, and decisions arising from these job-embedded activities. Frequently, the summation of these discussions would be posted so that all the teachers would be informed about what was discussed. The principals and vice-principals devoted a lot of time on a regular basis to visiting classrooms, often to view whether new practices were being implemented.

In all these aspects of fostering a learning culture, the principals were the key nexus, helping shape and resource professional learning (Gumus, 2013), helping problem-solve, and stimulating teams to take collective responsibility for the quality of the students' learning experience. Data were disaggregated to "drill down" to the specific needs of individual students, with charts, graphics, and whiteboards detailing the issues; pyramids of intervention became a popular technique to support individual students who were struggling. Principals encouraged teachers to share their pedagogical skills and innovations with colleagues, and these "champions," as one of our principals called them, set a trend in motion. Teachers began visiting and observing what other teachers were doing. In Steven's case, principals and teachers from other schools in the district visited and observed how the structures and supports he instituted had transformed the school culture with a marked impact on student learning and teacher competence.

Building school capacity means addressing "teachers' knowledge, skills, and dispositions; professional community; and program coherence" (Youngs & King, 2002, p. 647). Our principals understood this implicitly and put these pieces together to change the nature of the learning communities in their schools. They ensured their teachers encouraged meaningful parental involvement, informing parents of student progress and making them feel welcome within the school. Joan and Mary in particular, with large immigrant school demographics, transformed their schools to serve as hubs for community-related services. The more parents are engaged in their children's education—and distributive leadership also supports this value—the better the opportunity for the children to learn (Henderson & Mapp, 2002; Young, Austin, & Growe, 2013).

Providing Instructional Leadership

"The principal ensures that all students have ongoing access to quality teaching and learning opportunities to meet the provincial goals of education" (Alberta Education, 2009, p. 5). Principals kept their fingers on the pulse of learning-related activities in their schools by frequent observations of classroom learning, questioning students and teachers about the learning process, and getting feedback from and responding to team meetings. Thus studying *behaviours* is an important task of instructional leadership (Leithwood, Jantzi, & Steinbach, 1999). So too are defining school mission, managing the instructional program, and promoting school climate (Hallinger & Heck, 1997), and these are the levers by which principals exert their most direct influence.

John, the high school principal for 1200 students, was so convinced of the importance of instructional leadership he persuaded a reluctant superintendent to release the vice-principals from teaching duties so as a school leadership team they could focus collectively on instructional leadership, changing programming, and school climate issues. In Steven's context, the preferred route was modelling, monitoring, and professional dialogue (Southworth, 2002), as well as developing specific structures and supports to enhance capacity in quality teaching.

Most of our principals also invested much time in reading current literature about teaching and learning processes, and encouraging teachers to incorporate these readings into embedded professional learning and discussion in teams and PLCs. Principals and vice-principals also ensured teachers were familiar with the *Program of Studies* and their teaching activities were fully informed by the outcomes of the provincial curriculum.

John and Donald insisted teachers put specific learning targets of the lesson on display, and all students, even at the lower end of the elementary spectrum, were cognizant of learning objectives and standards (Sammons, Gu, Day, & Ko, 2010).

With an appreciably greater emphasis on instructional leadership and accountability over the last decade came the recognition that teachers in Alberta needed a serious upgrade in knowledge and skills regarding assessment *for* and *of* learning (AISI projects helped to identify and attend to this in significant ways). When interwoven, learning-focused leadership, assessment of student learning, and school improvement provide a framework for an aligned and coherent approach to developing and implementing strategies that can have a positive influence on sustained improvement in a school (Aitken, 2009; Webber, Aitken, Lupert, & Scott, 2009). Our principals understood explicitly the elements to weave together. PLCs were important structures within all schools to advance knowledge and skills about teaching and learning.

Principals need to "implement effective supervision and evaluation to ensure that teachers consistently meet the Alberta Teaching Quality Standard (TQS)" (Alberta Education, 2009, p. 5). Murphy, Hallinger, and Heck (2013) indicate that there is very little direct or indirect evidence supporting the notion that principal evaluation of teachers leads to school improvements, and in turn student learning. They do note, however, considerable support for the notion of what is referred to in Alberta as teacher supervision, whereby principals provide feedback to teachers (Hattie, 2009); develop communities of practice in which teachers share goals, work, and responsibilities for student outcomes (Wahlstrom & Seashore-Louis, 2008); offer abundant support for the work of teachers (Leithwood & Jantzi, 2005); and create systems in which teachers have the opportunity to routinely develop and refine their skills (Bryk, Sebring, Allensworth, Luppescu, & Easton, 2010). Several of our principals shared the sentiments of Murphy et al. (2013) and the other cited authors, and instead of treating teacher evaluation and supervision as an exercise focused on *individual teachers*, they began to invest more time and effort in assessing the quality and content of teacher team meetings, committees, and PLCs—for these were critical sites of embedded learning and the springboard to changing practices. Steven, for example, articulated how his participation in conferences and his reading of professional literature guided his orientation in this direction.

Principals also put greater emphasis on ensuring teachers developed competencies in new and emerging pedagogical technologies. The more technologically adept, and sometimes reluctant, teachers were encouraged to share their expertise at staff meetings, and this often stimulated a flow of teachers into particular classrooms where technological innovation was on the agenda. As well, particularly in the case of Mary and Joan, whose urban schools presented a number of community-based challenges, communication and collaboration with parents and community agencies were proactively attended to in order to support student learning.

Developing and Facilitating Leadership

Developing and facilitating leadership took several forms in our sample of schools. Principals often identified the admin team, with vice-principals and sometimes teacher leaders, as the primary locus for developing leadership. Individuals would also be invited to the admin team, and to serve as chairs of committees and teams. Katherine, Mary, and Joan discussed this at length in the case studies. In John's case, the conversion of vice-principals into full-time administration and leadership positions afforded them a whole-school perspective and inclusion in all principal-led discussions about issues and strategies. This was probably the most outstanding example of embedded professional development promoting leadership skills. Several of John's VPs later assumed the role of principal in other schools in the district. Timothy spoke of being absent from his school for several months. With no VP, he chose his most experienced and "master" teacher to coordinate activities in the school, and this strategy went off without a hitch. He credited the maturity and experience of his staff, many of whom had been at the school a decade or longer, and the collaborative culture of the school as promoting leadership without formal leaders during his extended absence.

Moolenaar, Daly, and Sleegers (2010) highlighted how often teachers seek out principals for advice as being an important indicator for innovative change. All our principals had an open door policy, were visible daily in halls and classrooms, developed trusting relationships, and engaged in "tough conversations" when necessary to ensure that teachers and teacher assistants were brought into the decision-making loop when appropriate. Transparency of decision-making, on an ethically-sound basis (Langlois & Lapointe, 2007), was a characteristic held in high regard by our principals.

Harris (2012) is well known for her expertise and research about distributed leadership, and she contends that school change and improvement without it cannot be sustained. Distributed leadership in our sample of schools was present in formal leadership roles, such as VPs and department heads, and in informal roles within teams and committees. Sackney and Walker (2006) related the importance of principals building leadership capacity through a culture encouraging trust, collaboration, risk taking, reflection, shared leadership, and data-based decision-making. These qualities were abundantly apparent in the lexicon and practices of our principals. Teachers mentoring newer teachers, in some cases over a five year period, became a powerful instrument in several schools, ensuring the induction process served to develop novice teachers in a step-wise and careful manner (Youngs, 2007).

Managing School Operations and Resources

"The principal manages school operations and resources to ensure a safe and caring, and effective learning environment" (Alberta Education, 2009, p. 6). Bush (2008) notes a connection between the importance of the management function of school leadership and the role it plays in keeping the school focused on the core process of student learning. This view is supported by Bryk et al. (2010) when they highlight how instructional leadership effectiveness depends on successful coordination of programs, people, and resources. Grissom and Loeb (2011) go one step further than Bryk et al. when they assert that a more holistic view of school leadership requires skills across multiple dimensions—in instruction, but also in management of the school as an organization. In other words, the management function of school leadership goes hand-in-hand with leadership, as both are required for establishing an environment that keeps student learning at its centre. We share this view, as did our sample of principals.

The degree to which principals handled administrative matters varied. Often other staff and administrative assistants, or in some contexts school managers, were tasked with ordering resources, tracking expenses, and reporting on a regular basis. All principals—with the exception of Ellen, who relied on her admin team and administrative assistant to complete this function—involved grade teams and departments (where applicable) in discussions about what resources were needed and within which budget allotments they were allowed to prioritize purchases. Several principals spoke of the need for transparency in these discussions and abandoned the practice of allowing staff to dip into another team's or department's surplus towards the end of the school year to fulfill wish lists. This provided more stability in the budgeting process and reduced a lot of the conflict related to resource "raiding." Budgets were designed to reduce class size (Timothy), to bolster different kinds of programming in order to attract and better serve students (James), and to feed students and clothe immigrant families with supplements from grants (Joan and Mary). Significantly, all principals mentioned the core function of the budget was to ensure quality education and support the developmental needs of students. Within the discretion they were allowed by centralized funding mechanisms based on student population—and by district policies, which varied district to district—the principals in our sample gave compelling narratives about the close correlation between the budgeting process, shared decision-making, and student learning and developmental needs.

Understanding and Responding to the Larger Societal Context

"The principal understands and responds appropriately to the political, social, economic, legal and cultural contexts impacting the school" (Alberta Education, 2009, p. 6).

School and community contexts matter and serve as an influence on the role of the principal, and the principal in turn influences them (Boyd, 1985; Boyd, 1992; Goldring, Huff, May, & Camburn, 2008; ten Bruggencate, Luyten, Scheerens, & Sleegers, 2012; Walker & Shuangye, 2007). If one competency stands out to underscore the role of principal as "boundary spanner," with an eye on global, national, and provincial trends impacting education, on what's happening in the community, and on relations with central office, this is the one that demarcates where formal leadership differs from informal leadership. The principal carries the heavy pail of water on this dimension.

Principal beliefs also lead to change in school structures, which leads to improved student results when aligned with their dispositions such as passion, persistence, and commitment to social justice (Jacobson, 2011). In Canada, the issues of ethnicity, race, language, religion, and sexual orientation often frame various perspectives on diversity. Our sample of principals, even in small towns and rural settings, are learning to grapple with the challenges.

Attending to the advocacy mandate, the principal makes every effort to impact student learning. Khalifa (2012) notes that the principal's role of community leader, when coupled with high visibility and advocacy for community causes, leads to trust and rapport between school and community. This sense of principal engagement, in turn, may lead to improved academic results for students. Mary, Joan, Timothy, and Katherine were particularly active on this front.

Riehl (2008) makes the point that schools are serving a more heterogeneous student population now than ever before. Reihl drew in normative, empirical, and critical literature to review the role of principals in responding to the needs of diverse students. Three tasks were highlighted: fostering new meanings about diversity, promoting inclusive school cultures and instructional programs, and building relationships between schools and communities. Principal work that "accomplishes these tasks can be thought of as a form of practice, with moral, epistemological, constitutive, and discursive dimensions" (Riehl, 2008, p. 183). Joan and Mary paid particular attention to new Canadian students and their parents, investing much time and creating structures and various media to frame an invitational tone in their relationships with these communities. As well, Joan ended the practice of physically separating special education students in an almost segregated part of the school, and John significantly upgraded support for inclusion of special education students in his high school. Katherine made a special effort to reach out to First Nations and Low German Mennonite students and their parents. Several of our principals recognized that school pathways in the past had a distinct bias for academic, post-secondary futures that pushed many students who preferred alternative routes out of school. They vigorously supported programming relating to preparation for a trades education and for the world of work. Mary, Joan, James, and John were particularly active in ensuring that new programming met the diverse needs of *all* students, not just the minority destined for university.

Several principals recognized that students vary in their learning styles, and much attention was paid—through professional learning sessions, embedded learning in teams, and presentations by passionate "champions"—to ensure their teachers developed a repertoire of teaching and learning styles. Joan and Mary were eloquent and insistent on this point.

Conclusions

Let us return to our research questions. We trust our 10 case study chapters and the findings chapter presented enough "meat on the bone" to allow readers to answer these questions in an independent manner. That being said, we think a short summary and synthesis at this juncture is appropriate.

The main research question in this study was: "How do 10 experienced and successful principals enact the seven professional competencies for Alberta School Leaders?" Our evidence suggests that the principals were the pivots who directed meaningful structures and supports for enacting the competencies. The enactment started with the perspective that exercising the competencies required informed consent and buy-in from everyone in the building. It was grounded in the belief that the work of school improvement and student achievement requires a fundamental shift in the direction of distributed leadership (Harris, 2012), and that collaborative teams and a plethora of committees needed to have their voices heard and their perspectives honoured by formal leadership. The net of leadership, formal and informal, was expanded out of necessity to adapt to the changing agenda. The principal in this new context was the chief change agent with a whole-school perspective connected to district and Alberta Education goals and policy. While much of the principal's influence on student learning may be classified as indirect, his or her power to address vision, mission, and the nature of programming (Leithwood et al., 1999), combined with passion, communication skills, and persistence, have a very direct influence on the motivation and work lives of teachers.

Waters, Marzano, and McNulty (2003) identified 21 specific leadership responsibilities significantly correlated with student achievement. Included in the list are:

- *Culture* – fostering shared beliefs and a sense of community and cooperation;
- *Focus* – establishing clear goals and keeping these goals at the forefront of the school's attention;
- *Communicate* – establishing strong lines of communication with teachers and students;
- *Outreach* – advocating and being a spokesperson for the school to all stakeholders; and
- *Affirm* – recognizing and celebrating school accomplishments and acknowledging failures.

The principals in our sample were at the nexus of all these core activities. Sub-questions included:

A) What roles does mentorship play in the preparation and development of these principals?

There was a strong connection between mentorship and the preparation of most of the principals in this study as they entered their new roles. These relationships continued well beyond the novice stage. In the large urban district the relationship was formalized by the district and closely related to internal preparation programs in which acquiring knowledge of the competencies and demonstrating leadership type tasks were critical variables in giving candidates for formal leadership the green light to advance. In a jurisdiction with a less formal approach, Katherine found mentors in her superintendent, other principals in her jurisdiction, and through her work with the Canadian Association of Principals. She has gone on to mentor other principals. Timothy was mentored years ago by a principal and presently is mentoring a young principal in his district. Timothy and his mentees' discussions are often competency-based, as the ATA took a strong lead in creating a competency-based development program with the cooperation of the district office. Steven received varying degrees of mentorship as he moved quickly into the principal's role in northern Alberta before moving to southern Alberta. He played an active role in devising structures and supports for teachers to impact student learning, and his school was visited on many occasions by other principals and teachers, some from outside his district, as an exemplar of how to get the job done and do it right. Donald, whose career as a principal is near its end, credits his mentors and peers in a small urban setting with allowing him to discuss sensitive matters in a confidential manner and talk about complex issues with those who have traversed the same road. Thomas applauded his last VP for helping him come to grips with his new school, and he characterizes his present VP as both a mentor to him and his mentee.

Hansford and Ehrich (2005) identify the following as positive outcomes for principal mentees: supports gained, greater levels of empathy noted, counselling availability, shared ideas, problem-solving help, professional development enhancements, and a sense of improved confidence in one's ability to do what has become a very demanding job. Except for one individual (Ellen) who received all of *four minutes* of advice from the outgoing principal, the other principals spoke of the benefits of mentorship in the language of Hansford and Ehrich and, as we noted above, mentorship provided a strong emotional anchoring for several of our principals. While the initial emphasis in the mentorships certainly could be described as procedural and administrative in orientation, our evidence supports the idea that mentorship was also strongly oriented to all matters under the umbrella of leadership.

B) How do the strategies for enactment compare when juxtaposed among similar and dissimilar school organizational types?

Many strategies could, without stretching the truth, be described as similar, with trust building, vision, collaboration, and the capacity for strategic thought being the foundational ingredients. The strategies employed were also tightly correlated with community contexts, student characteristics, and the prevailing cultures of the schools. Several principals took a "look, wait, listen, and see" approach before devising strategies for change, and at a later date were not shy about shaking up the culture and attitudes of certain individuals, if these were deemed impediments to change. That being said, the principals shared an unswerving commitment to distributed leadership, widening the net of leadership through team-, grade-, and committee-based structures on a K-12 basis. In this respect, when we hypothesized that the scale and scope of the schools would change the mechanisms of leverage possessed by the principal, we were pleasantly surprised to find that the ways principals leverage their influence, direct and indirect, have more commonality than we first supposed.

C) To what degree are the competencies formalized within their school districts?

While all our principals had knowledge of and respected the utility value of the competencies, the large urban district was the only one in our sample that used the competencies for the variety of functions envisaged by the Stakeholders' Committee for Recommendation 76. The competencies (see Appendix A) were prepared to guide the recruitment, preparation, development, and assessment of formal school leaders. While the principals used the *Guideline* as *de facto* policy to orient their professional activities, several were disappointed when district supervisors showed little interest in engaging them in competency-based conversations, or in looking at portfolios structured around evidence of competency attainment. Other than Joan and Mary, principals had little or no knowledge of whether or not the competencies entered into discussions about the qualifications of principals new to the district or plans for their ensuing professional development. In another district, the competencies played a significant role in the assessment of formal school leaders because of an ATA initiative in designing a protocol for the supervision and evaluation of principals. But other than that, use of the competencies as a robust document that included a number of functions did not appear common practice. Mombourquette (2013) researched how visibility of the *Guideline* in district websites was largely hit-and-miss. Our subsequent data would tend to support this contention. We think that for the competencies in their full range to be taken seriously on a provincial scale, they need to have the same regulatory and legal status of the *Teaching Quality Standard for the Provision of Basic Education in Alberta*.

D) How do principals account for leadership practices before *and* after the introduction of the *Guideline* in 2009?

In the introduction of this book, we foreshadowed the answer to this question. In short, we worked with a sample of experienced and successful principals who had knowledge of, and enacted, the competencies after their introduction as "unofficial policy." Lack of district buy-in in several cases seemed to be irrelevant in this regard. The seven competencies, articulated at length by the Stakeholders' Committee from 2005 to 2006 within the confines of Alberta Education's Teacher Development branch, had wide and deep support within the Committee. That support was grounded in the values of 20 or so representatives of stakeholder organizations. They believed the competencies were in essence a description of some, not all, key tasks of excellent school leadership. They knew, chapter and verse, what they recognized as the hallmarks of excellent school leadership, and they also knew when these standards, as they were then called, were not being met by formal leadership. They envisaged a role for the ministry, faculties of education, and district central offices in helping flesh out the applicability and substance of these competencies in their programming. The Committee's wish was that the competencies serve as a province-wide policy to spread expectations for better school leadership. As of yet, this has not come to pass.

But what our data says to us is that our sample of principals, experienced and successful as they are, can now describe their beliefs, values, dispositions, and actions in the lexicon of the competencies. From what they told us, on and off the record, their pre-competencies practices were not much different from their post-competencies behaviours. In other words, the Alberta school leadership competencies, which were grounded in the American ISLLC standards, are a realistic description of significant functions of experienced and successful principals. This may be somewhat tautological, but what our 10 principals who generously donated their time to share their professional experiences told us was: their practices reflect the competencies and the competencies reflect their practices. The 17 other principals, all seasoned and successful, whose interviews did not make it into this book, were of a similar mindset. We will make use of their data and wisdom in future research articles. We thank all 27 for agreeing to speak with us at length!

REFERENCES

Aitken, E. N. (2009). Effective leadership and assessment working together for school improvement: Hitching the horse to the cart. *International Journal of Learning, 16*(3), 151-165.

Alberta Education. (2003). *Alberta's commission on learning. Every child learns, every child succeeds: Report and recommendations.* (LC91.2.A3.A333 2003). Edmonton, AB. Retrieved from http://education.alberta.ca/department/ipr/commission/report/printable.aspx

Alberta Education. (2009). *Principal quality practice guideline: Promoting successful school leadership in Alberta.* (LB2831.926.C2 A333 2009). Edmonton, AB: Alberta Education. Retrieved from http://education.alberta.ca/admin/resources.aspx

Aydin, A., Sarier, Y., & Usyal, S. (2013). The effect of school principals' leadership styles on teachers' organizational commitment and job satisfaction. *Educational Sciences: Theory & Practice, 13*(2), 806-811.

Barnes, C., Camburn, E., Sanders, B., & Sebastion, J. (2010). Developing instructional leaders: Using mixed methods to explore the black box of planned change in principals' professional practice. *Educational Administration Quarterly, 46*(2), 242-262. doi: 10.1177/1094670510361748

Bedard, G., Mombourquette, C., & Aitken, A. (2013). Calgary Catholic School District. In J. Brandon, P. Hanna & K. Rhyason (Eds.), *Vision in action: Seven approaches to school system success* (pp. 165-231). Edmonton, AB: College of Alberta School Superintendents.

Bennis, W., & Nanus, B. (1985). *Leaders: The strategies for taking charge.* New York, NY: Harper & Row.

Bottoms, G., & Schmidt-Davis, J. (2010). The three essentials: Improving schools requires district vision, district and state support, and principal leadership (pp. 1-53). Southern Regional Education Board.

Bowers, A. J. (2009). Reconsidering grades as data for decision making: More than just academic knowledge. *Journal of Educational Administration, 47*(5), 609-629. doi: http://dx.doi.org/10.1108/09578230910981080

Boyd, V. (1992). *School context: Bridge or barrier to change.* Austin, TX: Southwest Educational Development Laboratory.

Branson, C. M. (2010). *Leading educational change wisely.* Sense Publishers Rotterdam.

Brown, K. M., Anfara, V. A., & Roney, K. (2004). Student achievement in high performing, suburban middle schools and low performing, urban middle schools: Plausible explanations for the differences. *Education and Urban Society, 36*(4), 428-456. doi: 10.1177/0013124504263339

Bryk, A., Sebring, P., Allensworth, E., Luppescu, S., & Easton, J. (2010). *Organizing schools for improvement: Lessons from Chicago.* Chicago, IL: University of Chicago Press.

Bush, T. (2008). From management to leadership: Semantic or meaningful change? *Educational Management Administration & Leadership, 36*(2), 271-288. doi: 10.1177/1741143207087777

Camburn, E., Rowan, B., & Taylor, J. E. (2003). Distributed leadership in schools: The case of elementary schools adopting comprehensive school reform models. *Educational Evaluation and Policy Analysis, 25*(4), 347-373. doi: 10.3102/01623737025004347

Chappuis, S., Chappuis, J., & Stiggins, R. (2009). The quest for quality. *Educational Leadership, 67*(3), 14-19.

Copland, M. A. (2003). Leadership of inquiry: Building and sustaining capacity for school improvement. *Educational Evaluation and Policy Analysis, 25*(4), 375-395. doi: 10.3102/01623737025004375

Datnow, A., Park, V., & Wohlstetter, P. (2007). Achieving with data (pp. 1-84). Los Angeles, CA: Center on Educational Governance.

Elfers, A., & Stritikus, T. (2013). How school and district leaders support classroom teachers' work with English Language Learners. *Educational Administration Quarterly, 20*(10), 1-40. doi: 10.1177/0013161X13492797

Friedkin, N. E., & Slater, M. R. (1994). School leadership and performance: A social network approach. *Sociology of Education, 67*, 139-157.

Goldring, E., Huff, J., May, H., & Camburn, E. (2008). School context and individual characteristics: What influences principal practice? *Journal of Educational Administration, 46*(3), 332-352. doi: http://dx.doi.org/10.1108/09578230810869275

Grissom, J. A., & Loeb, S. (2011). Triangulating principal effectiveness: How perspectives of parents, teachers, and assistant principals identify the central importance of managerial skills. *American Educational Research Journal, 48*(5), 1091-1123. doi: 10.3102/0002831211402663

Gronn, P. (2002). Distributed leadership as a unit of analysis. *The Leadership Quarterly, 13*(4), 423-451. doi: http://dx.doi.org/10.1016/S1048-9843(02)00120-0

Gumus, S. (2013). The effects of teacher- and school-level factors on teachers' participation in professional development activities: The role of principal leadership. *Journal of International Education Research, 9*(4), 371-380.

Hallinger, P., & Heck, R. (1997). Exploring the principal's contribution to school effectiveness. *School Effectiveness and School Improvement, 8*(4), 1-35.

Hansford, B., & Ehrich, L. C. (2005). The principalship: How significant is mentoring. *Journal of Educational Administration, 441*(1), 36-52.

Harris, A. (2012). Distributed leadership: Implications for the role of the principal. *The Journal of Management Development, 31*(1), 7-17. doi: 10.1108/02621711211190961

Hattie, J. (2009). *Visible learning: A sysnthesis of over 800 meta-analyses relating to achievement*. Oxon, UK: Routledge.

Hays, P. S. (2013). Narrowing the gap: Three key dimensions of site-based leadership in four Boston charter public schools. *Education and Urban Society, 45*(1), 37-87. doi: 10.1177/0013124511404065

Henderson, A. T., & Mapp, K. L. (2002). *A new wave of evidence: The impact of school, family, and community connections on student achievement*. Austin, TX: Southwest Educational Development Lab.

Higgins-Norman, J., Goldrick, M., & Harrison, K. (2009). Pedagogy for diversity: Mediating between tradition and equality in schools. *International Journal of Children's Spirituality, 14*(4), 323-337.

Jacobson, S. (2011). Leadership effects on student achievement and sustained school success. *International Journal of Educational Management, 25*(1), 33-44.

Khalifa, M. (2012). A re-new-ed paradigm in successful urban school leadership: Principal as community leader. *Educational Administration Quarterly, 48*(3), 424-467. doi: 10.1177/0013161x11432922

Knapp, M. S., Copland, M., & Swinnerton, J. A. (2007). Understanding the promise and dynamics of data-informed leadership. In P. A. Moss (Ed.), *Evidence and decision making. 106th yearbook of the National Society for the Study of Education: Part I* (pp. 74-104). Malden, MA: Blackwell.

Kutsyuruba, B., Walker, K., & Noonan, B. (2011). Restoring broken trust in the work of school principals. *ISEA, 39*(2), 81-95.

Lambert, L. (2005). Leadership for lasting reform. *Educational Leadership, 62*(5), 62-65.

Langlois, L., & Lapointe, C. (2007). Ethical leadership in Canadian school organizations: Tensions and possibilities. *Educational Management Administration & Leadership, 35*(2), 247-260. doi: 10.1177/1741143207075391

Leithwood, K., & Jantzi, D. (2005). A review of transformational school leadership research 1996-2005. *Leadership & Policy in Schools, 4*(3), 177-199. doi: 10.1080/15700760500244769

Leithwood, K., Jantzi, D., & Steinbach, R. (1999). *Changing leadership for changing times.* Buckingham: Open University Press.

Luo, M. (2008). Structural equation modeling for high school principals' data-driven decision making: An analysis of information use environments. *Educational Administration Quarterly, 44*(5), 603-634.

Marzano, R., Waters, T., & McNulty, B. (2005). *School leadership that works: From research to results.* Alexandria, VA: Association for Supervision and Curriculum Development.

Mintzberg, H. (1979). *The structuring of organizations.* Englewood Cliffs, NJ: Prentice-Hall.

Mombourquette, C. (2013). Principal leadership: Blending the historical perspective with the current focus on competencies in the Alberta context. *Canadian Journal of Educational Administration and Policy, 1*(147), 1-19.

Moolenaar, N. M., Daly, A. J., & Sleegers, P. J. (2010). Occupying the principal position: Examining relationships between transformation leadership, social network position, and schools' innovative climate. *Educational Administration Quarterly, 46*(1), 623-672. doi: 10.1177/0013161X10378689

Murphy, J., Elliott, S. N., Goldring, E., & Porter, A. C. (2007). Leadership for learning: A research-based model and taxonomy of behaviors. *School Leadership & Management, 27*(2), 179-201. doi: 10.1080/13632430701237420

Murphy, J., Hallinger, P., & Heck, R. (2013). Leading via teacher evaluation: The case of the missing clothes. *Educational Researcher, 42*(6), 349-353. doi: 10.3102/0013189X13499625

Naseer, A. S. (2011). Successful leadership practices of head teachers for school improvement. *Journal of Educational Administration, 49*(4), 414-432. doi: http://dx.doi.org/10.1108/09578231111146489

Reynolds, A. J. (1999). Educational success in high-risk settings: Contributions of the Chicago Longitudinal Study. *Journal of School Psychology, 37*(4), 345-354. doi: http://dx.doi.org/10.1016/S0022-4405(99)00025-4

Richmond, G., & Manokore, V. (2011). Identifying elements critical for functional and sustainable professional learning communities. *Science Education, 95*(3), 543-570. doi: 10.1002/sce.20430

Riehl, C. (2008). The principal's role in creating inclusive schools for diverse students: A review of normative, empirical, and critical literature on the practice of educational administration. *Journal of Education, 189*(1/2), 183-197.

Sackney, L., & Walker, K. (2006). Canadian perspectives on beginning principals: Their role in building capacity for learning communities. *Journal of Educational Administration, 44*(4), 341-358. doi: 10.1108/09578230610676578

Sammons, P., Gu, Q., Day, C., & Ko, J. (2010). Exploring the impact of school leadership on pupil outcomes. *International Journal of Educational Management, 24*(1), 83-101. doi: 10.1108/09513541111100134

Seashore-Louis, K., Dretzke, B., & Wahlstrom, K. (2010). How does leadership affect student achievement? Results from a national US survey. *School Effectiveness & School Improvement, 21*(3), 315-336. doi: 10.1080/09243453.2010.486586

Seashore-Louis, K., & Wahlstrom, K. (2011). Principals as cultural leaders. *Phi Delta Kappan, 92*(5), 52-56.

Southworth, G. (2002). Instructional leadership in schools: Reflections and empirical evidence. *School Leadership & Management, 22*(1), 73-91.

ten Bruggencate, G., Luyten, H., Scheerens, J., & Sleegers, P. (2012). Modeling the influence of school leaders on student achievement: How can school leaders make a difference? *Educational Administration Quarterly, 48*(4), 699-732. doi: 10.1177/0013161x11436272

Timperley, H. (2011). Knowledge and the leadership of learning. *Leadership and Policy in Schools, 10*, 145-170. doi: 10.1080/15700763.2011.557519

Wahlstrom, K. L., & Seashore-Louis, K. (2008). How teachers experience principal leadership: The roles of professional community, trust, efficacy, and shared responsibility. *Educational Administration Quarterly, 44*(4), 458-495. doi: 10.1177/0013161x08321502

Walker, A., & Shuangye, C. (2007). Leader authenticity in intercultural school contexts. *Educational Management Administration & Leadership, 35*(2), 185-204. doi: 10.1177/1741143207075388

Waters, T., Marzano, R., & McNulty, B. (2003). *Balanced Leadership: What 30 years of research tells us about the effect of leadership on student achievement.* Mid-Continent Research for Education and Learning, Website: http://www.mcrel.org.

Webber, C., Aitken, N., Lupert, J., & Scott, S. (2009). The Alberta student assessment study: Final report. Edmonton, AB: Alberta Education.

Westley, F., & Mintzberg, H. (1989). Visionary leadership and strategic management. *Strategic Management Journal, 10*, 17-32.

Ylimaki, R. M. (2006). Toward a new conceptualization of vision in the work of educational leaders: Cases of the visionary archetype. *Educational Administration Quarterly, 42*(4), 620-651. doi: 10.1177/0013161x06290642

Young, C. Y., Austin, S. M., & Growe, R. (2013). Defining parental involvement: Perception of school administrators. *Education, 133*(3), 291-297.

Youngs, P. (2007). How elementary principals' beliefs and actions influence new teachers' experiences. *Educational Administration Quarterly, 43*(1), 101-137. doi: 10.1177/0013161x06293629

Youngs, P., & King, M. B. (2002). Principal leadership for professional development to build school capacity. *Educational Administration Quarterly, 38*(5), 643-670. doi: 10.1177/0013161x02239642

Appendix A:
Professional Practice Competencies for School Leaders in Alberta

THE ALBERTA SCHOOL LEADERSHIP FRAMEWORK:
Building Leadership Capacity in Alberta's Education System

Framework Vision

All Alberta schools are served by educational leaders who are accomplished teachers, demonstrate the *Professional Practice Competencies for School Leaders in Alberta* throughout their careers, and are dedicated to achieving the essential purpose of educational leadership, i.e., to ensure that each student has an opportunity to engage in quality learning experiences that lead to achievement of the goals of education and address the student's learning and developmental needs.

In this context, "student engagement" refers to three dimensions of the learning experience—social, emotional, and intellectual—that result in students becoming engaged thinkers and ethical citizens, and their development of an entrepreneurial spirit. "Quality learning experiences" are school-sponsored activities that foster students' capacities to think critically, be resilient, adaptable and confident in their abilities, take personal responsibility for life-long learning, and collaborate to achieve a common purpose.

Framework Purposes

1. There is a common, consistent understanding of effective school leadership in the Alberta context, as defined in the *Professional Practice Competencies for School Leaders in Alberta.*

2. Effective teaching and leadership practices that are already in place in many Alberta schools and classrooms are identified, shared, and implemented across the province to promote equity in the quality of education that all Alberta students receive.

3. All Alberta school leaders demonstrate the applicable *Professional Practice Competencies for School Leaders in Alberta* throughout their careers.

4. The new generation of school leaders is effective "out of the gate" in demonstrating the applicable *Professional Practice Competencies for School Leaders in Alberta*, and experience career-long success in achieving the essential purpose of educational leadership.

5. Teacher efficacy is enhanced with the support of school leaders so that:
   - teachers become experts in learning, not just teaching;
   - collaborative, generative learning at the community, school, and classroom levels is promoted; and
   - all students are engaged in their education and are well-prepared to fully participate in Alberta's prosperous future and to contribute meaningfully to society.

6. School leaders foster teachers' instructional efficacy by promoting their professional learning and reflective practice.

7. School leaders have equitable access to programs that reflect the *Indicators of Quality of School Leader Development Programs in Alberta* and experience career-long success in demonstrating the *Professional Practice Competencies for School Leaders in Alberta.*

8. School leaders participate in a province-wide community of learning with access to professional networks, on-line resources, and expert advice.

9. Albertans are assured that Alberta's school leaders have the knowledge, skills, and attributes to fulfill their roles and responsibilities.

10. The school community understands the challenges faced by school leaders, actively supports them in their practice, and embraces a shared leadership model.
11. Education stakeholders have a common foundation and language for the development of school leadership policies and development programs that are aligned with the *Professional Practice Competencies for School Leaders in Alberta* and are effective in supporting and guiding school leaders.
12. Education stakeholders use the *Indicators of Quality for School Leader Development Programs in Alberta* to enhance the content, design, and delivery of school leader preparation, induction, and career-long professional learning programs and activities.

Framework Elements

The Alberta School Leadership Framework elements define effective school leadership in the Alberta context, promote quality school leader development programs, and identify roles and responsibilities of Alberta's education sector stakeholder organizations and post-secondary institutions (that offer school preparation programs) for fulfilling the Alberta School Leadership Framework vision.

The essential purpose of educational leadership is to ensure that each student has an opportunity to engage in quality learning experiences that lead to achievement of the goals of education and that address his or her learning and developmental needs.

Every school leader must be an accomplished teacher and is responsible for fulfilling the essential purpose of educational leadership.

Every school leader is expected to:

a. fulfill the applicable provincial requirements,
b. demonstrate the applicable *Professional Practice Competencies for School Leaders in Alberta* (*Competencies*), and
c. meet the school authority's requirements for school leaders.

The **Competencies** are interrelated and are not presented in rank order. The **Indicators** that accompany each competency describe how it is demonstrated. School authorities may interpret, refine, and add to the *Indicators* to reflect the local context.

The *Competencies*:

a. apply to Alberta's principals as well as assistant principals, associate principals, and vice-principals;

b. identify the basic competencies for effective school leadership applicable to all Alberta school contexts;

c. frame a school leader's career-long responsibility to fulfill the essential purpose of educational leadership;

d. represent a professional curriculum for school leadership preparation, induction and professional learning programs; and

e. facilitate province-wide consistency in school authority policies and processes for school leader professional growth, supervision, and evaluation.

Principals are accountable for the demonstration of all the *Competencies* throughout their careers. Assistant principals, associate principals, and vice-principals are accountable for the demonstration of those *Competencies* that are directly related to their assigned role and leadership designation.

Reasoned, evidence-based, professional judgment must be used to determine whether the applicable *Competencies* are demonstrated by a school leader.

Definitions

In the context of this document,

"**Competencies**" constitute an interrelated set of knowledge, skills, and attributes that is drawn upon and applied to a particular context for successful performance. They are the provincial requirements for the practice of school leadership for which Alberta school leaders are accountable throughout their careers.

"**Notice of Remediation**" refers to the written statement issued to a school leader by the individual undertaking the evaluation process if he or she concludes that the school leader does not demonstrate one or more of the applicable *Alberta Professional Practice Competencies for School Leaders in Alberta* and/or does not fulfill one or more of applicable provincial and school authority requirements.

"**Principal**" refers to an individual who holds a valid Alberta teaching certificate, is designated by a school authority, and is responsible for the provision of educational leadership as set out in provincial legislation.

"**School authority**" refers to a school board, a person, or society that operates a charter school or an accredited private school.

"**School community**" refers to students, teachers and other staff, parents, school council, and others who have an interest in the school.

"**School leader**" refers to a principal as set out in provincial legislation and to an assistant principal, associate principal, or vice-principal subject to the responsibilities assigned to the designation by the school authority.

"**School leader evaluation**" refers to the formal process of gathering and recording information and evidence over a period of time, and the application of reasoned professional judgment in determining whether or not a school leader demonstrates the applicable *Professional Practice Competencies for School Leaders in Alberta*.

"**School leader professional growth**" refers to a career-long learning process whereby a school leader develops and refines the knowledge, skills, and attributes related to the *Professional Practice Competencies for School Leaders in Alberta*.

"**School leader professional growth plan**" refers to the document that each school leader annually develops, implements, and reports on, in accordance with the school authority's policy and processes.

"**School leader supervision**" refers to the ongoing process by which the individual assigned to undertake this responsibility by a school authority supports and guides school leaders in demonstrating the applicable *Professional Practice Competencies for School Leaders in Alberta*.

PROFESSIONAL PRACTICE COMPETENCY #1
Fostering Effective Relationships

A school leader must build trust and foster positive working relationships within the school community on the basis of appropriate values and ethical foundations.

Indicators

A school leader:

a. acts with fairness, dignity, and integrity;

b. demonstrates a sensitivity to—and genuine caring for—others, and cultivates a climate of mutual respect;

c. promotes an inclusive, safe school culture that respects and honours diversity;

d. demonstrates responsibility for all students and acts in their best interests;

e. models and promotes open and collaborative dialogue;

f. uses effective communication, facilitation, and problem-solving skills;

g. supports processes for improving relationships and dealing with conflict within the school community; and

h. adheres to applicable professional standards of conduct.

PROFESSIONAL PRACTICE COMPETENCY #2
Embodying Visionary Leadership

A school leader must involve the school community in creating and sustaining shared vision, mission, values, principles, and goals.

Indicators

A school leader:

a. communicates and is guided by an educational philosophy based upon sound research, personal experience, and reflection;

b. provides leadership that leads to achievement of the school's vision and mission;

c. meaningfully engages the school community in identifying and addressing areas for school improvement;

d. ensures that planning, decision-making, and implementation strategies are based on a vision shared by the school community and an understanding of the school culture;

e. facilitates change and promotes innovation consistent with current and anticipated school community needs;

f. analyzes a wide range of data to determine progress towards achieving school goals; and

g. communicates and celebrates school accomplishments.

PROFESSIONAL PRACTICE COMPETENCY #3
Leading a Learning Community

A school leader must nurture and sustain a school culture that values and supports learning.

Indicators

A school leader:

a. engages the school community to promote the success and development of all students as a shared responsibility;

b. promotes and models life-long learning for students, teachers, and other staff;

c. fosters a culture of high expectations for students, teachers, and other staff;

d. fosters and sustains an inclusive school environment, where diversity is celebrated, students are encouraged to take risks in learning, and each student is equally valued as a contributing member of the school community;

e. promotes and facilitates meaningful, collaborative, professional learning for teachers and other staff;

f. ensures that parents are informed and have opportunities for meaningful input into how their children's learning and developmental needs will be addressed; and

g. fosters the use of local community resources and agencies to enhance student learning and development.

PROFESSIONAL PRACTICE COMPETENCY #4
Providing Instructional Leadership

A school leader must ensure that each student has access to quality teaching and the opportunity to engage in quality learning experiences.

Indicators

A school leader:

a. implements supervision and evaluation processes to ensure that all teachers consistently achieve the *Teaching Quality Standard Applicable to the Provision of Basic Education in Alberta* and/or other provincial requirements;

b. demonstrates a sound understanding of effective pedagogy and curriculum;

c. ensures that teachers use appropriate pedagogy to respond to various dimensions of student diversity;

d. ensures that students have access to appropriate programming based on their individual learning needs;

e. implements strategies for meeting the standards of student achievement;

f. ensures that student assessment and evaluation practices throughout the school are fair, appropriate, and balanced;

g. recognizes the potential of new and emerging technologies and enables their appropriate integration in support of teaching, learning, and reporting; and

h. ensures that teachers and other staff effectively communicate and collaborate with parents, and with appropriate local community agencies, to support student learning and development.

PROFESSIONAL PRACTICE COMPETENCY #5
Developing and Facilitating Leadership

A school leader must promote the development of leadership capacity within the school community for the overall benefit of the school community and education system.

Indicators

A school leader:

a. demonstrates informed decision-making through open dialogue and consideration of multiple perspectives;
b. promotes team-building and shared leadership among members of the school community;
c. facilitates meaningful involvement of the school community in the school's operation, where appropriate, using collaborative and consultative decision-making strategies; and
d. identifies and mentors teachers with the potential for educational leadership roles.

PROFESSIONAL PRACTICE COMPETENCY #6
Managing School Operations and Resources

A school leader must manage school operations and resources to ensure a safe, caring, and effective learning environment.

Indicators

A school leader:

a. effectively plans, organizes, and manages the human, physical, and financial resources of the school, and identifies areas of need;

b. ensures that school operations align with provincial legislation, regulations, and policies, as well as the school authority's policies and processes; and

c. applies principles of effective teaching, learning, and student development, as well as ethical leadership to management decisions.

PROFESSIONAL PRACTICE COMPETENCY #7
Understanding and Responding to the Larger Societal Context

A school leader must understand and appropriately respond to the political, social, economic, legal, and cultural contexts impacting the school.

Indicators

A school leader:

a. advocates for the needs and interests of children and youth;

b. demonstrates a knowledge of local, provincial, national, and global issues and trends related to education;

c. assesses and responds to the community context in fulfilling the school's vision and mission; and

d. advocates for community support of education at the school, system and provincial levels.

Master of Education in Educational Leadership

The Master of Education (Educational Leadership) program reflects recent shifts in the knowledge base and in the restructuring of educational leadership programs world-wide using a 21st Century professional practice competencies approach which integrates theory and practice. This program particularly reflects the Faculty of Education's commitment to prepare leaders for schools and school jurisdictions.

This leadership preparation program is consistent with acknowledged professional practices to meet anticipated demands for competent and committed school leaders.

The purpose of the Master of Education (Educational Leadership) program is to provide the knowledge and skills for candidates who wish to develop a leadership focus within their teaching career. This content includes:

- A critical examination of leadership models, theories, skills, and contexts.
- Significant opportunities to integrate local district issues and communities of practice through the fulfillment of two school-based leader internships.
- Choice of exit requirements: capstone or thesis.

The program features three themes considered central to developing educational leaders:

- Leaders as Moral Stewards,
- Leaders as Educators, and
- Leaders as Community Builders.

Courses address the *Professional Practice Competencies for School Leaders* and develop these competencies in:

- Establishing vision and addressing school-based change,
- Developing positive school culture,
- Managing the organization,
- Facilitating community engagement,
- Leading school-based professional learning,
- Integrating curriculum studies into instructional practices,
- Using research practices to promote school growth,
- Coming to know the foundations of educational leadership,
- Utilizing collaborative decision making processes,
- Understanding the wider context of schooling, and
- Using leadership theory to lead school-based internships.

Here is what a current school leader had to say about the program:

> *"The instructors of the program are experienced, knowledgeable, and wise. Their enthusiasm for educational leadership ignited my passion to become an effective school leader, competent in leading school change and improvement."*

Erin Hurkett (M.Ed 2011) Principal, Lethbridge Public School District.

FOR MORE INFORMATION ABOUT THIS COMPETENCIES BASED LEADERSHIP PREPARATION PROGRAM GO TO EDGRADSTUDIES.CA

Index